The
Caribbean Legion

The Caribbean Legion

Patriots, Politicians, Soldiers of Fortune

1946-1950

Charles D. Ameringer

The Pennsylvania State University Press
University Park, Pennsylvania

Library of Congress Cataloging-in-Publication Data

Ameringer, Charles D., 1926–
   The Caribbean Legion : patriots, politicians, soldiers of fortune,
1946–1950 / Charles D. Ameringer.

      p.   cm.
   Includes bibliographical references and index.
   ISBN 0-271-01451-2 (cloth)
   ISBN 0-271-01452-0 (paper)
   1. Caribbean Legion.   2. Caribbean Area—Politics and
government—1945-   3. Conspiracies—Caribbean Area—History—20th
century.   4. Caribbean Area—Foreign relations—United States.
5. United States—Foreign relations—Caribbean Area.   I. Title.
F2183.A42   1996
972.905'2—dc20   94-39178
                                                            CIP

It is the policy of The Pennsylvania State University Press to use acid-free paper for
the first printing of all clothbound books. Publications on uncoated stock satisfy the
minimum requirements of American National Standard for Information Sciences—
Permanence of Paper for Printed Library Materials, ANSI Z39.48-1992.

Contents

List of Figures   vii

Acknowledgments   ix

List of Abbreviations   xi

Introduction   1

1946:   Mr. Braden Stirs the Pot   11

1947:   Cayo Confites   27

1948:   Costa Rica   61

1949:   Luperón   95

1950:   The OAS Puts on the Lid   117

Appendixes   141

Notes   149

Selected Bibliography   171

Index   175

List of Figures

1. A partial listing of "Cayo Confites" arms seized by the Cuban government in September 1947.

2. Reproduction of wall chart depicting the organization of the air forces of the Liberation Army of the Caribbean. Prepared by Brigadier General Miguel A. Ramírez, July 29, 1948.

3. Reproduction of wall chart depicting the organization of the naval forces of the Liberation Army of the Caribbean. Prepared by Brigadier General Miguel A. Ramírez, July 29, 1948.

4. Copy of Octavio Arana Jiménez's request for an investigation of charges of espionage against him; submitted to the OAS Investigating Committee by the government of Nicaragua.

5. Document prepared by Charles Hauch of the U.S. State Department for the OAS Investigating Committee verifying that fifteen submachine guns captured at Luperón were originally approved for export from the United States to the Ministry of Defense of Guatemala.

6. The survivors and weapons of Luperón after their capture in the Dominican Republic, June 1949.

To Jean

Acknowledgments

I am indebted to the Department of History and the Research and Graduate Studies Office of the College of the Liberal Arts of the Pennsylvania State University for their generous support in the preparation of this book. I also wish to thank Dr. Benjamín Núñez of Costa Rica and Licenciado Bernardo Vega of the Dominican Republic for their assistance and friendship in facilitating my research and travel in their respective homelands. The people of the Caribbean are long-suffering, and I like to think that their spirit rubbed off and provided the inspiration for this work.

List of Abbreviations

ACNA	Cuban-North American Airways
AD	Democratic Action party (Venezuela)
ADC	Caribbean Democratic Action
APRA	American Popular Revolutionary Alliance
ARA	American Republics Affairs (U.S. State Department)
BAGA	Alemán-Grau-Alsina bloc (Cuba)
CTAL	Latin American Workers Confederation
CTC	Cuban Confederation of Labor
CUDD	University Committee for Dominican Democracy (Cuba)
FEU	University Students Federation (Cuba)
FULD	United Front for Dominican Liberation
IAPC	Inter-American Peace Committee
JD	Democratic Youth (Dominican Republic)
LCI	landing craft, infantry
LCT	landing craft, tank
MSR	Revolutionary Socialist Movement (Cuba)
OAS	Organization of American States
PRC-A	Cuban Revolutionary party-*Auténtico*
PRD	Dominican Revolutionary party
PSD	Social Democratic party (Costa Rica)
PSP	Popular Socialist party (Cuba) (Dominican Republic)
PT	patrol torpedo boat
RAF	Royal Air Force
RAMSA	Mexican Airways
RCAF	Royal Canadian Air Force
TACA	Central American Air Transport
UDAD	Dominican Antifascist Democratic Union
UDC	Central American Democratic Union
UIR	Revolutionary Insurrectional Union (Cuba)

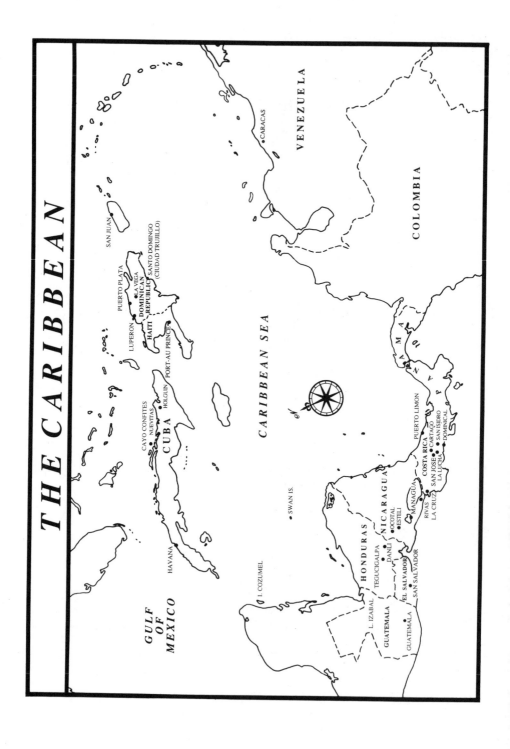

Introduction

The end of World War II was not the best of times for the strongmen of the Caribbean. The generals/presidents of Cuba, the Dominican Republic, Guatemala, Honduras, Nicaragua, and Venezuela, despite having joined the winning side, seemed to be ending up as losers. The wartime rallying cries of freedom from fear and want directed against Hitler and Mussolini had placed them in the bull's-eye as well. In the Caribbean during most of the war, opposition elements moved by patriotism put politics on hold, but by 1944, encouraged by the rising tide of democracy, they became active again.

Though the democratizing trends of World War II accelerated the pressure for change in the Caribbean, the process was more evolutionary than sudden. It began with the erosion of power of the rural elites during World War I, when the shortage of manufactured goods stimulated industrial development and urbanization and created new social structures comprised of rural and urban workers and middle-sector entrepreneurs, managers, professionals, and intelligentsia.[1] The changes over the next two decades were greater in some states of the region than in others, but all were influenced to some degree by large events in the world around them.[2] The Mexican Revolution, Russian Revolution, University Reform, and the Great Depression and New Deal of the United States each helped to shape the thinking of political leaders in the Caribbean seeking to organize the evolving economic and social order. They perceived these movements as socioeconomic in nature in that the purpose of political power was to achieve the redistribution of wealth and provide for the general well-being. Toward the mid- to late 1930s, the region witnessed the formation of a number of national political parties that shared the goals of democracy, nationalism, and socialism.

These parties owed a particular debt of gratitude to Víctor Raúl Haya de la Torre, a Peruvian exile who founded the American Popular Revolutionary Alliance (APRA) in Mexico in 1924. In synthesizing his program, Haya went through the same agonizing experience as the political leaders of the Caribbean, first flirting with communism and then rejecting it because of its advocacy of class conflict and subservience to Moscow. Haya placed his faith in the democratic political order as the means for achieving economic well-being and social justice. Once the popular classes achieved political power, Haya foresaw the creation of the anti-imperialist state placing the agricultural production and mineral resources of the nation in the service of the people through economic planning, an expanded public sector, and regulation of foreign capital. He proposed land reform in combination with state programs for credits, modernization, and marketing. With the wealth of the nation secured, Haya envisioned the opportunity to underwrite an extensive social program providing housing, health care, labor reform, and education. He stressed that this would be done without sacrificing essential individual freedoms and rights and without class warfare.[3]

In the Caribbean, Haya's ideas influenced the programs of two new political parties, one in Cuba and the other in Venezuela. The Cuban Revolutionary party-*Auténtico* (PRC-A), founded in 1934, adopted Haya's concept of economic and social reform without sacrificing democracy. As a leader of the University Reform movement, Haya helped found the José Martí People's University in Havana, where he addressed the student Generation of '30, the principal founders of the PRC-A. While certain circumstances special to Cuba also shaped the *Auténtico* program, among them a powerful nationalistic sentiment against all forms of U.S. intervention and the experience of the violent struggle during 1930–33 against the dictator Gerardo Machado, the *Auténticos,* like the *Apristas,* denounced the class struggle, adopting the multiclass (*policlasista*) concept, and chose to wean organized labor from the Communists by supporting improved working conditions and collective bargaining. Owing to patient, grass-roots organization, the *Auténticos* played a critical role in the drafting of the Cuban Constitution of 1940, providing for electoral reform and social guarantees.

In Venezuela a contemporary student generation organized the Democratic Action party (AD) in 1941, another *Aprista*-style party adapted to local realities. They began their movement in 1928 as students at the Central University in Caracas demonstrating against the "tyrant of the Andes," Juan Vicente Gómez, who had been in power since 1908. They attacked his rule as authoritarian and corrupt and accused him of a sellout of the nation's oil riches to foreign interests. However, their protest was suppressed, and many spent the following years in exile until the dictator died in 1935, among them Rómulo Betancourt, the most influential leader of the Generation of '28, who took refuge in Curaçao, Costa Rica, and Chile. Like Haya, these exiles discovered certain truths in Marxism but eventually turned away from the "stereotyped formulas" and "internationalist dogmas" of the Third International, preferring to seek "Venezuelan" solutions within a democratic order.[4]

In defining AD's program, Betancourt revealed the *Aprista* influence, proclaiming "[we are] defenders of economic nationalism, agrarian democracy, and social justice, ardently debating possible means whereby the country [may] recover and strengthen a regime of public liberties."[5] Also adopting Haya's multiclass thesis, Democratic Action denied that it was a "labor party," though, in fact, much of its strength derived from its liaison with organized labor.[6] The party was uniquely Venezuelan as well in that everything it promised depended upon the largess of oil. Unlike Lázaro Cárdenas in Mexico, however, AD did not propose to nationalize petroleum but to dominate oil production and "sow the oil" in order to deliver the Venezuelan masses from poverty and ignorance.[7] Having served as a loyal opposition during most of World War II, the AD and PRC-*Auténtico* parties were in a strong position to take advantage of "the shift from conservative or authoritarian rule toward democracy" occurring in "many parts of Latin America in the 1940s."[8]

On June 1, 1944, just five days before the D-Day landings in Normandy, Cuba elected Dr. Ramón Grau San Martín, the *Auténtico* candidate, as its president. Grau defeated Carlos Saladrigas, the hand-picked candidate of the retiring president, Fulgencio Batista. Batista had dictated Cuban affairs since 1934, first, governing as a military strongman through puppet presidents, then, as constitutional president himself from 1940 to 1944. While he had tried to appear more democratic during the war years, the *Auténticos* were the real democrats, and the Cuban people gave them a landslide victory. Grau was not of the Generation of '30, but he was its hero, having served as president in the hundred days between Machado's fall and Batista's rise. He was dean of Havana University's medical school when the students went underground to fight Machado and had been forced to flee into exile for defending their struggle. Grau's victory in 1944, in the midst of expanding Allied success, "raised enormous popular expectations" that the revolutionary promise of a decade earlier would at last be fulfilled.[9]

With Allied victory final in the following year, Venezuela's AD achieved power under circumstances similar to those in Cuba. Democratic Action collaborated with a group of junior army officers in October 1945 in overthrowing Venezuela's wartime president, General Isaías Medina Angarita, because of his efforts to impose a successor, thus reneging on his promise to hold democratic elections. Coming from the Andean state of Táchira, Medina was the third of the "Táchira clique" to be president; Gómez was the first (1908–35), followed by General Eleazar López Contreras (1935–41). Reform-minded junior officers, better educated and more professionally oriented than the *andino* generals, were determined that there would not be a fourth. Though participation in a military coup contradicted fundamental AD doctrine, Betancourt explained that AD "wanted to govern, . . . to contribute . . . to the building of a new order, based on effective democracy, with economic nationalism and social justice."[10] It seized what it rationalized was its only opportunity at the moment to achieve power, with Betancourt becoming provisional president and presiding over a junta of civilians and soldiers. Without letup he and AD endeavored in the next two years to create a functioning democracy and activist state, climaxing in the reform Constitution of 1947.

The democratic message of World War II also undid Jorge Ubico, the dictator of Guatemala, even though economic and social conditions were not as complex there as in Cuba and Venezuela. General Ubico had run the country since 1931 and his rule "might well have continued for some years longer, had it not been for the impact of World War II."[11] Several thousand U.S. troops maintaining air bases in Guatemala during the war spread democracy's message, including the Four Freedoms. "In the Guatemala of Ubico," Professor Richard Adams has noted, "one did not generally advertise any freedoms, much less four of them, without evoking some invidious comparisons, and younger Guatemalans were quick to respond."[12] The revolution taking place in neighboring Mexico also evoked a restlessness in Guatemala.

Urban workers, the middle class, even the landed elite, and rebel army officers collaborated in forcing Ubico to resign in July 1944, achieving definitive victory over his would-be successor, General Federico Ponce, in October. Lacking a political organization and without a program, they improvised, adopting the Atlantic Charter as a statement of principles and reading it aloud on street corners. Moreover, the evolving movement soon had a leader "not tainted" by service to Ubico.[13] History professor Juan José Arévalo arrived from exile in Argentina and appeared to be everyman's candidate for president. Arévalo was hard to figure from an ideological standpoint, but he "looked every inch" a president (being six feet tall) and he was "a master of politics."[14] He spoke vaguely of "spiritual socialism," placing the liberation of the human spirit above the distribution of material goods, and he called for Central American federation in order to overcome despotism and imperialism.[15]

As these events unfolded in the Caribbean, the dictators left standing, Rafael Trujillo of the Dominican Republic, Tiburcio Carías Andino of Honduras, and Anastasio Somoza García of Nicaragua, watched in horror. Carías in Honduras had the least to worry about, presiding over a society classified as "seriously undeveloped."[16] Only the banana plantations on the north coast were "new," dating from 1900 and contributing the major share of the nation's income. But Carías kept this development isolated, cooperating with American-owned banana companies in stifling efforts to organize the workers. In the highlands, where most of the people lived, a feudalistic society persisted, with little change since the Spanish imposed their will during the colonial era. The landed elites, "living on their remote estates,"[17] did not take the time to govern the country; they paid the generals to do the job, and Carías was one of the most effective in doing it up to then in the twentieth century.

Carías was elected president in 1932 and remained in office for the next sixteen years without bothering to hold further elections. He continued in office first by rewriting the constitution and later by amending it. He achieved order in a country accustomed to a steady succession of presidents and juntas, but he did it without excessive brutality and made "slight" economic gains through "a program of public works and road construction."[18]

In November 1943, with the liberalizing effects of World War II reaching even Honduras, Carías experienced a rare but futile challenge to his power. Jorge Rivas Montes, a twenty-three-year-old officer of the presidential guard and graduate of the military school in Guatemala, attempted a coup that collapsed within hours. Condemned to death, but released after serving two and a half years in jail, Rivas fled to Guatemala, where he volunteered his services to Arévalo, who placed him under his personal command for use in special operations. With little chance of altering the political situation in Honduras, a half-dozen junior officers joined Rivas Montes in exile to form a small but active element in the intrigue in the Caribbean in the second half of the 1940s. In the meantime, although Carías was the least affected by the changes in the region, Somoza and Trujillo realized that their greater notoriety made their situations more dangerous. They were sensitive especially to external factors with regard to U.S. opinion and policy and to the new circumstances of democratic neighbors sheltering dissident elements in exile.

The Dominican Republic and Nicaragua experienced economic and social change beginning in the World War I era, but the defining factor of political control in each of these countries was U.S. intervention. American troops occupied the Dominican Republic from 1916 to 1924 and were present in Nicaragua off and on between 1912 and 1933. During these periods, in each country, the United States armed and trained a constabulary force for the purpose of maintaining internal order and upholding constitutional government. But, as an unwelcome result, these armed elements became tools of personalist politics, enabling Trujillo in the Dominican Republic and Somoza in Nicaragua to seize political power. Each instituted an authoritarian rule that enforced social order and controlled economic activity for regime enhancement and personal gain.

Somoza had been in power since 1936. His control over the U.S.-trained National Guard enabled him to keep everybody in line. He was ruthless and greedy, but, given the history of U.S. interest in Nicaragua, he courted Washington's favor and strove for the appearance of constitutionality. He governed through the Liberal party, a traditional party extending back to the nineteenth century, much like the Conservative party, the main opposition, whose leaders either acted discreetly or resided in exile, principally in Mexico. During World War II, Somoza outdid himself in his pro-U.S. position, declaring that he considered "every Nicaraguan aviator and soldier as a potential fighting man for the United States."[19] Nonetheless, when the war ended, the United States exerted pressure on Somoza to permit a free election for president, scheduled for February 1947. He appeared to comply, but when his handpicked candidate exhibited too much independence, Somoza removed him, defying even the United States in maintaining the dictatorship.

Just like Somoza, Trujillo was the product of a United States policy gone wrong. And like Somoza, he endeavored to show that he was exactly what the Americans wanted in a leader. He had more difficulty proving this because he was essentially evil. Coming from a lower middle-class background, he had contempt for the traditional elites, especially the membership of the exclusive Club Unión, which once had blackballed him.[20] Amid much grandstanding and in a paternalistic fashion, he started a number of programs and projects to improve the conditions of the mass of the people, but he exercised absolute power, tolerating no criticism, much less opposition.

He showered favors on the armed forces, which had been his avenue to power, and he employed a network of spies and agents that terrorized the

Dominican people. His megalomania was legend, to the extent of renaming the capital city for himself, and he amassed a fortune for himself and his family, treating the nation and its resources as his fiefdom. In order to conceal his venality, he expended large sums on propaganda and public relations, especially in the United States, and took special care to cultivate influential Americans, including retaining as advisors or consultants retired U.S. military officers who had served as attachés in the American embassy in Ciudad Trujillo. In 1946, with all the talk of democracy and freedom, Trujillo faced no serious internal threat, but the circumstances for opposition elements who had managed to escape abroad were much improved, causing the autocratic leader to feel the urge to act against them and against any foreign leader giving them comfort.

Whereas Somoza's opposition usually fled to Mexico, which generally discouraged exile political activity, Trujillo's enemies were concentrated in Cuba and Venezuela, where the new democratic governments exhibited sympathy, even support, toward efforts to organize against him. Under the best of circumstances, Trujillo showed little respect for international borders, but if Betancourt and Grau were going to be trouble, he was prepared to intervene to crush them first. In December 1945 he directed Presidential Secretary José Almoina to send a circular dispatch to Dominican diplomatic missions instructing them to invite Venezuelan exiles, "enemies of the Revolutionary Junta of Caracas," to come to the Dominican Republic, where they could expect "a warm reception, hospitality, and protection, both personal and political."[21] Former President López Contreras and the journalist José Vicente Pepper accepted Trujillo's offer and willingly collaborated in preparing the first of Trujillo's aggressions against Betancourt, which occurred in November 1946.

The action consisted of provoking an uprising in Táchira, the western state contiguous with Colombia and a *gomecista* stronghold, as noted. Using the Dominican embassy in Bogotá as a staging area and provided with a large sum of money from Trujillo, followers of López Contreras crossed into Venezuela. They controlled some roads and blew up a few highway bridges, which caused a "partial uprising," but, lacking wide popular support, the movement quickly fizzled.[22]

In the meantime Trujillo sent a team of spies to Havana. He instructed Major Henry Gazón, posted as military attaché, and his wife, Evangelina, described as a "Mata Hari type,"[23] to enlist the Cuban army chief of staff, General Genovevo Pérez Dámera, in a plot to overthrow Grau San Martín.[24] The wooing of the general proved inconclusive; he was too cagey to be taken in by the Gazóns, but he left the door ajar for future dealings with Trujillo. The Gazóns and their successor, José Sanz de Lajara, a man notorious for scandalous behavior,[25] had better luck with disaffected military officers residing in Miami. In October 1946 certain generals hoping to restore the good old days agreed to stage an uprising at Camp Columbia, Cuba's main military base, if Trujillo would supply them with the necessary arms. The plot included an overflight of Havana by Dominican warplanes disguised as Cuban military aircraft. The movement was postponed when Trujillo's plot against Betancourt failed in November 1946.[26]

Thus, just as the United States was finishing one war, its Caribbean neighbors were circling one another menacingly, in anticipation of starting another. Trujillo and Somoza were in a powerful position militarily, which dictated caution on the part of the democratic states, whose strongest card was propaganda to discredit the dictators and to rally hemispheric opinion for collective action. In July 1946 Betancourt accused Trujillo of "oppressing and terrorizing" his people and affirmed that "the police have the right to break down the door of a house where a crime is being committed."[27]

Few American states were willing to break down any doors. They would not even support a modest proposal set forth by Uruguayan Foreign Minister Eduardo Rodríguez Larreta in November 1945 advocating "multilateral collective action" in defense of democracy and human rights.[28] Recognizing the contradiction between his proposal and the principle of nonintervention, Rodríguez Larreta stated incisively the fundamental issue that was to divide the Caribbean for the next five years, that is: "nonintervention cannot be converted into a right to invoke one principle in order to be able to violate all other principles with impunity."[29] The fact that the United States appeared to favor the Rodríguez Larreta proposal frightened off even those countries that showed some interest in collective action. But U.S. sympathy for the Rodríguez Larreta proposal cut two ways. Whereas it caused Latin American governments to cling more tightly to the principle of nonintervention, it emboldened political groups in exile to intensify their revolutionary efforts.

The exiles took as their inspiration the spectacular invasions of World War II that liberated occupied territories from abroad. They had reason to expect that they might be successful. The governments of Cuba, Guatemala, and Costa Rica (after May 1948) provided springboards for attack; arms dealers had plenty of "war surplus" material available for purchase, anything from jeeps and bazookas to landing craft, P-38 Lightning fighters, and B-24 Liberator bombers; and a substantial number of Cubans and Dominicans had combat experience, having volunteered to serve in the armed forces of the United States. Other war veterans added to the mix: Spanish Republicans and U.S. fighter and bomber pilots still thirsting for action. The icing on the cake was the appointment of Spruille Braden in September 1945 as assistant secretary of state for inter-American affairs. He was the sort that broke down doors.

Caribbean exiles of various nationalities organized military operations against certain states in the region, setting in motion a series of three events: the Cayo Confites affair in 1947, an attempt to invade the Dominican Republic by sea from Cuba; the Costa Rican civil war and Nicaraguan liberation movement in 1948, wherein the Caribbean exiles assisted the Costa Rican rebel José Figueres in his war of national liberation in return for his promise to aid them against Somoza and Trujillo; and the Luperón attack in 1949, the site of an unsuccessful airborne invasion of the Dominican Republic from Guatemala. Although these events differed in many respects, a core group of the same individuals participated in each. This fact gave rise to the myth of an army of exiles under the banner of the Caribbean Legion. There was no army—no permanent body of troops—only a "general staff" that called itself the Liberation Army of the Caribbean and also adopted the name Caribbean Legion in 1948 during the fighting in Costa Rica. The more romantic "Caribbean Legion" caught on and came to represent the antidictatorial struggle in the Caribbean in the post–World War II years.

At the same time, the Caribbean Legion appeared real enough to be the title of an intelligence estimate prepared by the U.S. Central Intelligence Agency in March 1949. However, the report essentially discussed "conspiracies" in the Caribbean, failing to describe the Legion in any detail or establish a cause and effect relationship. In a dissent with the report's general conclusion, the intelligence bureau of the Department of State argued, "The conflict which has made the Legion possible is a more persistent factor in the political relationships of the area than the Legion itself which might at any time fall apart as an organization."[30]

Real or not, the common thread that ran through the conflict in the Caribbean was the presence of Dominican exiles. In 1946 Trujillo was halfway through his thirty-one-year reign. Though no one could predict with certainty that he would govern for another fifteen years, the absolute nature of his rule and his seemingly entrenched position provided little hope then that the end was in sight, and those who despised him were willing to resort to desperate measures. In January of that year General Juan Rodríguez García, an aging don and wealthy rancher, fled the Dominican

Republic and became the principal leader and financial backer of the armed expeditions. Although all nationalities of the Hispanic Caribbean took part, Dominican exiles in particular determined the action of the Caribbean Legion. In tracing the specific movements of the Caribbean Legion, one has only to follow the trail of the arms provided by Rodríguez from Cayo Confites to Costa Rica and on to Luperón. At the same time, the Caribbean Legion had a place in the larger flow of events.

The fate of the Caribbean Legion was influenced by general trends taking place in Latin America from the end of World War II to the onset of the Cold War. Although the Caribbean exiles were independent actors and able to affect events, their early success coincided with the "democratic opening and reformist initiatives" occurring in parts of Latin America (1944–46), and their ultimate failure paralleled the "collapse of the reformist initiatives and political closing" happening in Latin America in general from the end of 1946 to 1950.[31] These periods were, in turn, influenced by U.S. policy. Whereas immediately after World War II the United States appeared willing to support an interventionist policy in the hemisphere on behalf of democracy, by the end of the decade it placed a premium on stability out of concern that the Communists might exploit situations of unrest and uncertainty. To put it another way, a "nudge to the left" occurred in Latin America in 1944–47,[32] but by 1948–50 the "military and traditional elites successfully neutralized the new forces."[33]

The story of the Caribbean Legion, then, is unique, but the outcome is roughly predictable when placed in the broad context of contemporary events. Essentially the activities of the Caribbean Legion provide valuable insights into a part of what a number of scholars conclude represented "a crucial historical bridge" in modern Latin America, "the period coinciding with World War II and the beginning of the Cold War."[34]

1946

Mr. Braden Stirs the Pot

The Braden Corollary

As an aspect of their claim to legitimacy as chiefs of state, Anastasio Somoza and Rafael Trujillo relied upon the appearance of approval by the United States. Each had risen to power as the commanding officer of an American-trained military force following a period of U.S. occupation, and each took care to remain identified with U.S. policy and to have influential friends in Washington. When Spruille Braden became the assistant secretary of state for inter-American affairs in September 1945, their luck ran out.

Braden was a firm believer in positive action to attain the goal of democracy in the Americas. He proposed a "so-called" corollary to the Good Neighbor policy, insisting that the principle of nonintervention ought not prevent the United States from fulfilling its responsibilities on behalf of free elections and human rights. Warning against "intervention by inaction," he declared that the United States "must distinguish between legitimate governments and those usurping power from the people."[1]

Braden had been born and reared in the mining camps of Montana and took pride in his tough, two-gun cowboy image. His interventionism was based on his wartime experiences as ambassador in Colombia, Cuba, and Argentina, where he fancied himself as an anti-Nazi paladin. He was determined to stand up for democracy in Latin America whether "they wanted it or not."[2] Braden's effort to topple Juan Perón in Argentina constituted the major test of his policy, but he applied it to other dictators as well, including Somoza and Trujillo.

The essential features of the Braden corollary were stated in a confidential aide-mémoire addressed to the Dominican government on December 28, 1945, wherein the United States denied a request for the purchase of a large quantity of munitions. The memorandum declared that such materiel "could only be used for one of two purposes," either against a neighboring republic (Haiti) or against the people of the Dominican Republic. Neither purpose, it affirmed, "would contribute to the cause of peace." It explained, moreover, that "the government and people of the United States have a warmer feeling of friendship for and a greater desire to cooperate with those governments which rest upon periodically and freely expressed consent of the governed." And it concluded, the United States "has been unable to perceive" the observance of democratic principles in the Dominican Republic, "in theory or in practice."[3]

This harsh note characterized U.S. policy toward the Dominican Republic in the coming year. United States policy "did not favor" the Trujillo government and blocked every effort of Trujillo to acquire arms on the grounds that "it did not want to aid, or appear to be aiding," his continuation in power.[4] When Trujillo appeared to be working a deal to acquire arms in Brazil in February 1946, Secretary of State James Byrnes instructed Adolf Berle, the U.S. ambassador in Brazil, to look into the matter, repeating the concern that Trujillo would only use such weapons against Haiti or his own people.[5]

Although the Braden policy of denying arms sales to dictators extended to Argentina, Honduras, and Nicaragua also, and Braden's conflict with Perón received more publicity, the policy tended to come down hardest on Trujillo and the Dominican Republic. This stemmed not only from Trujillo's own aggressive behavior but also from the influence of Braden's chief deputy, Ellis O. Briggs, the director of the Office of American Republics Affairs (ARA). Briggs, a career foreign service officer, had been ambassador to the Dominican Republic from June 1944 to January 1945. While there, his practice had been "to treat the odious tyrant of Santo Domingo with chilly formality and to touch his bloodstained paw as infrequently as possible."[6] This attitude contributed to his "replacement" within only six months, which the Dominican Republic regarded as a "diplomatic victory."[7]

Briggs, like Braden, who saved his career, viewed dimly both the "moral judgment" school and the "butter-up-the-dictator" school,[8] suggesting that "the care and feeding of dictators should not be left to nature lovers, however well-intended, but to professional animal trainers."[9] More formally, Briggs had advised the State Department in June 1944 "that the Trujillo dictatorship represented the denial of many of the principles to which the United States was committed, but that the promotion of its overthrow was not the responsibility of the American government, and it would be inconsistent with the existing commitments with respect to nonintervention."[10] However, he felt that the United States "ought to stop supporting" the Trujillo dictatorship and "refuse to allow the policy of the United States to be identified with it."[11]

Briggs's earlier difficulties in the Dominican Republic were related to the changeover from Cordell Hull to Edward Stettinius as secretary of state, but now the new secretary of state Byrnes seemed to support the policy of open contempt for Trujillo. In March 1946 Byrnes wrote to President Harry Truman that Trujillo was the hemisphere's "most merciless" dictator "and we ought scrupulously [to] avoid even the appearance of giving him any support."[12] In this regard the United States did not post an ambassador to Ciudad Trujillo (Santo Domingo) for about ten months after November 1945; that is, during almost one-half of Braden's tenure as assistant secretary. Trujillo observed "that he and Perón were in the same doghouse."[13]

When George H. Butler arrived in Ciudad Trujillo as U.S. ambassador in September 1946, he firmly supported the policy in place. The three B's (Braden, Briggs, and Butler) spoke in unison as far as Trujillo was concerned. Nor had the embassy's chargé d'affaires, George F. Scherer, given Trujillo any relief in the interim; he had observed in a confidential memorandum in February 1946 that there was not much difference "between Santo Domingo under Trujillo and Germany under Hitler."[14] He defined U.S. policy as "correct, but distant, avoiding any unnecessary cordiality."[15] Butler picked up on this quickly in his first official act, rejecting an invitation to attend a parade in celebration of the sixth anniversary of the signing of the Hull-Trujillo Treaty and to honor Trujillo as well. Butler regarded the event as "a political demonstration in support of Trujillo's reelection" (upcoming in May). At the same time he informed local American businessmen and companies that the State Department "disapproved and opposed" participation on their part in "the political activities of another American republic."[16]

Butler was just as direct in explaining Braden's policy to Trujillo face to face. In an interview in the Presidential Palace at the end of October, Butler told Trujillo bluntly "that the Government and people of the United States have a greater feeling of friendship for and a stronger desire to cooperate with those governments that rest upon the freely expressed wishes of the governed."[17] Trujillo, visably shaken and "seated on the edge of his chair," responded that he and his government "were deeply wounded" by the treatment they were receiving from the United States. He complained that he had cooperated "one-hundred percent" with the United States during the war and that "now he was being treated like a Hitler or a Mussolini." He blamed Braden for the "unjust" change in attitude and cited the aide-mémoire of December 1945, issued just after Braden became assistant secretary.[18]

Butler persisted, observing that Trujillo's opinion "seemed harsh and not totally justified." He stated that Braden was a personal friend and that he "respected and shared" his points of view. Braden, he assured Trujillo, "acted from conviction, not prejudice," being convinced of the need to promote democratic principles as the basis for the proper functioning of the inter-American system. He declared that the United States did not have a discriminatory policy toward the Dominican Republic, "that it was simply applying a general policy."[19]

Butler continued to turn up the heat. In accordance with the policy of nonintervention, he told Trujillo, the U.S. embassy would take no position in the forthcoming elections, "neither for or against him unconditionally." Trujillo did not comment, but, Butler reported, he appeared displeased, "probably realizing he had more to lose than gain." After all, Butler reasoned, Trujillo made "constant efforts" to create the impression that he had the support of the United States. As an indication of the way the meeting went, Trujillo, "half smiling," remarked at the end, "We are still your friends, even if we are your mistreated friends."[20]

On November 1, a few days after meeting with Trujillo, Butler addressed the American Chamber of Commerce in Ciudad Trujillo. There he publicly affirmed the Braden policy, citing Braden at length. Though he spoke in general terms about the principles of democracy and nonintervention in inter-American relations, he stressed America's commitment to the promotion of democratic principles, mentioning specifically freedom of speech and religion, which, he conceded, could result in different treatment for different states. "It is not an inconsistency in policy," he explained, "when our attitude and action in one country may differ from that in another."[21] Further, he told the businessmen not to participate in local politics, including making campaign contributions. Butler's speech was highly provocative, and the local press ignored it completely, but he was delighted to learn later that it made Trujillo "furious."[22]

Despite his strong stance, Butler was increasingly frustrated in his post.

As hard as he and embassy personnel tried, Trujillo and his minions were very skillful in exploiting the slightest contact for political advantage. Moreover, Butler noted, these contacts involved disreputable persons and were "personally very disagreeable." Consequently, believing that the "long interval" between his arrival and the departure of his predecessor (Joseph McGurk) had had "a salutory effect," Butler raised the idea of again having no ambassador in residence. "In small countries, like the Dominican Republic, that suffer the consequences of anti-democratic dictators," Butler suggested on November 18, "our interest would not suffer under a chargé d'affaires."[23] He added that Scherer had done a good job before as chargé.

Only days after the dispatch of this note, Ciudad Trujillo was abuzz with rumors of a possible coup against Trujillo. Butler personally received Dr. Viriato A. Fiallo, who warned him about likely disturbances in the upcoming weeks and hoped that the embassy would act "to mitigate" the severity of whatever repressive measures Trujillo might take. Fiallo headed an opposition group, Popular Union. He was one of the few persons to survive in opposition to Trujillo, probably because he exercised the utmost discretion, meaning that Trujillo could showcase him when it suited his purpose, and possibly because he was the nephew of General Federico Fiallo, the army chief of staff. Fiallo mentioned that Ambassador Briggs had given "great moral support" to liberal and democratic elements during his stay in the Dominican Republic and he indicated that Butler's Chamber of Commerce speech had done the same thing.[24]

Butler was moved by what Fiallo had to say and, though he recognized that he could not act unilaterally, he raised the possibility of multilateral action in the event of a crisis or violence in the Dominican Republic. "It would not be in accord with our principles," he wrote Washington, "to ignore a brutal suppression of civil liberties and individual rights."[25] As these events were unfolding the Dominican foreign minister, Manuel A. Peña Batlle, summoned Butler and the British ambassador on November 29 in order to give them copies of an intelligence report that described preparations for an armed invasion by Dominican exiles proceeding from Cuba and Haiti. The report proved to be false, and Butler, figuring that its real purpose was to justify a crackdown on opposition elements, as well as to divert attention from Trujillo's own plots against the governments of Rómulo Betancourt in Venezuela and Ramón Grau San Martín in Cuba, repeated his suggestion for an inter-American consultation.[26] He did not get the response he expected.

Drafting a note for Byrnes, State Department officer John C. Dreier asserted that there was no support among the American republics for multi-lateral action in defense of human rights. To prove his point he cited the "definitive rejection" of the proposal by Uruguayan Foreign Minister Eduardo Rodríguez Larreta that had called for collective action against dictatorial regimes. He stated that acts of brutality in the Dominican Republic might be the basis for consulting with other American republics but doubted, given the obsession with the doctrine of nonintervention, that anything would come of it "other than a pious expression of hope that the Dominicans would behave like good boys."[27] Briggs himself observed later that the best the United States could expect was an agreement "to beat Santo Domingo over the head with a toothpick."[28]

There were strong indications at the end of 1946 that Braden was losing influence. His policy of confronting dictators served in the afterglow of World War II, but with the outbreak of the Cold War it appeared risky. Braden himself indicated that he sensed this by the way he reacted to a lengthy dispatch from Butler on December 24. Butler reiterated his disgust for the Trujillo regime but, recognizing the difficulty in achieving collective action, proposed that the president and secretary of state issue a policy statement in the form of a press release treating specifically the problem of democracy and dictatorship in inter-American relations. By issuing a general statement to be applied impartially to all governments, Butler reasoned, the United States could promote democratic principles and finesse the outcries of "interventionism, discrimination, and personal prejudice."[29] Briggs agreed "totally" with Butler's ideas for a press release,[30] but Braden, though "in favor," suggested holding off "until we arrive in tranquil waters."[31] Braden's situation did not improve, it only got worse.

The Argentine Question

Braden's wish for tranquil waters was frustrated by his losing battle with Juan Perón. It was one thing to scorn the tyrant of Santo Domingo but quite another to take on the populist dictator of Argentina. The twenty months (September 1945-June 1947) that Braden served as assistant secretary were dominated by the Argentine question. Nelson Rockefeller, Braden's predecessor, had let Argentina off the hook by sponsoring its participation in the Act of Chapultepec (February 1945), provided it declare war on the Axis countries and purge its territory of Nazi influence. But Braden was not as forgiving, particularly as long as Colonel Perón remained in power.

Braden served as ambassador to Argentina from May to August 1945. During his stay he was an outspoken critic of Argentina's wartime collaboration with Nazi Germany and he vowed to dig out fascism "by its roots."[32] Telling Perón to his face that he would receive no U.S. military assistance while Nazi advisors remained in his government, Braden earned the title of "colonel tamer" and became the champion of Argentine democrats, who admired "his fearless preaching of democracy, his door-slamming toughness."[33] When he left Argentina, *The New York Times* editorialized, "Well done, Mr. Braden: Probably never before in so short a period did an Ambassador do so much for the country to which he was accredited as did Spruille Braden for Argentina."[34]

Braden was promoted to assistant secretary, some said "kicked upstairs," because, although his strong condemnation of Argentina's wartime behavior was popular, there were misgivings about his style, meaning that he was a throwback to the era of the big stick. Sumner Welles, the architect of the Good Neighbor policy, complained that Braden's policy violated the principle of nonintervention and, moreover, that it was helping Perón more than it was hurting him.[35] In an effort to overcome this criticism, Braden sponsored the proposal of the Uruguayan foreign minister, Rodríguez Larreta, for multilateral action against dictatorships.

Whatever chance this proposal had for success was lost in February 1946, when Braden interfered in Argentina's presidential election in a clumsy effort to defeat candidate Perón. Two weeks before the election, the U.S. State Department (Braden) published the "Blue Book on Argentina," a 131-page booklet based on captured German documents, which presented evidence that Perón and other high officials of the Argentine government were "so seriously compromised with the [Nazi-Fascist] enemy" that they were unworthy of "trust and confidence." This was an obvious act of intervention, and Perón turned it to his advantage, informing the voters that the choice was "Braden or Perón."[36] With Perón elected to a six-year term, Braden's policy started a slide from whence American public opinion had applauded his refusal to forgive Perón to where forgiveness was deemed a small price to pay for inter-American unity in the face of the new Soviet threat.

Along that slide Braden saw his anti-Perón policy slip from the effort to unseat Perón to mild pressure aimed at achieving Argentina's compliance with its pledges to eradicate Nazi influences. Despite the embarrassment

Braden had caused, Secretary Byrnes resisted calls to dismiss him. He insisted that if there were to be a change, Argentina must make it, and that Argentina would be judged "by deeds, not words."[37] At the same time he posted career diplomat George Messersmith to Buenos Aires with instructions to conciliate Perón in order to achieve Argentina's participation in a permanent defense pact in accordance with the Act of Chapultepec.[38] Given this ambiguous situation, Braden and Messersmith became bitter enemies and the principals in an undiplomatic controversy that made the cover of *Time* magazine. Braden condemned Messersmith for "appeasing" Perón, but the best he could do was to postpone the conference for an inter-American reciprocal assistance treaty, set for Rio de Janeiro, keeping the pressure on Perón long distance.

By holding the Rio conference hostage, Braden placed his entire antidictatorial policy in jeopardy. Within the U.S. Congress, Senators Tom Connally of Texas, Owen Brewster of Maine, and Arthur Vandenberg of Michigan accused Braden of "preventing the post-war reconstruction of the hemisphere" and "throwing Argentina and some other republics into the arms of the Russians."[39] Vandenberg, in particular, pointed out that Braden had "been dealing not only with the Argentine problem but also with the Rio Conference on a purely unilateral basis," failing to consult as required with other American republics.[40]

Braden's days as assistant secretary were numbered. The Republicans won the congressional elections in November 1946, elevating Vandenberg to the chairmanship of the Senate Foreign Relations Committee, and two months later General George C. Marshall succeeded Byrnes as secretary of state. Preoccupied with the growing challenge of the Soviet Union, and recognizing that Braden was a definite political liability, Marshall "decided that the [Rio] conference had been postponed long enough" and told Braden to get on with it.[41] With no serious concessions on Perón's part, the State Department announced on June 10, 1947, that Argentina had satisfied its Chapultepec commitments and that plans were moving ahead to hold the Rio conference. The Braden corollary was dead, and Braden was "permitted" to resign.[42]

Trujillo Feels the Heat

In the meantime, while the Braden policy remained in effect, Trujillo tried desperately to defend his regime. Deeply offended and troubled by the aide-mémoire of December 1945, Trujillo was heartened by Braden's feud with Juan Perón, but while it played out he could not risk being a passive observer. Though Trujillo's relations with the State Department and U.S. embassy in Ciudad Trujillo were unusually strained during Braden's tenure, Trujillo had a history of employing special agents in Washington, bypassing diplomatic channels and taking his case directly to high U.S. government officials, members of Congress, the public at large, and even to the President of the United States.[43] Among his most influential lobbyists was Joseph E. Davies, best known for his wartime "Mission to Moscow," who was a close friend and confidant of President Franklin D. Roosevelt. Davies served Trujillo as general counsel from 1933 to 1945, reportedly receiving $480,000 in 1934 alone as a commission for work in refunding the Dominican debt.[44]

Davies quit as general counsel at the end of 1945 in protest over the State Department's refusal to permit Trujillo to purchase arms in the United States. He made a kind of farewell visit to the Dominican Republic in February 1946, accompanied by his daughter, the wife of Senator Millard Tydings of Maryland.[45] On that occasion he stated publicly, "I have seen men in all parts of the world, in politics, in administration, in business, and I can tell you that you have here one of the greatest men in the world, a man who would be great in any age."[46] In retiring, Davies recommended that Trujillo retain Homer Cummings to succeed him. Cummings was another New Dealer who had been instrumental in achieving Roosevelt's presidential nomination in 1932 and who served as FDR's attorney general during his first two terms.

Cummings did indeed accept the position as Trujillo's general counsel in 1946, despite being seventy-six years old. Before doing so, he came to the Dominican Republic in February, just before Davies, and met with Chargé Scherer. Though Cummings did not use the same hyperbole as Davies, he definitely was impressed with the "material progress" being made under Trujillo and with the "high quality" of Dominican administrative officials. He criticized U.S. policy toward the Dominican Republic as "disguised intervention," saying that he had encountered bitterness and prejudice toward Trujillo in the State Department. He affirmed that the United States could not force democracy on the Dominican people and that it ought to be "patient," claiming that democracy would "evolve naturally" under Trujillo.[47]

Cummings repeated these thoughts to Butler in August, just before the latter left for the Dominican Republic as ambassador. He told Butler that he hoped he would go to the Dominican Republic with an open mind and "form his own opinions." Conceding that Trujillo was a dictator, Cummings asserted that he was doing extremely well for his country "in regard to material progress, education, agricultural development, the well-being of the masses, and the maintenance of law and order."[48] He added that Trujillo was making progress toward democracy in the Dominican Republic. Neither Scherer nor Butler was moved by Cummings's arguments, adhering firmly to Braden's policy of cold formality toward Trujillo, but career foreign service officers found it difficult to ignore the intimidating effect of an influential person like Cummings who had access to the White House.[49]

This circumstance inspired Byrnes to write to President Truman deploring Trujillo's efforts to influence U.S. policy by employing lobbyists or "persons of high reputation," paying them well for their services. "It is obvious," he stated, "that Trujillo or any other Chief of State does not need anyone to plead his case if his objectives are legitimate."[50] In writing to Truman, Byrnes was concerned not as much about Cummings as about Dr. William A. Morgan and Manuel de Moya, both of whom were poker-playing friends of the President.[51] Morgan was a prominent ear, nose, and throat specialist in Washington who had treated Trujillo's son and who traveled to the Dominican Republic periodically, performing at least fifteen operations a day, "on the rich as well as the poor," with Trujillo footing the bill.[52] De Moya was a smooth operator, known to be the "right-hand man" of Trujillo, who frequently traveled to the United States carrying large sums of money to be used "to open doors."[53]

In January 1946 Morgan acted as Trujillo's agent in the purchase of the Canadian corvette *La Chute* and then used his influence in the White House to secure an export license for the vessel en route from Canada to the Dominican Republic.[54] This occurred shortly after Braden refused the Dominican Republic permission to export arms from the United States, causing State Department officers to observe that Trujillo was prepared "to use any and all means to achieve his ends in the United States and circumvent the Department, even if it means going directly to the White House."[55] Morgan and his family traveled on *La Chute* to the Dominican Republic, where it was rechristened *Colón*. The ship sailed to Brazil the following month to pick up arms that Trujillo had acquired there over the protest of the United States.

Braden's ban on Dominican arms purchases in the United States caused Trujillo to buy guns wherever he could. For purposes of procuring arms, he employed retired U.S. Marine Corps officers George H. Stamets and Charles A. McLaughlin who had served as attachés in the Dominican Republic and knew their way around, and for their services Trujillo paid them handsomely. Trujillo enjoyed good relations with active duty officers as well, particularly with General George H. Brett, the commanding general of the Caribbean Defense Command, who tended to ignore diplomatic channels in the same way as Trujillo. In late August 1944 Ambassador Briggs reported Brett's visit to the Dominican Republic: "[He] arranged [it] through personal correspondence with Trujillo, without reference to [the] Embassy until two days before [his] visit," and it involved discussions of matters "not previously treated with the Embassy or reported to it afterwards."[56] Briggs observed that the visit "was directly contrary" to the policy of keeping Trujillo at arm's length (but it was Briggs who was recalled soon afterwards). Brett enjoyed a similar cozy relationship with Somoza of Nicaragua,[57] and Braden blasted him for visiting Argentina and "making ardent love to Perón."[58]

Aware of the U.S. military's concern over the delay in completing the inter-American mutual defense pact, Trujillo exploited the growing criticism of Braden's Argentine policy and the related issue of nonintervention. On March 21, 1946, a month after Perón's electoral victory, the Dominican ambassador to the United States, Emilio García Godoy, called on Braden, essentially to torment him further. Braden insisted that the United States was not going to withhold recognition of the Perón government, but neither was it going to sign a military pact "with those elements that had cooperated with the enemies of the United States and the other countries of the United Nations."[59]

García Godoy persisted. He complained that there was an anti-Trujillo press campaign being waged in the United States and suggested that it was being fueled by the State Department's aide-mémoire of December 1945, implying that someone had leaked it. He requested that the aide-mémoire and the reply of the Dominican government be withdrawn; if not, the Dominican government "would be obliged" to publish the full exchange of notes. He conceded that the publication of the aide-mémoire would intensify the controversy surrounding Braden's policy but argued that the Dominican Republic had the right to defend itself.[60] Braden recognized an effort "to embarrass" him by provoking an argument in the midst of his other troubles and he informed García Godoy that the aide-mémoire "was not to be published under any conditions."[61]

This response did not satisfy García Godoy, and the Dominican government tried again to force the publication of the aide-mémoire on the basis that it was already known "by various persons in Ciudad Trujillo, despite its private character."[62] The Dominican Foreign Ministry delivered a note to this effect to Scherer on April 5, implying that the leak was in the U.S. embassy. Secretary Byrnes sent off a quick reply that there was no foundation to the implication that any member of the U.S. embassy had made an unauthorized disclosure of the aide-mémoire and that the position of the United States was unchanged; "the aide-mémoire is not to be published under any circumstances."[63]

Thwarted in this maneuver, Trujillo used his controlled press to engage in a vulgar and vicious campaign against Braden. Demanding Braden's resignation, Trujillo's editorial writers accused him "of interfering where he was not wanted" and of acting like a "gauleiter." He was described as "the fat Machiavelli with the silly ties."[64] At the same time Trujillo sent a high-level delegation to Perón's inauguration, hoping to secure an agreement to raise their respective diplomatic missions to the rank of embassy. Thus, even while Braden's policy was running into strong opposition, Trujillo was being affected, causing him to depart from his normal pro-U.S. stance. He resorted to other uncharacteristic measures as well.

In January 1946, as a direct result of the aide-mémoire, the presidential secretary (Armando Mieses Burgos) suggested to José Ramón Stella, the editor of *La Opinión,* that he begin an "opposition" campaign, with the caveat not to attack Trujillo or the armed forces.[65] Stella took him up on it but started cautiously, deciding to limit criticism to the letters page. But even that turned out to be a bad idea. On February 23 a puzzled George Scherer reported that *La Opinión* had published a letter by José A. Bonilla Atiles, a prominent attorney and dean of the law school of the National University, announcing that he did not intend to support the nomination of Trujillo for another term as president. He insisted that he was "not an enemy" of the President or a "conspirator" and that he would probably vote for Trujillo when the time came, but he did not wish to commit himself so far in advance and observed that "no man is indispensable."[66] Scherer did not know what to make of Bonilla's statement but remarked that it was "too good to be true" and noted suspiciously that its publication coincided with Joseph Davies's visit to the Dominican Republic. Still, he found it interesting that Trujillo felt the need "to play this dangerous game."[67]

As this affair evolved, Scherer became convinced that Stella and Bonilla were "sincere in their opposition."[68] Bonilla followed up his first letter in *La Opinión* with another in which he revealed that he had been offered a legislative seat and had turned it down, demonstrating that he had not been bought nor could he be bought. Stella told a member of the American embassy that "he intended to continue feeling out the situation gradually and see where it leads."[69] Where it led to was harassment and reprisal, causing Stella to cease publishing critical letters in early March and to consider leaving the country.[70] Bonilla was fired as law school dean, expelled from the local Rotary Club, physically attacked by an "unknown assailant" leaving a movie theater, and finally forced to seek asylum in the Mexican embassy. At the end of May, Bonilla and his family came to the American embassy to request visas for travel to the United States.[71] Bonilla told Scherer that Trujillo was a tyrant, but that he himself was confused about U.S. policy toward the dictator. He sensed an estrangement because of the long absence at the time of an American ambassador and the unusual presence of anti-American commentary in Trujillo's press, but he could not understand why the United States did not criticize Trujillo openly as it did Perón of Argentina and Franco of Spain.[72]

As Trujillo's clumsy effort to demonstrate freedom of the press was unraveling, the dictator tried another maneuver that was more inept and counterproductive. In May 1946 his representative, Ramón Marrero Aristy, flew to Havana and reached an agreement with Juan Marinello and Blas Roca of the Cuban Communist party (the Popular Socialist party, PSP) and Lázaro Peña and José Morera of the Communist-controlled Cuban Confederation of Labor (CTC). The comrades promised to cease their criticism of the Dominican government (indeed, they would endorse Trujillo) in return for Trujillo's pledge to relax restrictions on labor unions, to free imprisoned labor leaders, to permit the return of political exiles, and to lift the ban on the Communist party.[73] Trujillo hoped to show the world that the Dominican Republic was so democratic that it tolerated a functioning Communist party. At the same time he wanted to end the anti-Trujillo propaganda being printed in the PSP's Havana newspaper *Hoy* and broadcast over its powerful Radio 1010 (Mil Diez), which could be picked up in the Dominican Republic. And he may have wanted to smoke out local leftists in order to round them up when he was ready to end his flirtation.[74] Briggs saw the situation as "making a pact with the devil, on both sides!"[75]

Communist organizers and labor leaders arrived in Ciudad Trujillo from Havana in August, among them the Dominican exiles Ramón Grullón and Mauricio Báez. Non-Communist exiles, smelling a rat, stayed away, and the Communists denounced them as "reactionary adventurers."[76] The comrades went to work quickly, organizing a Dominican PSP and publishing a manifesto in Trujillo's newspaper, *La Nación,* that described the new party's fundamental ideology as that of Lenin and Stalin. Scherer wondered if Trujillo was using the Communists in an effort "to frighten" the United States.[77]

In September the PSP held a rally in Villa Francisca Park—the first of its kind in sixteen years—causing "almost all" Dominican officials to feel it was a mistake to have permitted the Communists to return and causing Trujillo's "ardor to cool."[78]

By the following month Trujillo was concerned that he had been "deceived." The PSP sponsored a rally and parade (passing before the foreign embassies) on October 26 that seemed to get out of hand, and a new opposition group, identified as Democratic Youth (JD), appeared in the line of march. The appearance of Democratic Youth especially "surprised" Trujillo because no such group had been part of his deal with the PSP.[79] Trujillo sent Marrero Aristy to Havana to confer with Blas Roca and point out that the Dominican Communists "lacked experience" (meaning they did not know how to play ball) and "that Trujillo was not pleased with them."[80]

The American embassy, on the other hand, did not perceive Democratic Youth to be a Communist organization, noting that its statement of principles was "relatively mild," with no criticism of Trujillo, nor did it contain "any phrase or idea that could be recognized as Communist in origin."[81] Butler reported that JD held a meeting on November 24 in a vacant lot near the municipal football field that not even a tropical downpour could disperse, and he expressed admiration for the group's courage, braving the rain and "publicly demanding rights that are being denied by the present government."[82] Nonetheless, JD experienced Trujillo's wrath along with the PSP.

In this context Butler suspected, as previously noted, that Foreign Minister Peña Batlle's report of an imminent invasion was a ruse to justify the renewal of acts of repression. Trujillo stated at the time that "he intended to take drastic measures to preserve order and that the Dominican government was determined to fight against Communist conspiracies."[83]

With the rumors flying, the PSP itself circulated a broadside denying any connection with preparations for an invasion and affirming its intention to act in compliance with the constitutional order. It viewed the invasion rumors as a "grave threat" to the hard-won "democratic guarantees" in place since August.[84] Democratic Youth likewise prepared a flier to express its intention to operate within the law and declare that it "had no relations of any kind with any other political organization, either within or outside the country."[85] But these disclaimers had no effect on Trujillo, resulting in a violent crackdown on opposition elements during the month of December and causing a "highly respectable Dominican" to tell Butler that "he doubted even Hitler had exercised an internal control in Germany as complete and cruel as Trujillo exercises here."[86] Within six months Báez and Grullón had fled the country and Trujillo had outlawed the Communist party (PSP) again and crushed Democratic Youth.

Although Trujillo's grip was never more firm, and Braden's policy was in recession, it was too early to affirm that Trujillo was out of the woods. Braden's policy had not only caused Trujillo to panic and make desperate efforts to appear democratic, but it had raised expectations among the Dominican people and others, especially in the Caribbean region, who were enduring the trauma of authoritarian rule. The momentum created by Braden's policy may have been peaking when the policy itself was failing, but it was a real force nonetheless.

All Stirred Up

In January 1946 the U.S. embassy's legal attaché (FBI) speculated that "not more than eleven people in Santo Domingo" knew about Braden's aide-mémoire expressing disapproval of the Trujillo government.[87] In the following weeks and months there were strong indications that the word was getting out and that Braden's policy was encouraging opposition elements within the Dominican Republic and in exile. The problem became sufficiently acute for Braden to suggest a "policy line" in connection with "meetings and correspondence" with Dominican dissidents.[88] He instructed his people to reiterate that the United States would adhere to its treaty obligations and "avoid interfering in the internal domestic affairs of other American republics,"[89] but the genie was out of the bottle and working its magic. On February 6 a group of university students contacted Scherer to request photographs of Braden and former President Franklin Roosevelt, which, Scherer believed, they intended to use in an anti-Trujillo demonstration.[90] In May, Persio Franco, the uncle of Pericles Franco, a founder of the Dominican Communist party, visited the State Department and praised Braden and Briggs profusely, affirming that "they were the hope of Dominican people."[91]

Even as Braden's policy came under fire, a steady stream of anti-Trujillo Dominicans came to give him and his officers encouragement. Angel Morales, the leader of the Dominican Patriotic Union in exile, called at the State Department to express the hope that the American embassy in the Dominican Republic would continue "the correct but distant diplomatic relations with the Trujillo regime," for which he credited Ambassador Briggs. He added that he shared Braden's disappointment in the failure of the Rodríguez Larreta initiative.[92] In Ciudad Trujillo, Scherer attended a dinner party in the home of Mario Lluberes, a prominent architect, and became convinced that "he and his friends were well-informed about American policy," meaning they knew the contents of the supposedly secret aide-mémoire. Lluberes confided to Scherer that Braden's brief term as ambassador in Argentina "had been like a ray of sunshine for the oppressed people of the Dominican Republic."[93]

And Butler's stay in the Dominican Republic had let in more sunshine. His address to the American Chamber of Commerce of Ciudad Trujillo on November 1 gave many Dominicans a lift. When Viriato Fiallo visited him on November 20 to warn about a possible government crackdown on opposition elements, he referred to the heartening effect of Butler's speech and said that Briggs also, when he was ambassador, "had given great moral support to the democratic and liberal elements in opposition to the dictatorship."[94] Although Trujillo's press ignored Butler's speech, Democratic Youth reproduced it in full in its newsletter, being alone in making it available to the nation. One of its members, R. A. Roques Martínez, fired from his job in the Dominican Foreign Ministry for taking part in the November 24 rally, wrote to Butler expressing "his admiration" and saying that his speech "had made a favorable impression" on Democratic Youth.[95]

The firing of Roques Martínez (his two brothers were also dismissed from their jobs) marked the renewal of Trujillo's intolerance of opposition of any kind in the Dominican Republic. But in exile in New York, Bonilla Atiles, also fired from his job as law school dean, expressed the new state of mind that Braden, Briggs, and Butler had created among those who yearned to end the dictator's rule. Bonilla wrote to Braden declaring that his policy reflected "the hopes of the peoples of the hemisphere" and "achieved the honor of being criticized by the dictators and the elements that still think in nazifascist terms."[96] He would not dare state this in the Dominican Republic, he pointed out, but in exile he was free, and there were hundreds like him. Before he left the Dominican Republic in May, Bonilla had asserted that "no government can exist in the Dominican Republic without the backing of the Government of the United States."[97] On that belief Braden's disapproval of Trujillo helped set off a chain of events in the Caribbean that kept the region in turmoil for most of the post–World War II period.

1947

Cayo Confites

The Dominican Diaspora

In 1947 the largest concentration of Dominican exiles resided in Cuba. Some of them had fled the Dominican Republic in 1930, when Rafael Trujillo seized power; others came out in subsequent years, usually as the result of some run-in with the Trujillo dictatorship. A few settled down, but most yearned to return to their homeland. Those who wanted to go back believed that the best way to do it was to organize the exile community for action against the dictator.

The most serious effort to unite on the part of the Dominican exiles occurred on January 21, 1939, with the founding of the Dominican Revolutionary party (PRD). They met in the El Cano section of suburban Marianao, in the home of Dr. Virgilio Mainardi Reyna, a well-connected Dominican exile with an active law practice in Havana. Mainardi had enlisted in the Mariel expedition in 1934, the first exile operation against Trujillo from Cuba, which collapsed before it started. Among those present as founders of the party were Juan Bosch, Juan Isidro Jiménez Grullón, Enrique Cotubanamá ("Cotú") Henríquez, and Angel Miolán. Bosch was a young writer who in time became "perhaps the most prolific in the entire history of Quisqueya [Santo Domingo],"[1] and also president of the Republic. He was jailed in 1934 for his part in a conspiracy to assassinate Trujillo and went into exile in 1937. Jiménez Grullón, an intellectual and medical doctor, was the grandson of a former president. He presided over a political study group in the early thirties that led to charges of "communist activities" and expulsion in 1937. Cotubanamá Henríquez, also a physician, had deep Dominican roots and strong Cuban ties. He was something of a wild man and engaged vigorously in the politics of both Cuba and the Dominican Republic. Miolán was one of the "young rebels" of Santiago de los Caballeros (the study group led by Jiménez Grullón). He took part in the failed attempt against Trujillo in 1934 and escaped to Cuba.[2]

According to Miolán, Henríquez wrote the PRD's doctrine that was approved in the founding meeting. It was a hodgepodge of the revolutionary idealism of the times. Beginning with the patriotic rhetoric of the country's liberator, Juan Pablo Duarte, it continued with the basic concepts of the American, English, French, and Mexican revolutions, and ended up referring to "the great humanistic movements of universal character" inspiring the parties of the Latin American democratic left.[3] Among the latter the doctrine's models were the American Popular Revolutionary Alliance of Peru, Democratic Action of Venezuela, and the Cuban Revolutionary party-*Auténtico*. The Dominican Revolutionary party acknowledged especially the inspiration of Víctor Raúl Haya de la Torre, the founder of APRA. "Peruvian *aprismo*—the big brother of [the parties of the democratic left]—had a decisive impact upon the political direction of the PRD, influencing its theory and action."[4]

At the same time Henríquez spurned the idea that the PRD's doctrine was a carbon copy of that of the Cuban *Auténtico* party, of which he was also an author in 1935. If there were similarities, he explained, it was because the circumstances that gave rise to "revolutionary nationalism" were similar, but, he insisted, each country interprets its own realities and proposes its unique solutions. The PRD doctrine "was conceived and constructed especially for the Santo Domingo that had to endure the tyranny of Trujillo."[5] With a program as broad and idealistic as that of the PRD, it would seem that unity was readily attainable, but that was not the case.

The failure of the PRD to unify the exile community stemmed largely from the rivalry between Bosch and Jiménez Grullón—"los dos juanes." For about four years they were close collaborators and even good friends, but each wanted to be president and their ambition soured their relationship, political and personal. Henríquez foresaw the outcome of their rivalry: "'Los juanes' will lead us to failure in the long run."[6] In the meantime they traveled to Mexico in November 1941 to organize the Mexico section of the PRD and attend the Congress of the Latin American Workers Confederation (CTAL). They met with the Mexican labor leader and *criollo* Communist

Vicente Lombardo Toledano and received a tremendous boost with a resolution of solidarity between "the workers of America and the oppressed
people of the Dominican Republic."[7]

The PRD established sections in other countries of America, but Cuba
was the hub of *perredeísmo* in exile. It held its First Congress in Havana
(March 29 to April 7, 1943), even though at the time it had been forced to
change its name to the Dominican Antifascist Democratic Union (UDAD),
bowing to pressure from the government of Fulgencio Batista, which in
turn sought to appease Trujillo. But there was a war on, and in recognition
of that fact the First Congress, in condemning *caudillismo,* put on hold the
removal of Trujillo until the war's end. After the Congress closed, many of
the delegates volunteered for service against the nazifascist enemy in the
U.S. armed forces.[8]

The PRD/UDAD was the dominant Dominican exile organization during
the war years, but, as previously noted, it could not achieve the general
unity of the exile community. Though it claimed to represent the unifying
goal of eliminating Trujillo, it could not overcome partisanship and personal rivalry. Because 1944 was the centennial of Dominican independence,
PRD tried again in October to create a broad-based organization by sponsoring the First Congress of Exile Unity. Instead of achieving its purpose, the
congress precipitated the inevitable break between Bosch and Jiménez
Grullón: when Bosch emerged as the PRD's nominee for president in a
post-Trujillo Dominican Republic, Jiménez Grullón bolted the party.[9]

The Congress created the United Front for Dominican Liberation (FULD),
but with Jiménez Grullón gone it represented little more than the PRD.
Angel Morales signed on for the Dominican Patriotic Union, Ramón de Lara
did the same for the Dominican Democratic Front, and José Ramón Kings-
ley did likewise for the Independent Association for Dominican Liberation,
"but the unity was undermined by passions and partisanship, and did not
work."[10] Part of the failure was the PRD's fault, since it tended to be sec-
tarian and was fairly rigid with reference to party discipline, requiring its
membership to recognize PRD as "the only legitimate political institution of
the Dominican people" in the struggle against Trujillo.[11] Bosch, moreover,
declared Morales a "has-been."[12]

According to Miolán, the FULD also malfunctioned by naming Leovigildo
Cuello as a general delegate to the Supreme Council. This action took him
from his exile in Mayagüez, Puerto Rico, where he headed the PRD section
and was "well-connected," and moved him to Havana, where he was not as
effective. Likewise, by making Juan Bosch a special envoy for negotiations

with sympathetic governments and leaders in the region, he was no longer in charge of affairs in Havana, where he was the exiles' most influential person and enjoyed "a very close friendship" with Cuba's new president Grau San Martín.[13] Bosch furthermore was on intimate terms with Cuban Prime Minister Carlos Prío Socarrás, being, in effect, part of his inner circle.

Nevertheless, a promising sign of the Congress was the participation of certain Cuban political activists who were slated to have strong influence in the newly elected *Auténtico* government. Among them Manolo Castro was important. President of the University Students Federation (FEU) at the University of Havana and leader of one of the student armed bands (*bonches*) —"groups of desperados who impose their will and pass their examinations at pistol point"[14]—Castro (no relation to Fidel) became national sports director in the Grau administration from whence he played a large role in the anti-Trujillo plotting. Another key activist was Rafael Díaz Balart, head of the University Committee for Dominican Democracy (CUDD), who cemented further the relationships between the Dominican exile community, on the one hand, and the Cuban intellectual, radical student, and "*pistolero*" (gangster) elements, on the other. These groups figured prominently in the political dynamic of the *Auténtico* governments.

Getting Rid of the Dictator

At the same time that the Dominican exiles struggled to achieve unity, they were divided over the means for getting rid of Trujillo. Their Cuban allies tended to favor a violent solution to the problem of Trujillo, but the Dominican exiles were not so sure. Many Dominicans in exile possessed "an attitude *garibaldiana*," disposed to return to the homeland by organizing a filibustering expedition.[15] Some wished to emulate Ghandi;[16] that is, to follow the tactic of passive resistance, eschewing violence and bloodshed. Still others considered returning home to begin an underground resistance movement. Manuel "Pipi" Hernández, a Dominican exile employed at the American naval base at Guantánamo, wrote in 1945 that the only thing to do "was to transfer the struggle to the fatherland, since fighting by remote control was not right." "The only way that you can defeat the regime," he maintained, "is by pressuring it, by confronting it with the popular mobilization of the workers, students, peasants, and professionals. We believe that this is the right way."[17] Pipi Hernández wanted to make use of emerging social forces in the Dominican Republic, especially the organized sugar workers, spurred by wartime economic activity.

Bosch, who had tilted toward an armed invasion, revised his thinking as the result of a visit to Venezuela in October 1945. He traveled to Caracas to congratulate Betancourt, who had seized power on the eighteenth of the month, hoping to secure "as much support as possible" in the struggle against Trujillo and "to act as liaison" in establishing "an informal understanding" among AD of Venezuela, the *Auténticos* of Cuba, and Juan José Arévalo of Guatemala.[18] Betancourt welcomed his friend warmly but counseled him against "a reckless adventure," being of the opinion that Trujillo had too much firepower for any force that the exiles might put together. He advised Bosch to do what AD had done; that is, seek out and cooperate with dissident elements in the armed forces, especially junior officers, in order to carry out a coup d'état against Trujillo.[19] In the meantime he pledged financial and moral support to Bosch for organizing a propaganda campaign to discredit Trujillo and achieve sympathy for his cause in the hemisphere.[20]

Betancourt's strong admonition persuaded Bosch to try the coup option. He traveled to Haiti in November where he met with President Elie Lescot who regarded Trujillo as a personal enemy and pledged discreet assistance in the effort to remove him, giving Bosch $25,000 of his own money for that purpose.[21] He also shared intelligence with Bosch, revealing that Trujillo was very worried about possible unrest, causing him to quarter troops "for long periods of time," with the result that their morale was low. He also disclosed that Trujillo was short of arms and ammunition.[22] This conformed with information that Bosch was receiving from his own sources inside the Dominican Republic.[23]

Confident of his support from Betancourt, Lescot, and Prío, and collaborating with Viriato Fiallo, one of the leaders of the clandestine opposition in the Dominican Republic,[24] Bosch organized a coup for February 1946, to be triggered by an attempt on Trujillo's life. The American embassy in Caracas reported that Bosch met with rival exile leaders Morales and Jiménez Grullón in Caracas on February 19, 1946, to set into motion a plan to assassinate Trujillo sometime between February 24 and March 8. They intended to ambush the tyrant on Avenida George Washington, "near the monument," when he drove to one of his "nocturnal trysts."[25] (Oddly enough, this is precisely the way that Trujillo was slain on May 30, 1961.) The plot allegedly involved a cabinet member and a high-ranking army officer. On February 25, George Scherer cabled from Ciudad Trujillo that an assassination plot indeed was in the works and might happen "within two weeks." He added that Bosch was in Port-au-Prince "awaiting the opportunity to enter the Dominican Republic."[26]

The plot to kill Trujillo did not materialize. Four men armed with Thompson submachine guns planned to eliminate Trujillo on February 27 (National Independence Day), but the plotters canceled the action.[27] The explanation given was the rise of a "momentary hope" that a peaceful change of government was possible, citing the publication of José Bonilla Atiles's letter in *La Opinión* (the leaking of Braden's aide-mémoire may also have been a factor); more likely someone got cold feet. Also, Trujillo's secret service may have gotten wind of the operation.[28] In support of the latter probability, throughout the following month the U.S. embassy reported a government crackdown, observing that Trujillo was "moving heaven and earth" to destroy "the opposition clandestine movement."[29] The situation was especially bad in La Vega Province, where two persons were reported killed and another forty were thrown in jail.[30]

The overthrow of Lescot in Haiti in January may also have sabotaged the operation. On March 9, Jiménez Grullón traveled to Haiti hoping to persuade the succeeding military junta of government to honor Lescot's promise to cooperate with Bosch, but he had no luck. He asked the Haitians to permit an advance team of twenty "well-trained" Dominican exiles to take up positions at "strategic points" along the border, stockpiling arms, and to authorize a landing "at a point near the frontier" from which to launch an armed attack against Trujillo, to take place "within the next two months."[31]

In tracking these events U.S. representatives in Ciudad Trujillo confirmed the existence of a "well-organized" clandestine movement and asserted that it possessed funds amounting to approximately half a million dollars.[32] The "angel" putting up this money was General Juan Rodríguez García, who had fled the Dominican Republic on February 1, 1946. Bosch, in organizing the conspiracy, had sent an emissary to Rodríguez who influenced his decision to go into exile.[33] Though "Juancito" Rodríguez, as he was generally known, had only a supporting role in the February plot, in time he became a major player in the antidictatorial struggle in the Caribbean.

General Rodríguez Takes Charge

There is a general consensus that Rodríguez was the "spark" that united the Dominican exile leaders and groups.[34] Rodríguez was a wealthy cattle rancher in La Vega, with holdings valued at three to four million dollars, making him the second richest man in the Dominican Republic, just behind Trujillo.[35] He had the title of general, having led troops in the revolution of 1912, but at age sixty-five he was essentially retired and was trying to stay out of Trujillo's way. As a member of Trujillo's Dominican party, he had served as a deputy from La Vega in the National Congress (1934 to 1942) and was among those voting in 1936 to change the name of the capital city from Santo Domingo to Ciudad Trujillo.[36] As late as November 18, 1945, Rodríguez organized a demonstration in La Vega in support of Trujillo against the "insulting behavior" of the "Communist" Rómulo Betancourt (the Venezuelan junta of government refused to have diplomatic relations with the Dominican government),[37] but it was a game of cat and mouse in which Trujillo watched closely for any sign of disloyalty on the part of this high-profile citizen. In addition, Rodríguez had something Trujillo wanted: the greedy dictator was rustling his cattle.[38] Rodríguez's situation was becoming untenable, and he was already thinking about fleeing the country when Bosch's agent contacted him.

Clearing his plans with legal confidants and leaders of the Internal Front, namely, Viriato Fiallo, Rodríguez devised a scheme to leave the country and take a sizable fortune with him. He called on Trujillo in January to inform him that he needed to go to Puerto Rico for treatment of an ailment affecting his mouth and, while there, also wished to purchase some special breeds of cattle to restock his diminishing herds, requesting approval to withdraw $200,000 for that purpose.[39] Trujillo, who was delighted to get the chance to steal some more cattle, willingly permitted Rodríguez to go and authorized the necessary transfer of funds abroad. Once in Puerto Rico, Rodríguez resettled in Havana and began to bankroll the exile conspiracies. Before his deception was revealed, Rodríguez allegedly withdrew a total of $500,000.[40] Trujillo finally grew suspicious about his activities in October 1946, causing Juancito's son, José Horacio, a graduate of Harvard Law School, to deny any wrongdoing and to offer to go abroad and return with his father, "on his word of honor," also escaping the dictator's clutches in this way.[41]

In the meantime Rodríguez, "the wise, old 'angel,'"[42] was busy purchasing arms for an invasion of the Dominican Republic. The filibustering option was on again. Rodríguez, with a big bundle of cash, Bosch, with covert relationships with three Caribbean presidents, and Morales, with well-established political assets and friends in Washington (Sumner Welles), met during the summer of 1946 and achieved a "working agreement," uniting them at least in the effort "to pull down Trujillo from his throne."[43] Before the year's end they had elaborated a grandiose plan for overthrowing Trujillo consisting of a principal force attacking by sea from Cuba; a second front opened by armed elements proceeding from Haiti; air strikes from Cuba against such targets as the Ozama Fortress, General Andrews Airport, and the Sans Soucí Naval Base; and fifth-column activities by the Internal Front in collaboration with dissident military elements.[44]

Even though Bosch and Morales each expected to be the next president of the Dominican Republic, Rodríguez exercised the role of commander in chief of the liberation army, without question. He established his headquarters in the Hotel San Luis in Havana, whose proprietor, Cruz Alonso, a Spanish refugee, served as innkeeper for virtually every Caribbean Quijote in those times.[45] General Rodríguez worked "day and night—at all hours" to create a movement "so large that it came to be spectacular."[46] Through the intervention of President Arévalo of Guatemala he acquired at least a thousand Mauser rifles from, of all people, Juan Perón of Argentina, along with at least a million rounds of ammunition.[47] Arévalo, who had lived in exile in Argentina for about ten years, apparently deceived Perón, telling him that he needed the weapons to defend his government against "the Yankee imperialists," but once the guns arrived in Puerto Barrios he forwarded them to Rodríguez in Cuba, who had put up the cash for them.[48]

Bosch likewise busied himself shopping for arms for the expedition, using Rodríguez's money plus the funds he got from Lescot.[49] He organized a small air cargo service as cover, Aerovía Cubana Norte Americana (ACNA), and initially acquired three aircraft, a DC-3, a Cessna, and an AT-13, enabling him to airlift "war surplus" arms purchased in the United States.[50] Though "large quantities" of arms were brought into Cuba through "regular channels" with the connivance of Cuban customs officials,[51] Bosch and a hired pilot, Edward William Murphy, used a small, private airfield at Santa Fé for clandestine flights carrying "to and from the U.S. arms and men, especially emissaries who needed to act in secret."[52] Bosch further called upon his partisans in the PRD section in New York City for help in the arms buildup.

Nicolás Silfa, one of the PRD leaders in New York, who had just completed three years of service in the U.S. armed forces, collected and stored bombs and high explosives in Manhattan during 1946 and 1947, endangering the lives of thousands of innocent people.[53] Though he tended to be melodramatic, Silfa told about having forty-eight "high-powered aerial bombs" in a warehouse at 67th Street and West-End Avenue in December 1946, when a fire broke out in the adjoining building. The fire was extinguished before it spread to Silfa's cache, but he visualized "entire families being blown to bits and flying through the air in the city of New York."[54] As the result of Silfa's work, two vessels sailed from New York for Cuba at the beginning of 1947 loaded with weapons and carrying "a good number of men, almost all of whom were World War II veterans."[55] Silfa followed them in June, but in the meantime he continued to drive around Manhattan in an unmarked truck loaded with high-powered explosives and to store bombs and other dangerous devices in crowded neighborhoods.[56]

The Arms of the Expedition

By the time that what came to be the Liberation Army of America was ready to set sail and take off (August–September 1947), it had amassed an arsenal that had no equal in the history of filibustering in the Caribbean. For the amphibious assault on the Dominican Republic, the expedition consisted of a fleet of seven vessels, not all of which actually took part in the operation, as follows: *Aurora,* identified as a landing craft, tank (LCT), that Cruz Alonso purchased in the United States on behalf of Rodríguez and that arrived in Cuba in mid-July 1947; *Berta,* a 100-foot, diesel-powered "assault ship" of the type used by the U.S. Army during World War II for air-sea rescue, this one built in 1944 by the Ventnor Boat Works of Atlantic City, New Jersey; *Máximo Gómez* (nicknamed *Fantasma*), identified as a landing craft, infantry (LCI), a 158-foot, seagoing vessel capable of carrying 200 troops, that arrived in Cuba on August 29, 1947, sailing from Elizabeth City, North Carolina; *Maceo,* formerly the *Angelita,* a 120-foot, steel-hulled, Dominican schooner seized by the expeditionaries in international waters off Cuba and pressed into auxiliary service; *La Victoria,* a 75-foot schooner, an auxiliary vessel that was lost at the end of July, running aground in Nipe Bay; and *R-41* and *R-42,* two patrol torpedo (PT) boats committed to the expedition by the Cuban Navy and moored at the Mariel Naval Base.

Then there was the ship that wasn't: *Patria,* an LCI purchased by Rodríguez's agent, Cruz Alonso. U.S. customs officers impounded the vessel in Baltimore, Maryland, at the beginning of August 1947, at the behest of the State Department. The missing *Patria* affected critically the outcome of the expedition.[57]

For its planned air raids, the expedition assembled a variety of aircraft that, if truly armed and operational, could do a lot of damage, coming to a total of sixteen: six P-38 Lightning fighters; one B-24 Liberator bomber; two

B-25 Mitchell bombers; two Vega Venturas (an updated version of the B-14 Hudson bomber); one C-46 Curtiss Commando troop carrier and cargo plane; two C-78 Cessna cargo planes; and two C-47 Skytrain/"Goonie" paratroop and cargo planes (military version of the Douglas DC-3).[58] Silfa, who was a pilot, recalled that the movement had a few other planes, including three P-51 Mustang fighters, but no other source supports this claim (see Fig. 1).[59]

For the main assault, the Liberation Army possessed enough arms, ammunition, and equipment to outfit two thousand men if necessary. As in the case of the planes and ships, 1946 and 1947 provided Rodríguez and his cohorts with an unprecedented opportunity to procure serious weapons at bargain prices. The thousand Mauser-type rifles (possibly 1,500) acquired from Perón through Arévalo were the core element.[60] But the inventory of armaments (including appropriate ammunition) contained just about everything needed for a successful revolution: fifty machine guns, Danish Masden design, manufactured in Argentina; at least 200 Thompson submachine guns; Colt .45 automatic pistols ("enough for everyone"); ten automatic rifles (probably obtained in the Arévalo-Perón gambit); fifteen bazookas, with 300 bazooka rockets; several hundred bombs of various types and sizes, from 5 to 300 pounds, and, according to Silfa, even some 500-pound bombs, or "blockbusters"; three 81mm. mortars; three 37mm. antitank guns; 2,000 hand grenades; and enough U.S. Army-style steel helmets to equip the force, plus miscellaneous equipment ranging from generators, radios, and jeeps to field glasses, walkie-talkies, and machetes.[61]

The Cuban Allies

Rodríguez accumulated this stockpile of weapons and organized the Liberation Army with the "complete knowledge and cooperation" of high officials of the Grau administration.[62] President Grau "knew all about the expedition" and gave it his "blessing."[63] Moved by sentiments of personal ambition, hatred for Trujillo, and the wish to repay Cuba's debt to Máximo Gómez (the Dominican general who fought for Cuban independence), Grau's lieutenants embraced the movement to the point of suffocating it.[64] Grau's principal agent in channeling aid to the Dominicans was José Alemán, the minister of education, who was the President's favorite and heir apparent. Alemán was part of the BAGA (Bloque Alemán-Grau-Alsina), the

El Jefe de Estado Mayor
General del Ejército MEMORANDUM

al

Honorable Sr. Ministro de Estado.

De acuerdo con la petición verbal que usted hubo de hacerme, tengo
el honor de informarle que el material de guerra ocupado a los expedi-
cionarios de "Cayo Confites" y que actualmente se encuentra en el Cuer-
po de Aviación y distribuido en otras Unidades del Ejército, es el que
a continuación se relaciona:

        1 B-24, ocupado en Rancho Boyeros.
        6 P-38, ocupados 5 en el Mariel y 1 en Campo Brihuegas
        1 C-46, ocupado en el Mariel.
        2 B-34, ocupados en Rancho Boyeros.
        2 B-25, ocupados en el Mariel.
      130 fusiles "Argentinos"
        5 fusiles automáticos.
       50 fusiles "Kraggss" …
   27,000 cápsulas calibre 30.
        9 cajas de lata portátiles conteniendo granadas
          de 81 m.m. En total: 27 (3 vacías)
        4 cajas de granadas para morteros de 81 m.m. En
          total: 153
        2 cajas de cargas fraccionarias para morteros -
          de 81 m.m. (Una de las mismas incompleta)
        3 Morteros de trincheras, con sus trípodes y planchas.
        3 picos.
        3 palas de hierro.
        9 granadas para Morteros de 3 pulgadas (81 Mmts)
        2 cargadores para morteros.
        1 estuche para Morteros.
        1 Baqueta para Morteros.
        3 placas para Morteros.
        4 Bazzokas.

                    De usted respetuosamente,

                        R. Cabrera

Fig. 1. A partial listing of "Cayo Confites" arms seized by the Cuban government in
September 1947.

corrupt inner circle that was destroying the soul of the Grau administration,
and he headed the Revolutionary Socialist Movement (MSR), one of the
most powerful and dangerous *pistolero* groups functioning in Cuba. Alemán
reportedly siphoned off three million dollars of his ministry's funds to support the buildup of the Liberation Army, and he provided buildings, trucks
and buses, and other facilities for the operation.[65]

Alemán's chief aide, in turn, was Manolo Castro, the national sports director (Ministry of Education). As a star athlete (indicating that his appointment was not exclusively political [*botella*]), the former president of the
Havana University Students Federation and MSR gunman, Castro signed up
hundreds of Cuban youths for the anti-Trujillo adventure, using the José
Martí Sports Park and other school sites for recruiting stations.[66] He took on
the job of buying airplanes in the United States and of hiring veteran American pilots, leading to his conviction (posthumously) in U.S. Federal Court in
Jacksonville, Florida, in March 1948, charged with the illegal export of
arms.[67]

Convicted with Castro and Miguel Angel Ramírez (whose story will unfold) was Hollis B. Smith, an American citizen, World War II veteran, and
explosives expert. In July 1946 Smith started working for Silfa and Ramírez,
the Dominican exiles in New York, manufacturing and preparing bombs
and rockets. Smith, Castro, and Ramírez carted a quantity of explosives to
Baltimore in July 1947, intending to transport them to Cuba on board the
LCI *Patria,* but instead flew them to Cuba one step ahead of U.S. authorities when the ship was seized, leading to their subsequent conviction on
gunrunning charges.[68]

Smith swore that Alemán "bragged" to him about "personally" organizing
the liberation movement, which enabled him to learn a great deal about
Alemán's role and that of the MSR in preparing the expeditionary force. He
claimed that Alemán promoted the invasion plan as a means of winning
popularity and improving his chances for the Cuban presidency.[69] Alemán
stored a portion of the Liberation Army's weapons on his finca, América,
just outside Havana, and he assigned MSR *pistoleros* Castro and Rolando
Masferrer virtually full time to the conspiracy. Masferrer, described as "one
of the leading schismatic Communist intellectuals in Havana,"[70] had been
thrown out of the Communist party in August 1945, helping then to organize the MSR. He had served in the International Brigade in the Spanish
Civil War and at the time was editor of the weekly magazine *Tiempo en
Cuba.*[71]

Another Cuban Spanish Civil War veteran, who was MSR and had an
active part in preparing the expedition, was Eufemio Fernández, the chief
of the national secret police. The odd thing about Fernández was that,
although he was MSR, he was much closer to Carlos Prío Socarrás, the
minister of labor, than to Alemán. Over time, despite whatever official position he held, Fernández's main function was to serve as Prío's bodyguard.[72]
Prío was Alemán's principal rival for the *Auténtico* presidential nomination

in 1948 and, although not as active in the filibustering scheme as Alemán, he clearly was not going to let the Education Minister get the upper hand on him. He rendered assistance and monitored the situation, obviously through Fernández, but also through Bosch, whom he kept on retainer (*botella*) and relied upon as "an idea man," and through his brother-in-law, Enrique Cotubanamá Henríquez, the Dominican-Cuban who served as his "liaison man" with the expedition.[73]

President Grau also had a "liaison man" with the expedition: Captain Jorge Felipe Agostini of the Cuban Navy and chief of the Presidential Palace Guard. Agostini also had fought in Spain and his activities on behalf of the Dominican exile movement demonstrated the deep involvement of the navy in the conspiracy.[74] Commodore José Aguila Ruiz, the navy's commanding officer, "knew about the movement from the beginning" and assisted it every step of the way. He provided intelligence reports and officially intervened in Cruz Alonso's efforts to purchase landing craft in the United States.[75] Smith claimed that he landed at the Mariel Naval Base when he made his illegal flight and that the munitions on board were then taken to Alemán's finca in navy trucks driven by navy personnel.[76] Most of the expedition's P-38s were parked at Mariel, as were the two PT boats mentioned before, and the American pilots had use of Mariel's facilities.[77]

Mobilizing the Force

By July 1947 everything seemed to be falling into place. The Dominican exiles had been meeting weekly in the clinic of Dr. Romano Pérez Cabral, which Miolán described as the "cradle" of the anti-Trujillo movement in the "land of Martí," and about two hundred of them were ready to go.[78] Now, Rodríguez and his Cuban and Dominican allies and backers agreed, was the time to complete the finishing touches and get it all into writing. They met from July 10 to July 17 to draft a formal statute and elect the Dominican Revolutionary Central Committee to lead the invasion and serve as the junta of government. Angel Morales, Juan Rodríguez, Juan Bosch, Leovigildo Cuello, and Juan Isidro Jiménez Grullón accepted election to the Central Committee and pledged "to carry out an armed revolution in the Dominican Republic" for the purpose of overthrowing the "tyrant" Trujillo and establishing a revolutionary government that "will guarantee the well-being of the Dominican people . . . and collaborate in the struggle for the establishment of democracy in all the countries of America."[79] Morales was elected president of the Central Committee, and Rodríguez was named commander in chief and chief of staff of the Liberation Army, with the Dominicans Alexis Liz and Luis Bordas appointed executive officer of the general staff and adjutant to the chief of staff, respectively.[80]

At this point Alemán, Masferrer, and Castro shifted into high gear, stepping up the recruiting and raising a force of twelve- to thirteen-hundred men.[81] An overwhelming number of the volunteers were Cubans, identified as MSR, though a few members of the rival *pistolero* group, the Revolutionary Insurrectional Union (UIR), also joined up, including Fidel Castro Ruz, a twenty-one-year-old Havana University student leader beginning to make his mark. Young men like Fidel Castro and José Luis Wanguemert, another Havana University student, showed up at the José Martí Sports Park, the Hotel San Luis, or the Sports Palace anxious to enlist and begin training. Students, workers, and professional men answered the call to arms, "along with simple men from the fields."[82] In fact, so many answered the call that Alemán authorized the encampment of the expeditionary force on the spacious and more remote campus of the Polytechnic School in Holguín in order to permit training in one place at one time. Wanguemert, who traveled to Holguín by rail on July 22, wrote in his diary: "The State provided *guaguas* (buses), automobiles, and railroad tickets, making possible the transportation of almost 1,200 men in less than a week. The American Liberating Revolution was on the march."[83]

But something else prompted the move to Holguín: the Liberation Army was attracting too much attention. Rumors about preparations for an exile invasion of the Dominican Republic were flying all over Havana. The Dominican chargé in Havana, Héctor Incháustegui Cabral, whose dispatches were always colorful, if not reliable, asserted that he did not need "special sources" (spies) to find out what was going on, because he heard it "on the street, in cafés, from bootblacks and taxi drivers," and read it in the newspapers "everyday."[84] He reported that the mothers of the volunteers had published a petition calling on the Cuban government to stop the expedition from sailing.[85] And now Trujillo knew.

The Diplomatic Front

The first diplomatic note of protest from Arturo Despradel, the Dominican foreign minister, to Rafael P. González Muñoz, the foreign minister of Cuba, was dated July 23, 1947. It is odd that this was the Dominican government's first reaction since November 1946 to what was going on; yet it shows how fast things were moving since the formation of the Revolutionary Central Committee and the mobilization of the expeditionary force. Despradel related in the most careful diplomatic language what the Dominican government knew about the preparations for an armed invasion and expressed confidence that the Cuban government would attend to the matter appropriately.[86] González Muñoz replied that the Cuban government would look into it.

Despradel, obviously not satisfied, decided to turn up the heat. He instructed the Dominican ambassador before the United Nations to bring the matter to the attention of UN Secretary General Trygve Lie and requested Ambassador Julio Ortega Frier in Washington to make a call at the State Department. Ortega told Assistant Secretary Norman Armour (Braden's successor) about the "imminent invasion" of the Dominican Republic by a "well-armed" revolutionary force proceeding from Cuba and complained that the "anti-Trujillo" attitude of the United States was encouraging the movement.[87] Armour rejected the idea that U.S. policy was a factor in stirring up dissident elements and related that the United States had been receiving reports for the past six months about revolutionary plotting in the Caribbean, one of which concerned an armed attack against Venezuela based in the Dominican Republic, with evidence that U.S. citizens had abetted the movement through illegal arms exports, and that indictments were likely.[88]

As Armour said, the United States had been tracking revolutionary activities in the Caribbean all year. Oddly, the reports from Frank P. Corrigan, the U.S. ambassador in Caracas, had more to say about these conspiracies than those from R. Henry Norweb, the U.S. ambassador in Havana. This was probably the case because the most intense activity during the first half of the year, especially during March and April, involved the plotting by Trujillo and Eleazar López Contreras against Rómulo Betancourt, and because C. M. Lamarche, the key Dominican exile leader in Caracas, had a bad habit of sharing secrets with U.S. embassy personnel. For example, he told First Secretary Thomas J. Maleady on March 30 that he had "abandoned all hope" of overthrowing Trujillo by force because "Juancito" Rodríguez was having trouble acquiring arms and raising a large enough force.[89]

The embassy in Ciudad Trujillo also had special sources. Butler cabled the Secretary of State on January 29, six months before Trujillo's alarm, that Viriato Fiallo had visited and related that Juan Rodríguez was active in exile "organizing a powerful movement against Trujillo."[90] And a May 24 intelligence report filed by the Third Army's G-2 field office in Miami contained certain pieces of the puzzle related to Cruz Alonso's arms shopping trip to Argentina and the acquisition of the assault ship *Berta* by Rodríguez.[91] On the same day, the Guatemalan ambassador to the United States, Jorge García Granados, told Braden that President Arévalo was "so disgusted" with Trujillo's rigged reelection of May 16 that he intended to "quietly" send the Dominican ambassador packing, in effect rupturing relations.[92] American officials had not yet put it all together, but these documents fixed the timing of Arévalo's decision to aid Rodríguez and gave a clue to the use of the *Berta* for transferring Perón's rifles from Guatemala to Rodríguez in Cuba.[93] Norweb seemed to get wind of these events belatedly (though still ahead of Trujillo), calling on González Muñoz on July 17 to inquire if there was any truth to the rumors of an armed invasion being prepared in Cuba against the Dominican Republic.[94] He cabled two days later that Bosch was reportedly in Santiago with 150 men ready to set sail "toward Haiti" in order to overthrow Trujillo.[95]

From the standpoint of U.S. policy, Rodríguez, Bosch et al. had picked a bad time to finally launch their invasion. Braden, in eclipse for most of 1947, had resigned in June. Ellis Briggs, concerned that Secretary of State Marshall might relax Braden's policy of not selling arms to dictators, sent a memo to the Secretary on July 7 describing Trujillo as the "most despicable and least principled dictator in the hemisphere" and recommending "no change" in the arms policy. He also advised against the sending of a special delegation to Trujillo's inauguration in August, even if requested.[96] Briggs's concerns were justified; Marshall was already fighting the Cold War and his focus in Latin America was on the upcoming conference (August 15) in Rio de Janeiro to conclude the Inter-American Reciprocal Assistance Treaty. Seeing a parallel between the filibustering activities in the Caribbean and the armed incursions from neighboring countries occurring against Greece, which had evoked the Truman Doctrine,[97] Marshall conceded that sending a special delegation to Trujillo's inauguration might be inappropriate but "for practical reasons" approved lifting the absolute ban on arms sales to Trujillo, effectively scrapping the Braden corollary.[98]

Thus, when the Dominican Republic lodged its protest on July 23 and Ambassador Norweb submitted a detailed report two days later exposing the conspiratorial activities of Bosch, Rodríguez, Manolo Castro, and certain Cuban naval officers,[99] Marshall reacted forcefully. He instructed Norweb to go directly to President Grau and express U.S. concern about a possible breach of the peace in the hemisphere. After the usual polite disclaimers, specifically, "we are certain he shares our preoccupation" and "we in no way believe his Government has anything to do with the alleged revolutionary conspiracy," Marshall was insistent that Grau must investigate the plot, "leaving no stone unturned," with the expectation that if he discovered its existence "he would crush it rapidly and effectively."[100] The Cuban government denied any knowledge of the worst-kept secret in Havana but recognized the need to do a better job of covering its tracks.

The Move to the Cay

Following the express orders of President Grau,[101] the Liberation Army of America evacuated Holguín on July 28 and retreated to Cayo Confites, a tiny isle off the east coast of Cuba, to complete its training and organization. Cayo Confites is too small to appear on most maps, other than the most detailed of navigation charts, but it put a label on the expedition ; . last. A parcel of land about 800 meters long and 200 meters wide at its widest point, and just barely sticking out of the sea, Cayo Confites is located northeast of Nuevitas at 77° 39′ west longitude, 22° 12′ north latitude.

Exposed to the tropical sun and rain, none of the expeditionaries had anything good to say about the place. Miolán noted its lack of cover and its scarce vegetation, namely, a few sickly mangrove trees and "some stretches of grama grass and purslane, barberry, half a dozen coconut palms, a lone pine tree on the dockside, next to a small natural beach."[102] Silfa called it "Devil's island, the most inhospitable place on the Cuban coast."[103]

In truth, it was home for an old fisherman, Ismael Montenegro, and his family and a few goats, but it was not intended to accommodate a thousand-plus inhabitants. With no fresh water or shelter (not even tents), the leaders erred if they meant to keep the men there for any length of time. They showed a lack of experience in maintaining a force in the field, especially with reference to sanitary facilities and waste disposal. Silfa said the men "refused to imitate the cat," to make holes in the sand to relieve themselves and cover it up. "They preferred to go in the bushes at one end of the island."[104] The place became a stinking mess in no time, breeding hordes of mosquitoes and flies, and raising the spectre of disease. "Some persons, Cotubanamá Henríquez among them, had to be taken to the mainland, ill with gastroenteritis or typhoid fever."[105] In order to eat their rations, the men went into the water waist-deep to escape the flies.

Giving evidence of the hastiness of the retreat to Cayo Confites, the expedition ran dangerously short of food and water in the first week, before the *Berta* established a regular run to Nuevitas and the Cuban Navy began bringing supplies and even delivering the mail.[106] Once the troops started eating and had improvised rustic shelters ("*chabolas*"), little more than a frame cover of branches and thatch, life settled into a routine. Miolán, Silfa, Wanguemert, and Tulio Arvelo, a Dominican volunteer who also wrote about the adventure, all told the soldier's story of lousy food, miserable conditions, gruelling training, and boredom. "We recall only those days when something important happened," wrote Wanguermert. "The rest is a blur, consisting of marches and drills and formations, which we did over and over again until we did it mechanically."[107] Silfa related that the training was "fierce," practicing "hitting the beach" from the landing craft, that the sand caused blisters on his feet, and that the heat, day and night, was "oppressive."[108]

The force formed four battalions, each named for a revolutionary hero, with a lieutenant colonel commanding: "Antonio Guiteras," under Eufemio Fernández, the Spanish Civil War veteran and Prío's top gunsel; "Luperón," commanded by Jorge Rivas Montes, a Honduran national and professional military officer, who fled to Guatemala after spending two and a half years in jail following the unsuccessful coup attempt against Tiburcio Carías in November 1943 (Hollis Smith claimed Rivas Montes held the rank of captain in the Guatemalan Army and was on active duty with pay[109]); "Máximo Gómez," led by Diego Bordas, one of the principal Dominican exile leaders in Puerto Rico and, according to Miolán, a graduate of West Point[110] (though he may have confused him with his brother, Luis Manuel, also living in Puerto Rico and on active duty in the U.S. Army[111]); and "Sandino," in the charge of Rolando Masferrer, the highest-ranking MSR leader on the island.

Certain Dominican volunteers rallied to form a fifth battalion, not as large as the others, which they called the "José María Cabral" and placed under the command of Miguel Angel Ramírez. Ramírez had been living in exile in New York since 1930, where he had been a vice consul at the time Trujillo seized power and "refused to return home to serve the dictator."[112] He earned his living as a commission merchant, wholesaling bananas, but dabbled in exile politics and got swept up in the anti-Trujillo movement. In an effort to discredit him, the Dominican government claimed that when the

United States entered World War II he tried to get a Dominican passport for his wife, a German citizen. Being refused the passport, Trujillo's spokesman alleged, "was motive enough" for him to begin "subversive" activities against the Dominican government.[113] The formation of this exclusive unit revealed the growing apart of the Dominicans and Cubans on the island.

As the month of August waned, and no one among the troops had any idea of when D-day would be, morale sank, tempers were on edge, and factionalism became a problem.[114] In order to maintain discipline, Masferrer, whom Silfa nicknamed "the Tiger," took over the movement and became "the absolute dictator" of Cayo Confites.[115] Alexis Liz, the chief of staff, upbraided Rodríguez for letting this happen, and the two men actually drew their pistols for one tense moment.[116] Juan Bosch, a personal and political enemy of Masferrer, was especially affected by this situation. He isolated himself at one end of the island in order to avoid Masferrer, and Miolán and Ramírez set up an around-the-clock vigil to protect him from possible assassination.[117] Even so, according to Silfa, Masferrer was determined to punish Bosch for his "insubordination" and, though he did not get Rodríguez's approval to shoot Bosch on the spot, allegedly the General agreed to it "as the first order of business" upon reaching the Dominican Republic.[118]

In assessing the Cayo Confites affair after it was over, the U.S. embassy staff in Havana cited this divided leadership as a powerful factor in causing the eventual failure, noting that the leadership passed from the "idealistic" Dominicans, Rodríguez and Bosch, to the Cuban "gangsters," Alemán and Masferrer.[119] "What's in it for me?" was the way the embassy described the latter's attitude. Down at the soldiers' level the Dominican Arvelo had these same doubts about the Cubans, recalling rumors about some of them having maps of Ciudad Trujillo on which they had marked the locations of the banks and principal jewelry stores. The Dominicans, feeling outgunned, were fearful that the "criminal elements" among the Cubans planned to go on a "looting spree" under cover of the liberation movement.[120] But the truth was, no one was going anywhere. They had become prisoners of a sort—castaways—marooned on a desert island.

The expedition's move to Cayo Confites on July 28 disrupted the timetable for invading the Dominican Republic. D-day may have been intended for mid-August, prior to the Rio Conference and Trujillo's inauguration. The move was a setback, and the confusion surrounding it contributed to the detention of the LCI *Patria* in Baltimore in the first week of August. This vessel was vital to the operation; without it the movement was stuck. The Cuban ambassador in the United States and high-ranking naval officers tried vainly to have the *Patria* released,[121] but it remained in Baltimore, paralyzing the expedition and giving time for other elements to come into play and ultimately threaten the operation.

Enter the Villain

Diplomatic pressure by the United States and the Dominican Republic influenced Grau's decision to order the expedition to leave the mainland, but internal politics had much to do with it as well. On July 23 General Fausto E. Caamaño, the Dominican Army chief of staff, took the extraordinary step of communicating directly with General Genovevo Pérez Dámera, the Cuban Army chief of staff, stating, "Although I assume you are aware of the military preparations taking place in Cuba for the purpose of invading our territory, I wish to notify you officially for the record."[122] There was an earlier unconfirmed report in April that Trujillo had contacted Pérez Dámera seeking his collaboration in preventing Dominican exiles from using Cuba as a base of operations against the Dominican Republic, but, if so, it had no effect, because the army's role through mid-year had been generally passive, and Pérez Dámera apparently was not in the loop.

Now, with this message in hand, Pérez Dámera confronted Grau, who appeared surprised that he did not know more about what was going on and, in a "teasing" manner, asked Alemán "to bring the General up-to-date."[123] Pérez Dámera was close to Grau and loyal, but he detested Alemán, probably because he also had presidential ambitions and also because he was outraged over the behavior of *pistolero* groups like the MSR; besides, Grau erred in making sport of the General in front of his bitter enemy. Making the best of his humiliation, he reportedly declared that the expedition "ought to leave Cuba soon" or he would disband it as a "threat to the peace,"[124] which, in addition to other pressures, may have triggered the move to Cayo Confites, where the navy exercised jurisdiction. But Pérez Dámera still had reach; on August 23 he seized a rebel P-38 that missed the Mariel airfield and landed at the army airport at Camp Columbia by mistake.[125] For good reason, the expeditionaries felt uneasy and "concerned" about the army chieftain's potential to do them harm.[126]

The United States in "Watchful Waiting"

The developing rift within the Cuban government relieved Ambassador Norweb, but he became alarmed anew at the beginning of August, when he and the U.S. Navy lost track of the expedition on-the-move, which caused him to believe that President Grau had betrayed him. Norweb had been assured by Grau on July 28 that he would take "energetic measures" to stop the exile revolutionary activity,[127] but in follow-up meetings with Foreign Minister González Muñoz, the Ambassador ran into a stonewall. He possessed evidence that the expedition had departed Nipe Bay "in three vessels" and concluded bitterly that Cuba was unwilling to cooperate with the United States on this or any matter.[128] Adding to Norweb's frustration was the fact that he had no idea of the whereabouts of the expedition, and González Muñoz was not telling.[129] Under Secretary of State Robert Lovett was upset over the lack of intelligence about these developments and complained to Roscoe Hillenkoetter, the director of the newly created Central Intelligence Agency.[130]

On August 1 Secretary of State Marshall requested Secretary of National Defense James Forrestal to have the navy provide "reconnaissance service" to monitor the "reported expedition" and keep State "continuously advised." He wanted "no show of force" and suggested the use of PT boats "to tail each of the three vessels."[131] But they searched in the wrong place; on the assumption that the expedition was en route to the Dominican Republic or else to Haiti in preparation for a land incursion, the navy patrolled to the east of Nipe Bay, whereas the Liberation Army had actually sailed in the opposite direction to Cayo Confites.

Ciudad Trujillo was under the same assumption, causing a state of high anxiety. The U.S. army attaché reported the sounds of machine gun fire for several minutes around the Ozama Fortress on August 3, and the scrambling of two aircraft, but he could only speculate that the cause may have been nervous sentries or a provocation to smoke out the suspected underground.[132] Not even Trujillo's crack agent in Havana, Alfonso Luis Fors, a private detective and former police official under Gerardo Machado, knew the whereabouts of the expedition, but he tried too hard to find out and was killed by "*pistoleros*" on August 5 in a drive-by shooting.[133] Amidst the confusion the State Department knew where only one ship was, the *Patria* in Baltimore, and was determined to keep it there.[134]

On the evening of August 6, Juan Bosch called at the home of an officer of the American embassy in Havana to try to persuade him to secure the release of the *Patria,* declaring that "it was vital for the success of the movement."[135] In an effort to show his seriousness and absolute confidence in the success of the movement Bosch outlined the plans for the invasion and overthrow of Trujillo, including information that they intended to come ashore in five different places and the conviction that the majority of the army would come over to their side "once the attack began."[136] How much of this was true is speculative; what was certain, however, was that even if the location of the expedition was still unknown, the embargo on the *Patria* in Baltimore gave the United States more leverage. Bosch's revelation that there were to be five landing sites, among them two on the south coast, was partially confirmed by Wanguemert, who talked about advancing up George Washington Avenue in the capital city.[137] However, years later, Miolán scoffed at the idea. "Look at the map," he suggested, implying that the only feasible sites were on the north coast.[138]

In any case, the amphibious landings were to be accompanied by air strikes, and there is evidence that the planes were not ready to go. The expedition's aircraft were too sophisticated for the available personnel; the P-38 airplane is a weapons system that requires not just pilots but a great deal of ground support for maintenance, arming, mounting bomb racks, etc. Norweb reported that the rebels would have been better off using "transport planes" and tossing their bombs out the door. "They could have been ready in a matter of days," he observed, "instead of weeks."[139]

After almost two weeks of being in the dark Norweb reported the location of the expedition on Cayo Confites. The break came not from reconnaissance flights but from the British minister in Havana. Four British subjects, crew members of the LCT *Aurora,* jumped ship in Nuevitas on August 6 and made a sworn statement in the British Legation in Havana two days later. The minister gave Norweb a copy on August 11 (there was no explanation for the apparent delay in notifying Norweb).[140] The men had signed on in New York at the end of June with "M.A. Ramírez, an importer of tropical fruit" and sailed for Cuba on the *Aurora* (actually, the *Libertad* at the time) on July 9. After arriving at Nipe Bay, instead of loading bananas, they spent their time transferring munitions to their ship from another (the *Berta*) and then, on July 31, transported the weapons and four hundred armed men in uniform to a place called Cayo Confites. They remained there about five days, virtual prisoners, observing the military training, which they described as strict. When the *Aurora* sailed to Nuevitas on August 5 for provisions, they managed to escape "with only the clothes they were wearing" and sought out the British vice-consul, who listened to their story and arranged for them to travel to Havana.[141]

Shortly after receiving this report, the U.S. Navy at Guantánamo began daily reconnaissance flights over the rebel base at Cayo Confites, observing the figures below like creatures in an ant farm. Norweb forwarded to Washington two aerial photos taken on August 14 showing "the encampment, some of the personnel, and an LCT on the beach."[142] The reports became routine: on August 16 "the revolutionary forces were still there."[143] And a week later: "Still there, . . . practicing landings."[144] Looking up at the planes, the men on the ground were demoralized; being watched in this way filled them with an overwhelming sense of failure.[145] Norweb also monitored the status of the rebel P-38s parked at Mariel, with some of the intelligence coming from overflights, without protest from the usually sensitive Cuban government. He was certain that the lack of readiness of the P-38s was now (as of August 23) the "principal cause" holding up the invasion.[146]

The men hired to fly the planes were a problem, too. Manolo Castro and others recruited them mainly in the United States for $10,000 ($5,000 up front; $5,000 after the mission).[147] Some allegedly were former Flying Tigers, with colorful names (probably fictitious) like Tex Talbot and Buck Templeton.[148] One pilot landed a B-24 Liberator at Rancho Boyeros, Havana's principal airport, on July 31, without clearance, giving his name as Chester Pickup, though "Hiccup" would have been more appropriate because he was drunk, having consumed a fifth of whisky and started on another.[149] A Sports Palace bus took him to the Hotel Sevilla Biltmore, where the pilots were staying and where he registered as "John Brown of Rio de Janeiro."[150] The Sevilla was swank quarters in those days, a short stroll to Sloppy Joe's and La Floridita.

These sorts of high jinks and the apparent failure of the expedition to complete its organization led U.S. officials to believe that the crisis had passed. "Reliable sources" informed Norweb on August 23 that the men on the cay were "tired of the delay" and had given their commanders ten days to begin the attack or "they would desert en mass."[151] Only a few days later, the ambassador cabled that the expedition's chances for success "were deteriorating rapidly owing to the constant delays and falling morale."[152] On August 29 he even recommended scaling back the U.S. aerial reconnaissance. "It has been useful," he noted, but implied that he was now more concerned about a possible incident with the Cuban government.[153] In that context, after the expedition was discovered on Cayo Confites, Under Secretary Lovett reiterated to Norweb that there was to be no change in U.S. policy and that the United States expected Cuba to break up the expedition, though he softened his pronouncement with a caution against embarrassing Cuba or holding it accountable.[154]

Trujillo Contacts Grau

American officials may have been feeling relaxed, but the Dominican government remained apprehensive. It was gravely concerned over the presence of the exile revolutionary force on Cayo Confites in whatever shape. Dissatisfied with the results of protests through normal channels, Trujillo sent a cable directly to President Grau on August 20. He repeated the charges of the formation of an "international brigade" on Cuban territory, with intent to invade Dominican territory, and reviewed the diplomatic correspondence initiated on July 23 that had raised the issue and invoked traditional friendship and the inter-American conventions with reference to the rights and duties of states. He expressed bitter disappointment that the protests not only failed to stop the revolutionary activity but that it actually became "more feverish." He concluded that the Cuban Foreign Ministry, despite pledges to fulfill Cuba's international obligations, was unable to control the situation and that it would require the influence of the presidential office to obtain the cooperation of the appropriate Cuban officials. He appealed to Grau to "use his political and moral authority" to that end, warning that it would be unfortunate if "this lamentable question" could not be resolved by diplomatic means.[155]

Despite Trujillo's implied threat, Grau's response the next day was calm and noncommittal. After expressing the usual wishes for fraternal relations, he did not acknowledge what he and almost every Cuban knew, that there was an expeditionary force, but he said he would try to ascertain the facts and work to avoid an undesirable outcome.[156] This was not much to go on, but Trujillo took what he could, interpreting Grau's reply to mean, first, that Grau wanted peace; second, that Grau did not deny the charges; and, third, that Grau would seek to prevent the "outcome in question."[157] In transmitting this reading to the Cuban chargé in Ciudad Trujillo, Foreign Minister García Godoy further charged that the individuals making up the "anti-Dominican revolutionary expedition" were extremists of the "same kind that acted in favor of communism in the last Spanish war."[158] Hence,

Trujillo played the Communist card, but Joe McCarthy was still a judge in Appleton, Wisconsin, and it fell with little effect.

New Life

Trujillo may have called Grau's attention to Cayo Confites, but he did not get the result he wanted. In fact, despite the deplorable conditions on the island, the Liberation Army seemed to get a new life toward the end of August. Grau granted Alemán a sixty-day leave of absence on August 26, causing American officials to speculate that he was being given "an opportunity to devote more time to the solution of the Dominican problem."[159] An even bigger lift occurred with the arrival of the LCI *1006*, renamed the *Máximo Gómez*, at Mariel on August 29. This vessel sailed from Elizabeth City, North Carolina, on August 25, apparently without challenge; there is absolutely nothing in available documents to explain this inconsistency in U.S. policy in view of the handling of the *Patria*.[160]

The American explosives expert Hollis Smith traveled to Cayo Confites on the *Máximo Gómez* on September 7. He had returned to Miami on August 22, where he was questioned by customs officials, and several days later he called at the State Department, where he was told that he had been "deceived" if he believed that the United States supported the revolutionary movement and was warned not to return to Cuba.[161] Since he had not been paid for his services and was out about $6,000, he flew to Havana anyway on September 3, hoping to collect his money, but he may have been a spy, at least Masferrer thought so as time wore on.

Smith's return to Cuba may have been as casual as he described it, but it was fortuitous nonetheless because he was on hand to truck the munitions stored at Alemán's finca to the Mariel Naval Base and to load them on the *Máximo Gómez* for the voyage to Cayo Confites. On board with him were many of the chiefs: Angel Morales, Masferrer, Ramírez, and Rivas Montes, plus Captain José María Tercero (a former Nicaraguan National Guard officer in exile in Guatemala), and "a large number of Dominican exiles from New York."[162] When the vessel reached the island, greeted by "vivas" and widespread rejoicing, the troops dubbed it unofficially the *Fantasma*, because its arrival had been rumored for so long that they had come to doubt its existence.

Finally, the long-awaited invasion seemed imminent—even the rebel air force appeared to be taking shape, according to Norweb,[163] and a U.S. intelligence report expected D-day to come sometime during the week of September 14.[164] A clandestine radio broadcast originating in Cuba told the Dominican people to "take heart," that they would be liberated "soon."[165] Giving substance to these portents, Smith began the task of adding charges to the expedition's supply of rockets and shells. On September 11 he witnessed the capture of the Dominican schooner *Angelita,* which, rechristened the *Maceo,* was added to the invasion fleet and converted to a "munitions ship." Smith's explosives, to the relief of most, were placed on board.[166] Although the U.S. embassy in Ciudad Trujillo reported the belief that the invasion was coming by sea on the north coast,[167] the Dominican chargé in Havana, Incháustegui, suggested that at least part of the force might attack by land from Haiti, reporting that the "military leaders of the expedition" had traveled there to go "over the ground."[168] It was improbable that President Dumarsais Estimé would be as cooperative as Elie Lescot had been, but like any genuine Haitian leader he hated Trujillo for having ordered the massacre of thousands of Haitian squatters on Dominican territory in 1937, so it was possible that he might not be a problem either.

Opening the Haitian Front

Between August 14 and September 15, a total of twenty-six persons carrying official Cuban passports and connected with the Dominican exile movement arrived in Port-au-Prince, with the pace quickening especially after September 10. On that day Iván Ruiz, the brother of Fabio Ruiz, the Cuban chief of police, and two others arrived in Haiti reportedly "to make a final inspection of the revolutionaries' bases and liaisons" in order to determine the "form and date of the attack."[169] Closely on their heels came Juan Díaz, a naturalized U.S. citizen, one of the founders of the PRD and then head of its section in New York, and José Enrique Camejo, the former Cuban chargé d'affaires in Haiti and still an official of the Foreign Ministry, carrying an offical letter of introduction from President Grau to President Estimé.[170] Camejo was described as "Grau's representative in the group that went to Haiti."[171] Rounding out the group was Buenaventura Sánchez Félix, another of the "pioneers" of the PRD, having gone into exile in 1930, an author and intellect with connections throughout the Caribbean; he also came to negotiate with Estimé.[172]

Accompanying Sánchez Félix to Port-au-Prince on September 12 was George Osawa, a spy in the service of Trujillo. Osawa, an American-born Japanese, was a naturalized Cuban citizen and medical doctor who used his professional standing to gain the confidence of fellow physician Cotú Henríquez and penetrate the Dominican exile movement. However, the American embassy in Port-au-Prince possessed an intelligence report describing Osawa as "an opportunist and gangster" and learned that upon his arrival there he "immediately got in contact with" Manuel Arturo Peña Batlle, the Dominican ambassador to Haiti, who, as a consequence, notified his government about these efforts to organize a Haitian front.[173] If a Haitian front was indeed a possibility, the expeditionaries did not get the chance to use it because two unforeseen disasters struck the movement just as it seemed ready to go.

Disasters Strike from the Blind Side

The first disaster was natural. A severe tropical storm hit Cuba's Atlantic coast, pounding Cayo Confites for three days (September 12–14); the tiny isle was virtually inundated, the storm surge cutting it asunder in one place.[174] One wonders if the flooding helped wash away the muck that had piled up, or only made matters worse, but the force did not stay around long enough to find out.

The second disaster, man-made, began to unfold on the afternoon of September 15, when the men on the island picked up a "flash" on the radio reporting a fierce gun battle in the Orfila section of the Marianao suburb of Havana. Two rival units of uniformed police representing the competing *pistolero* groups MSR and UIR fought it out for two and a half hours, leaving six dead and eleven wounded. The fight, the equivalent of Chicago gangland's St. Valentine's Day massacre, had been building up for some time but was the immediate result of the shooting on September 12 of Captain Raúl Avila, an MSR chieftain and chief of the police of the Ministry of Health. The prime suspect in the killing was Major Emilio Tró, director of the National Police Academy and UIR top gun.

With a warrant for his arrest, Major Mario Salabarría, chief of the Enemy Activities Investigating Bureau of the National Police, MSR leader, close ally of Alemán and Manolo Castro, and active supporter of the Cayo Confites expedition, went to the home of Major Antonio Morín Dopico, chief of

police of the Marianao suburb, where Tró was in hiding.[175] The enmity
between Salabarría and Tró went back a long time, at least to their student
days at the University of Havana in 1939.[176] Tró resisted arrest, resulting
in the shootout that shocked even the *habaneros,* who had grown accustomed to *pistolero* violence, and causing the death of Tró and the wife of
Morín, among others, reportedly after the flag of surrender had been
raised.[177]

Only after the battle had been raging into the late afernoon did President
Grau, supposedly suffering "from grippe," "with great reluctance" order the
army to stop it and "ask" army Chief of Staff Pérez Dámera, who was in
Washington at the time, to return to Havana.[178] Pérez, "considerably dis-
turbed" over the reports he received from Havana, requested a special U.S.
Army plane in order to return to Cuba, since his "was not in operational
condition," and he arrived back in Havana at 3 A.M. on September 16.[179]

Pérez had been in Washington on a scheduled visit (in fact, the expedi-
tionaries may have planned to act during his absence[180]); he was there to
confer with his U.S. military counterparts and with James H. Wright
(Briggs's successor at State), who allegedly advised him to put an end to the
Cayo Confites affair. He may have met also with Trujillo's confidential agent
Arturo Despradel, who was present in Washington, supposedly carrying a
suitcase full of money for Pérez.[181] At the same time, according to Silfa,
Despradel bribed Pérez's traveling companion, National Police Chief Fabio
Ruiz Rojas,[182] which would mean that while one Ruiz brother was in Washington accepting money to stop the exile revolutionary movement, the
other (Iván) was in Haiti preparing the invasion of the Dominican Republic
by way of the land frontier. Pressure by the United States and Trujillo's gold
may have influenced General Pérez's suppression of the Dominican exile
movement, but there were other powerful factors moving him as well. The
shootout at Orfila provided him with the opportunity to dispose of a hated
political rival, Alemán, and purge the national police forces of gangster elements, something that he had been wanting to do for a long time,[183] the
disarming of the Cayo Confites expedition being part of the process.

Although Grau gave Pérez the green light "to restore order and round up
illegal arms," the General "ran away with the ball."[184] He appointed a military supervisor for the national police, furloughing Chief Ruiz. Pérez became the "man of the hour," arresting the "assassin" Salabarría and occupy-
ing the National Police Academy; the MSR was on the run.[185] These events
put the spotlight on the MSR and exposed the deep involvement of its
leaders (Alemán, Manolo Castro, and Masferrer) in the plot to overthrow

Trujillo. On September 20 the army raided Alemán's finca, América, seizing thirteen truckloads of arms and military equipment.[186] Pérez Dámera tried to give the "impression" that these weapons were to be used in a coup against the Cuban government, making him look like a patriot and not a villain breaking up the popular Dominican revolutionary movement.[187] Grau was outraged, unable to defend his "favorite" Alemán without admitting the true purpose of the impounded arsenal, but he was finally "made to see the light" and thereafter summoned Juan Rodríguez from Cayo Confites to inform him that he had twenty-four hours to leave Cuba.[188] Even Viriato Fiallo, the leader of the underground in Ciudad Trujillo, tipped off that the plan was going awry, took asylum with his family in the Colombian embassy.[189]

The Collapse of the Expedition

Meanwhile, on Cayo Confites, the situation was deteriorating badly, and Masferrer maintained discipline "under a reign of terror."[190] The men on the island were hoping for a "truce" in Pérez's persecutions while Grau and Rodríguez conferred and figured out what to do, but the radio continued to carry bad news: there was an order for the arrest of Manolo Castro; the army had searched the Sevilla; the Flying Tigers had flown.[191] Fearing that they would be next, Masferrer gave the order to abandon the cay on September 22. The men set fire to their accumulated junk and trash, leaving as a reminder of their presence an inscription on the wall of the fisherman Montenegro's shack citing Martí: "It is better to die standing up than to live on one's knees."[192] The *Aurora, Angelita,* and *Fantasma* (nee *Máximo Gómez*) sailed to the west, reaching Cayo Santa María on September 23 and spending the night there. The *Berta* was not in the line of ships, being in Nuevitas when Masferrer gave the order to set sail, and a Cuban Navy launch seized it on September 23. Arvelo, who was on board, thought it was "a joke" when a Cuban seaman, whom he had come to know well, "stuck a gun in his ribs" and announced, "Bueno, let's go, prisoner; the party's over."[193] "We were now prisoners of those who had treated us as friends and comrades," Arvelo lamented, speaking for the fourteen men on the *Berta*.

Hollis Smith claimed that Masferrer had sailed to the west, toward Havana, planning to reinforce Alemán and the MSR and restore the President's authority, but after radio contact with Grau had agreed to stop at Cayo

Santa María and await Rodríguez there.[194] Rupert Waddell, a former RAF officer who was the radio operator on board the *Fantasma*, related that Grau had said he "had gone along with the MSR long enough" but that if the expedition would leave Cuban waters in twenty-four hours "it was free to go wherever it wished."[195] Masferrer replied that they were short of food, water, and fuel, and Grau agreed to supply these needs, but away from Cuban territory. Two Cuban Navy frigates and a Coast Guard cutter brought Rodríguez on September 25 and escorted the rebel fleet out of Cuba and on to Cayo Güinchos, a deserted isle in the Bahamas. From the bridge of the *Fantasma*, Masferrer shouted, "Tomorrow, we sail for Santo Domingo," but the delay in loading the provisions on board—one of the frigates needed time to distill sufficient fresh water—caused a minor mutiny among the hungry and dispirited men. Masferrer declared that they had already sacrificed too much for them to give up now. After taking the arms and belongings of those whom he could not persuade, leaving three hundred men behind in their shorts, the invasion fleet set sail at midnight on September 26, for where was anyone's guess.[196]

Haiti was a possibility; Venezuela also—Manolo Castro and Eufemio Fernández had gone there for some purpose on September 18, just when things were starting to come undone. Masferrer told the men they were going to Port-au-Prince, where they had "six tanks and forty trucks" waiting for crossing the frontier and invading Santo Domingo.[197] But the expedition was now rudderless, and the rebels sailed along the Cuban coast, just outside territorial waters. The *Angelita*, too slow to keep up, put into Nuevitas on September 27, carrying, some of the expeditionaries thought, "the last messages for our families."[198] The other vessels sailed on to Antilla, where Cuban warships ended the odyssey on September 29, disarming the Liberation Army and loading the men, first in boxcars (messy with molasses), later on coaches, for the long trip to Camp Columbia, outside Havana.

Rodríguez claimed subsequently that he had cleared Cuban waters but turned back because Masferrer on the *Fantasma*, overtaken by a Cuban frigate, signaled that he was in "a jam." "I thought he had run aground," the General explained. "We were leading the way on the *Aurora*, with 400 men and sufficient arms and ammunition to equip another thousand men." The least Masferrer could have done, if he knew his cause was lost, "was let me continue."[199] One adventurer did avoid capture; Fidel Castro, fearing that he was a marked man, being UIR, had jumped into Nipe Bay and swam to shore.[200]

Despite their failure, the expeditionaries were treated as heroes. People lined the tracks all the way to Havana, placing grease on the rails in an effort to stop the train. But the men were enjoying the outpouring of support so much that they refused any opportunity to escape. "The MSR was more popular than ever," observed Smith, and the people threatened "to bomb the Capitol, if any harm came to the prisoners."[201] None did.

After examining the matter, Magistrate Evelio Tabio of the Supreme Court of Justice issued a decree on October 3 ordering the release of the expeditionaries incarcerated at Camp Columbia, finding that they had not threatened the constitutional order and that the armed forces erred in seizing their property and arresting them, some probably in international waters.[202] The advantage had passed to Alemán; Pérez Dámera was being depicted as a "Judas" who had betrayed the Dominican freedom fighters for two million dollars, selling out to the corrupt and corrupting tyrant Trujillo.[203] Norweb was convinced now that Pérez had gone too far, embarrassing the President and Alemán, and wondered how much longer Grau could keep together "such strange cats as the Minister without Portfolio [Alemán] and the portly Chief of Staff"[204] (Pérez was the original "Mr. Five-By-Five.") The Dominican government demanded that the Cayo Confites weapons be confiscated and turned over to it as reparations, but most were restored to Rodríguez instead.[205] Cuba kept the junk airplanes and landing craft, which Alemán had acquired with Ministry of Education funds, but Rodríguez recovered his rifles and machine guns and ammunition and flew them to Guatemala, where Arévalo was willing to give him refuge and support.[206]

The Force Scatters

On September 30 the Dominican Revolutionary Central Committee issued a statement vowing to fight on. They felt they had been betrayed, causing them "to lose the battle before it began," but expressed their profound gratitude to the Cuban people for their support and proclaimed that like Martí they would not permit one defeat to overwhelm them.[207] In truth, there was little left of the Dominican Revolutionary Movement besides Rodríguez and his guns. The political leaders (Bosch and Miolán) remained in Cuba, working to revive the PRD, which was shattered, and the military chiefs (Rodríguez and Ramírez) moved to Guatemala, where Central American intrigue provided new hope. The troops were left to fend for themselves.

The Cubans could go home, but some of the Dominican exiles, especially those from New York and Puerto Rico, encountered hard times. Bosch and his pilot friend Edward Murphy converted their arms smuggling operation into a channel for sneaking some of the exiles back into the States.[208] In order to avoid embarrassment, the U.S. embassy acted to get the American pilots out of Cuba. Lovett urged it to do so, and Norweb reported that they were "without a centavo."[209] Three days after the army raided the Sevilla on September 21 and searched their empty rooms, the embassy had the pilots on a Pan Am flight for Miami, providing a listing of their names, with the warning that they were probably phony.[210] The embassy also acted to extricate Hollis Smith.

Lieutenant Colonel Edward Casey, the acting U.S. military attaché in Cuba, met Smith as he cleared the gate of the Camp Columbia prison at 2:00 P.M. on October 5 and facilitated his departure (even paying for his ticket) on a "Q" Airways plane for Key West at 3:30 P.M.[211] Casey was very careful to explain to Smith that he would likely be arrested upon arriving in the United States but that the U.S. embassy had information "that his life was in danger if he remained in Cuba." Casey did not want to give the impression that the United States was protecting American citizens involved in Cayo Confites, or that he was "shanghaiing" Smith, but Smith got the picture and left of his own free will.[212] He was accompanied by two other adventurers, Rupert Waddell and Thomas Lawyer, whom Casey informed that he had no information they were in any danger but advised them to leave nonetheless (and Casey also purchased tickets for them). Casey spoke warmly about the "three chicos," calling them "crusaders" and concluding that "they would make excellent soldiers."[213]

If Smith was an American agent, as Masferrer believed (and hence the danger to his life), Casey's account provides no confirmation.[214] Smith was later indicted by a federal grand jury in Jacksonville, Florida, for gunrunning and convicted in a federal court in the same city in March 1948. He received a two-year suspended sentence and was placed on probation for three years.[215] Convicted with Smith were Ramírez and Manolo Castro, who had also taken explosives off the impounded *Patria* and flew them illegally to Cuba on August 16, but Ramírez did not return for the trial and Manolo was already dead. The latter had been shot outside the Cinema Resumén, which he owned, in downtown Havana on Sunday evening, February 22, 1948, in revenge for the slaying of Emilio Tró in the "battle of Marianao." Revolutionary Insurrectional Union gunsel Fidel Castro was picked up for questioning in connection with the killing but was released "for lack of evidence."[216]

Postmortems

Colonel Casey believed that the Cayo Confites expedition had a good chance of succeeding but principally blamed Manolo Castro for its failure. He concluded that Castro, who was responsible for organizing the revolutionary air force, failed to appreciate the urgency in getting the planes ready and "was too confident" of his ability to control Pérez Dámera. "I don't know why," Casey reported Castro as saying, "but Genovevo has always been afraid of me." This was his second big mistake, Casey said, because Pérez "was the man most responsible for the dissolution of the movement." He had been left out of the plot; "with a little bit of salesmanship," he could have been brought into the inner circle. But when he found out that he had been excluded, "his pride was wounded," and when he got the chance, he crushed the expedition, "without consulting the President and in deliberate violation of his wishes."[217] This is an interesting commentary, not only for what it states about Manolo and Pérez, but also because a U.S. military officer seriously concluded Cayo Confites might have succeeded if given the chance.

Perhaps. But the failure to coordinate key elements of the invasion plan—the training of the ground forces, the availability of the landing craft, and the preparation of the aircraft—caused delays that provided time for other factors to go wrong and for opposition to develop. The loss of Braden impacted in indeterminable ways. The divided leadership between the Dominican "knights in shining armor" and the Cuban "buccaneers," as Norweb described them, undermined the operation, not just because the MSR eventually took over but because the Cubans changed the entire character of the movement. The Dominicans started out with a modest plan—a surprise attack by a few hundred men designed to spark an internal uprising; the Cubans converted it into a noisy extravaganza, publicly recruiting over a thousand men and contemplating multiple amphibious landings, a land incursion, and air raids. While the U.S. embassy in Havana, echoing Colonel Casey, stated that the expedition "came within a hair of being carried out and probably would have succeeded,"[218] the history of the episode does not support such a conclusion. Clearly, the gun battle in Marianao was an unexpected event that precipitated the collapse of the expedition, but the plan, as envisioned by Manolo Castro, was never really ready to go.

Rodríguez Unbowed

Despite the frustrations and hardships, it is difficult not to put a romantic spin on Cayo Confites. It had everything: veterans of D-Day (Normandy), the South Pacific (Guadalcanal), North Africa (against Rommel), the French Resistance, the Flying Tigers, the Spanish Civil War (Loyalists, of course), the RAF, RCAF, and the French Foreign Legion. Even Ernest Hemingway made a cameo appearance; the first secretary of the Dominican embassy in Washington called at the State Department on August 25 to denounce the American author as one of the persons heading the invasion's "brain trust," and the Dominican government repeated the accusation in the press on September 30.[219] Rodríguez certainly was a romantic; at a time in his life when he could have been at home enjoying his grandchildren, he was getting ready to buckle on his armor again. He was not a man easy to defeat. Not only had Trujillo confiscated his estates, but he had placed his daughter under house arrest, with the threat that she would be executed if Rodríguez returned at the head of an invading force.[220] His son, José Horacio, told Colonel Casey in Havana on August 14 that his father would not rest until he had overcome Trujillo's tyranny, that he could have stayed in La Vega and lived "in luxury," but that would mean kowtowing to Trujillo, and that he could not do.[221]

Follow the trail of the guns.

1948

Costa Rica

The New Patron

The exile revolutionary activity continued but from a new principal base. The Cuban *ambiente* was not favorable. Ramón Grau San Martín had been humiliated in the Cayo Confites affair, and the failed expedition contributed to the decline of José Alemán's political career (though there was a golden exile in Miami in his future). The scene shifted to Guatemala, where President Juan José Arévalo "assumed center stage"[1] —or, more accurately, became the impresario, because he operated grandly off stage, choosing the script, doing the casting, and lining up the backers. Arévalo was driven by two central goals that complemented each other: the achievement of Central American federation and the elimination of dictators. Perceiving dictatorial government as the main obstacle to the attainment of a Central American union, his foreign policy had a unity of purpose, and he was a willing "champion" of the region's refugees from tyranny.[2] He belonged to the 1930s generation of exiles that opposed Gerardo Machado in Cuba, Jorge Ubico in Guatemala, Juan Vicente Gómez in Venezuela, Rafael Trujillo in the Dominican Republic, Tiburcio Carías in Honduras, and Anastasio Somoza in Nicaragua. In 1948 there were three down and three to go, and Arévalo, knowing the pain that Ubico had inflicted on his country, felt a moral obligation to aid those still struggling for liberation.[3]

Arévalo gave refuge to Juan Rodríguez García. He facilitated the transfer of Rodríguez's arms to Guatemala, transporting them from Cuba (with the connivance of Grau) in Guatemalan air force planes to Los Cipresales, the military airport near the capital city, and storing them in "secret places."[4] The weapons belonged to Rodríguez, but Arévalo exercised control over their use. For both internal and external reasons, Arévalo acted in secret. He had to walk a fine line between the two powerful colonels, Francisco Arana, the chief of the armed forces, and Jacobo Arbenz, the minister of defense, who were intense rivals in political tendency and ambition. Arévalo seemed to thrive on conspiracy, running a department of dirty tricks out of the Presidential Palace, though reserving such activity for after midnight.[5] He lodged Rodríguez in the nearby Pensión Toriello, with a direct telephone line to the palace, and gave the Dominican general the run of the place.[6]

A Gathering of Rebels

Like Penelope, Rodríguez was beset by suitors. It seemed that everyone had a revolutionary plan and wanted his guns. Aside from the Dominicans, who placed their revolutionary plans on hold—seeking only reciprocity from those whom they might aid—the dissident and exile elements that showed up in Guatemala were from Honduras, Nicaragua, and even Costa Rica.

The Nicaraguans were the most numerous and aggressive, comprised of leaders or respresentatives of virtually every political party and anti-Somoza faction of the country. The aged patriarch and former President Emiliano Chamorro personally made the pitch for the Conservatives, backed up by Gustavo Manzanares; General Carlos Pasos, who was almost picked to head the National Guard (Guardia) in January 1933, instead of Somoza, spoke for the breakaway Liberals; Rosendo Argüello, padre, and Rosendo Argüello, hijo, represented the Independent Liberals; and Toribio Tijerino, Pedro José Zepeda, and Juan Gregorio Colindres were old Sandinistas thirsting for revenge and keeping the flame.

The Hondurans were primarily young military officers like Jorge Rivas Montes, Francisco Morazán, Francisco "El Indio" Sánchez, Alfredo Mejía Lara, and Mario Sosa Navarro, who lacked a clear political program and appeared to be biding their time, ready to serve first wherever Arévalo might assign them. The Costa Rican was José Figueres, who at first impulse seemed out of place in the rough and tumble of Central American intrigue.

Most observers, Arévalo among them, set Costa Rica apart from the revolution and warfare that characterized the region. Whether deserved or not, Costa Rica had a reputation as a country of small farmers and freely elected, limited-term, civilian presidents who did not meddle in the affairs of neighboring republics and whose idea of governing was restricted to the building of bridges, roads, and schools. Costa Rica, "the Switzerland of the Americas," according to popular belief, had more schoolteachers than soldiers. Figueres declared that this was all wrong.

He claimed that Costa Rica had been a dictatorship since 1940, when Rafael Angel Calderón Guardia became president. According to Figueres, Calderón Guardia, allied with the Communist party and the Catholic Church, was a brutal authoritarian and demagogue who threatened the democratic traditions of Costa Rica. Combining "shock brigades" of Communist workers from the banana regions with electoral fraud, Calderón imposed Teodoro Picado as his successor in 1944 and was preparing to use the same tactics to steal the presidency again for himself in the elections scheduled for February 1948. The opposition parties had formed a National Opposition coalition and nominated moderate-liberal newspaper publisher Otilio Ulate as their candidate. Figueres supported the coalition but was convinced that Calderón would not accept defeat at the polls, if he permitted a free election in the first place, so he wanted to be ready to prevent four more years of Calderón, with guns if necessary. Prudent men regarded the feisty Figueres as "crazy."[7]

Don Pepe

Don Pepe Figueres was an agro-industrialist who had his first run-in with Calderón in July 1942. Figueres was not active in politics up to that time. He devoted the 1930s to the development of his finca, La Lucha Sin Fin, in the mountainous San Cristóbal region south of San José, thirty-five miles by line of flight, seven hours on horseback. Figueres developed a unique enterprise, growing the agave cabuya, processing the fiber and using it to manufacture rope and gunny sacks, and sharing the proceeds with the farmers and wage earners of La Lucha in the form of housing, schooling, and health and recreational facilities. In the words of a contemporary, "he was a 'socialist' before it was fashionable to be one."[8]

This life-style changed when Figueres delivered a radio address criticizing Calderón for his handling of a riot in San José on July 4, 1942. An Axis submarine torpedoed a United Fruit Company vessel in Puerto Limón harbor on July 2 that year. Then, using U.S. Independence Day as a pretext, demonstrators in San José went on a rampage and sacked the businesses of German and Italian residents of the city (Feoli, Musmanni, Reimers, Federspiel, Lehmann, etc.). Figueres was outraged over the destruction of scarce goods in wartime (Musmanni ran the city's largest bakery) and accused the government of orchestrating the entire affair. Calderón ordered Figueres's arrest and a few days later expelled him from the country, accusing him of Nazi sympathies. Figueres spent the next two years in exile in Mexico City.[9]

There he met the Nicaraguan Rosendo Argüello Jr., also an exile, and the two commiserated over the injustice of their situations. They concluded that since dictatorship was a common malady of Central America, a common remedy ought to applied, and pledged to collaborate to eliminate dictatorship entirely from the isthmus.[10] But Figueres rejected Argüello's suggestion that they join the Central American Democratic Union (UDC), saying that the group was all talk and no action. The UDC was made up of intellectual/literary expatriates like Pedro José Zepeda, who had been Sandino's chief adviser, propagandist, and theoretician, and Professor Edelberto Torres, the top Rubén Darío scholar in the Americas. Figueres convinced Argüello that armed action was the only way to go and furthermore that the struggle should begin in Costa Rica because it was the "weakest link" in the dictatorial chain. "From that base," Argüello agreed, "we could then proceed to liberate the whole of Central America."[11]

Figueres returned to Costa Rica in 1944 and, although he was active in politics, being one of the founders of the Social Democratic party (PSD) in 1945, he was hell-bent on armed revolution. Former president León Cortés, the principal opposition leader at the time, until his death in March 1946, informally appointed Figueres his "war chieftain," and the "loco" Don Pepe became the closest thing to a Costa Rican *pistolero*.[12] But he lacked arms. "You can't make chocolate without cacao," was the way Figueres put it.[13] He raised about $12,000 in Costa Rica, and Argüello contacted rich Nicaraguans in Mexico, being especially successful with Carlos Pasos, who contributed another twelve thousand.[14] By the end of 1946 they had accumulated about $60,000 worth of arms and were ready to carry out their "Sunday Plan"—an airlift of the arms from Mexico to Dominical on Costa Rica's Pacific coast.[15] Just as they were set to move, the very Mexican authorities to whom they had been paying protection money in order to carry on their illegal activity seized their cache and threw Argüello and Professor Torres in jail.[16]

Figueres was devastated by the loss. It could not have come at a worse time; the National Opposition was meeting in convention on February 13, 1947, and it probably ruined what slight chance he had for the presidential nomination. He believed that a showdown with Calderón was inevitable, and now he was not ready; the "prudent" men of the Opposition, he complained, would soak up all available funds in a political campaign that he "knew" was already "lost."[17] However, even if he had no faith in the process, he had to give it a chance to play out, and "he dedicated himself to making plans for the difficult days that were coming."[18] He needed principally to acquire arms.

The Competition for the Arms

The collapse of Cayo Confites was Figueres's salvation. Joining the mad scramble for Rodríguez's favor, Figueres claimed that he persuaded Juan Bosch first and then the old general that the best way to renew the revolutionary struggle was through Costa Rica.[19] But Costa Rica was a hard sell; not only was there a reluctance to put Calderón in the same category as the "three T's" (Trujillo, Tiburcio, and Tacho [Somoza's nickname]) but activists on the left viewed Calderón as a reformer who had enacted a labor code and established "social guarantees." From that point of view Figueres was seen not as a revolutionary but as a reactionary. Professor Torres proved to be Figueres's most influential advocate, arguing before Arévalo that Don Pepe's commitment to "federation and democracy" was solid.[20] Arévalo was not so sure, but even at the risk of supporting a "rightist" he seemed willing to take a chance if it expedited his goal "of getting at Somoza."[21] According to Argüello, however, the sudden appearance of Toribio Tijerino threw a monkey wrench into the proceedings.

Tijerino operated a soap factory in San Lorenzo, Honduras, just across the border from the Nicaraguan department of Nueva Segovia, which had been Sandino's stronghold and where the former Sandino General Colindres still lived, working a gold mine near Murra. Argüello described Tijerino as "a clever and quick-witted man," who had a plan with Colindres to start something of their own in Sandino country.[22] They began a competition for the arms, involving Chamorro and his clique and other Nicaraguan factions as well, that became unseemly and "even poisonous." They wined and dined anyone who might be helpful and organized "a committee of propaganda and defamation" that was "extremely effective."[23] The situation got so bad that Arévalo said enough was enough, informing the rival groups that if they could not agree to cooperate, he would wash his hands of the matter. Arévalo's ultimatum played into the hands of Tijerino, who had proposed a "Caribbean Pact" to place the direction of the antidictatorial struggle under a central command. Figueres did not like getting the arms with such strings attached, but he had been outfoxed and, because Arévalo was firm, he agreed to sign the pact with the others on December 16, 1947.[24]

The Caribbean Pact

A mixed bag of dissident leaders—Rodríguez for the people of the Dominican Republic; Chamorro, Manzanares, Zepeda, and Argüello Sr. for Nicaragua; and Figueres for Costa Rica—signed a Pact of Alliance (Caribbean Pact) dedicated to the overthrow of the dictatorships enslaving their respective countries. They pledged to form a single revolutionary team and to pool their resources for the achievement of the common goal. For that purpose the pact created a Supreme Revolutionary Committee comprised of Rodríguez and his son, José Horacio, representing the Dominican Republic; Argüello Sr. and Tijerino for Nicaragua; and Figueres and Argüello Jr. for Costa Rica. The signatories empowered the committee to coordinate the antidictatorial struggle, determine the contribution of each party, and carry out the common policies of the allies. They designated Rodríguez as president of the committee, as well as commander in chief of the allied armies, and authorized him to appoint a general staff to advise the committee on military matters.[25]

In yielding tremendous authority to a supranational body, the parties agreed that within each liberated country a junta of government was to be organized and to possess "complete autonomy" in internal matters but that with reference to "general affairs" it would follow the "instructions" of the Supreme Revolutionary Committee until the last dictator was eliminated. Moreover, they declared that the "reconstruction" of the Republic of Central America was a "fundamental necessity" and pledged to incorporate that principle into the new constitutions of the liberated states, committing the new states furthermore to the formation of a Democratic Alliance of the Caribbean. Swearing to absolute loyalty, discipline, and secrecy, the signatories agreed to submit any dispute over the interpretation or execution of the pact to the "irrevocable decision" of the president of Guatemala (Aré-valo).[26]

The Caribbean Pact was not very realistic, but it constituted an alliance of sorts and gave Rodríguez a commitment in writing. It was unlikely that any of the parties would or could fulfill the terms of the pact, except perhaps Rodríguez, who was last in line anyway. The lengthy courtship paid the Dominican had inflated his ego and led him to fantasize about heading "a great Caribbean federation."[27] As commander in chief, he created the Libera-tion Army of the Caribbean and Central America and named Miguel Angel Ramírez as his chief of staff and the Honduran colonels Rivas Montes and Morazán as deputy chiefs.[28] Figueres described the pact as a "lend-lease" treaty, which, in hindsight, appeared to be an attempt to water down his commitment.[29] Although the pact did not state it explicitly, there seemed to be agreement to follow the Figueres plan of "Costa Rica first." Figueres wanted the guns right away, but Arévalo and Rodríguez hesitated, prefer-ring to wait until the 1948 elections in February to see if Calderón would really try to continue in power illegally.[30] Figueres interpreted their attitude differently, remarking, "they did not believe the Costa Ricans would fight."[31]

The Sandino Mystique

In fact, there may have been a double-cross in the works. At least Arévalo and Rodríguez appeared willing to support a revolutionary movement in Nicaragua, despite Figueres's belief that they had committed the arms to him. While Figueres withdrew to La Lucha to prepare for armed action, counting on the shipment of weapons from Guatemala, Tijerino and Co-lindres planned to begin an armed insurrection in Nueva Segovia no later than February 8, not waiting for events in Costa Rica to develop.[32] After negotiating the pact, Colindres returned to Nicaragua sometime after the first of the year to arrange for the airlift of arms and men from Guatemala. According to the statement of José Ramón Espinosa, a captured rebel in the affair, Rodríguez promised "his full cooperation" to Colindres, making avail-able "all the materiel that he had."[33] Colindres allegedly told Arévalo that he could raise 500 men in twenty-four hours and that "he could put 5,000 under arms in eight days," intending to strike first in Jícaro, Ocotal, and San Juan de Telpaneca, all in the Segovia zone.[34] Arévalo and Rodríguez said that it was "essential" to have only Sandinista chieftains, "in order to raise the banner of Sandinismo," and Colindres gave them a list of forty such veterans, having already lined up Ramón Raudales, Heriberto Reyes, and Ismael Peralta. Colindres told his followers that Rodríguez had assured him he would not delay beyond February 8, having declared "that no one was more anxious than he."[35]

Having touched base with his people, Colindres traveled again to Guatemala via Danlí and San Lorenzo in Honduras and passing through San Salvador to confer with Tijerino and Rodríguez. He then returned to Nicaragua around January 18, with a small quantity of arms and a radio, and set up his camp in the vicinity of Los Encinos, gathering around him certain key lieutenants—Francisco Montalván, Gustavo Marín, José Angel, and Lino Moncada.[36] He had arranged with Rodríguez to have a pilot travel overland to Nicaragua to inspect the landing field for the arms airlift, planning to send a message by radio when he had pack animals ready at Ocotal for that purpose. After the pilot had viewed the site and returned to Guatemala, Colindres was set to use an open code, broadcasting the message "the *Revista Cultural* comes out today" as a signal to Rodríguez to send the planes loaded with men and arms.[37] However, his activity alerted residents in the area, who notified the National Guard, which in turn attacked Colindres's encampment. The rebels escaped, except for José Espinoso, a twenty-year-old farmer who was caught and told everything he knew, but they left behind personal effects and equipment and even code books.[38] Colindres's misfortune occurred just in time to bring Don Pepe back into the picture.

Figueres's War Plan

In truth, Calderón did try to steal the Costa Rican election. Otilio Ulate won the balloting on February 8, but Calderón cried foul and, when the National Electoral Tribunal failed to certify Ulate's election by a unanimous vote, Calderón's partisans in the Legislative Assembly, being in the majority, voted to annul the election on March 1. Learning that Ulate was meeting with his advisers, possibly to plan a protest rally, President Picado ordered his arrest, but the police killed Dr. Carlos Luis Valverde, a *Ulatista,* in the attempt, intensifying the crisis.

Figueres was at La Lucha; he told Ulate he was going there to be ready to defend the electoral victory with arms if necessary.[39] Still, he was ill-prepared. He was relying on Argüello to bring in Nicaraguan action types, although he had a few countrymen of his own who did not fit the peaceful *tico* (Costa Rican) stereotype. Edgar Cardona, Fernando Cortés, Max "Tuta" Cortés, Fernando Figuls, Frank Marshall Jiménez, Rodolfo Quirós, and Fernando Valverde Vega comprised the "original seven" and made up the core of Figueres's Army of National Liberation.[40] During the political campaign they had provided security at Opposition rallies, carried out dirty tricks and acts of sabotage (such as causing power outages), and even exploded a few bombs, just to keep the Calderonistas on their toes and to let them know "Basta!" ("Enough!").[41] Cardona and the Cortés brothers were fugitives at the time, wanted in connection with the midnight bombing of the parked car of Manuel Mora, the leader of the Popular Vanguard (Communist) party. Figueres did not feel comfortable politically with any of these men, but right now he needed their daring. From his mountain redoubt Figueres communicated with confederates in San José, Cartago, San Ramón, and elsewhere by means of a radio-telephone net put in place by Alexander Murray, a Canadian who grew up in Costa Rica, a "radioaficionado" who had served as a communications intelligence specialist in Great Britain during World War II.[42]

Figueres's war plan was simple; it counted on the natural barrier provided by the mountainous terrain south of the Central Plateau and on the small size (approximately three hundred men) and ineptitude of the Costa Rican Army. La Lucha was accessible by two routes, each of which traversed very steep ranges reaching altitudes of over 2,000 meters. One could travel the old route due south from San José on a dirt road via Desamparados and the towns of Santa Elena and Frailes, or take the new Inter-American Highway (still under construction and unpaved), leaving the valley floor at Cartago and El Tejar.

Relying on the physical features, Figueres planned to maintain a defensive position until he got the arms from Guatemala and equipped and trained a citizen army. The Inter-American Highway was the easier route to defend because certain high passes on the road were perfect choke points. Farther south on the highway, at Villa Mills, the U.S. Public Roads Administration, in charge of the construction, maintained its offices and facilities, including a clinic, garages, repair shops, trucks, and fuel supplies. This facility rendered Figueres invaluable aid during the conflict.[43] Beyond Villa Mills was San Isidro de El General, 136 kilometers (85 miles) from San José, with the most convenient airport on the highway south. Figueres also planned a "Northern Front" under Francisco "Chico" Orlich, his longtime friend and business partner, to carry out guerrilla operations in the San Ramón area.

The War of National Liberation Begins

The shooting of Ulate's adviser, Dr. Carlos Luis Valverde, sparked Figueres's decision to begin the War of National Liberation on March 12. The first action, which Figueres designated the "Maize Plan" ("Plan Maíz"), directed the seizure of the San Isidro Airport in order to fetch Rodríguez's arms from Guatemala. It went without a hitch, almost; resisting for a few volleys, the *jefe político* and his son were killed and a "communist individual" was wounded.[44] Max Cortés led thirty men in the raid that took the town a little after 5 A.M. and quickly controlled the airfield after that. Not more than an hour later a TACA (Central American Air Transport) domestic flight landed, and the rebels commandeered the aircraft and forced its startled passengers to deplane. By noon, before San José caught on to what was happening, they had hijacked a total of three TACA DC-3s.[45] Having now a tiny air force, Figueres sent two of his planes winging northward to establish the "air bridge" between San Isidro and Guatemala. "Some of our boys had never flown solo before," Figueres related, as Guillermo "Macho" Núñez and Otto Escalante (the future head of LACSA, the Costa Rican national airline) took off on the first of nineteen flights bringing men and especially arms and supplies that sustained Figueres's forces during the forty-day War of National Liberation.[46]

When Núñez and Escalante reached Guatemala the first time, things did not go as smoothly as planned. First of all, they landed at La Aurora, the commercial airport, causing a minor uproar. To add to it, Arévalo supposedly was having second thoughts, possibly influenced by Arbenz, who doubted Figueres's revolutionary credentials.[47] Finally, Argüello was vacationing in El Salvador, feeling the need for a rest after the exhausting struggle over the arms and possibly feeling the need to stay out of Rodríguez's way, whom he seemed to annoy.[48] According to Figueres, Colonels Francisco Cosenza, the air force chief of staff, and Arana saved the day, transferring the planes to Cipresales, the military field, and getting the arms loaded.[49] Rodríguez sent the arms in the custody of the staff officers of the Liberation Army of the Caribbean and Central America, the Dominicans Ramírez and Horacio Ornes, and the Hondurans Rivas Montes, Morazán, "El Indio" Sánchez, Sosa Navarro, Mejía Lara, and Presentación Ortega.[50] Noting that no Nicaraguans were included in this group, Argüello cursed his luck in not making it back in time to take part and complained that the Hondurans had wormed their way into Rodríguez's confidence using flattery.[51]

In all, eighteen officers comprised the foreign element in Figueres's fighting force. Argüello was among them, coming in on the next flight, accompanied by Nicaraguans José María Tercero (a Cayo Confites veteran) and Adolfo Báez Bone, among others. Figueres praised their contribution extravagantly but swore that they were the only ones who fought; "those who speak of mercenary troops in our struggle are lying."[52] He freely admitted that the foreign officers were critical in preparing his *tico* army. In need of more preparation time, Figueres abandoned La Lucha on March 14 and reestablished his headquarters at Santa María de Dota, thirty kilometers to the south, surrounded by lofty mountains.

In the "Free Territory"

The key to Santa María was El Empalme on the Inter-American Highway, a cattle crossing on a cloud-shrouded ridge (altitude 2300 meters) that cut off access from the north all the way to Panama. Frank Marshall and Rivas Montes set up a defensive line there on March 14 that withstood repeated assaults until the war's end. Marshall was a particularly fierce and reckless warrior, but he was also a controversial figure. He was the stepson of Ricardo Steinvorth, a German businessman, who sent him to Germany in the thirties for his schooling. When he returned, he was allegedly a "Hitler Youth"; at least he got in trouble in 1942 for shouting "vivas" for Hitler and Germany.[53] He had a grudge against Calderón for blacklisting Steinvorth during World War II, but, overlooking all that for the moment, Figueres described him as "the bravest of the brave."[54] The Honduran Rivas Montes was a happy-go-lucky individual, who later in 1954 was captured, hideously tortured, and murdered in the aftermath of a coup/assassination plot against Somoza.

Because the government forces could not break through at El Empalme, they tried an end run. A small force made up largely of banana workers from Golfito and under the command of Nicaraguan General Enrique Somarribas Tijerino and Costa Rican novelist-poet and Communist labor leader Carlos Luis Fallas landed at Dominical on the Pacific coast on March 20. They then advanced the thirty-eight kilometers up the side of the mountain to occupy part of the town of San Isidro. In this struggle Ramírez had his "finest hour," leading the rebel forces in a counterattack on March 21 and routing the loyalist troops completely two days later.[55] Anchored by Empalme and San Isidro, Figueres controlled an area of Costa Rica that he designated the "Free Territory," a sanctuary wherein he received arms and supplies flown in from Guatemala and recruits trudging in from the countryside. By early April the Army of National Liberation had swelled to about seven hundred men, and Ramírez, whom Figueres appointed chief of staff (he was already Rodríguez's chief of staff), oversaw its equipping and training.

In the meantime, with people like Marshall on his side and Fallas against him, Figueres had an image problem. In fighting Calderón and his Communist allies, Figueres needed to show that he had no intention of turning back the clock on social reform, nor that he was an agent of the "coffee barons." Figueres regarded himself as a socialist, though he did not have a clear idea of what that meant, only a broad concept of wanting "social progress with freedom."[56] From his headquarters in Santa María, Figueres issued two proclamations. On March 23 he broadcast an appeal to the Costa Rican people to support the army of National Liberation through acts of sabotage and to prepare for the army's "triumphal entry" into every town of the country, affirming that Calderón had destroyed the Republic and that "we shall create the Second Republic."[57] In the second proclamation on April 1, Figueres addressed the social issue explicitly, denying that his movement was "reactionary, bourgeois, or retrogressive." Those who say so, he declared, act in "bad faith." He reiterated his intention of creating the Second Republic, dedicated "to the greatest good for the greatest number," and ended with the promise, "The day that we end the war against bad faith, we shall begin a new war: the war against poverty."[58]

Figueres Takes the Offensive

Having launched the propaganda war, Figueres decided it was time to begin his planned offensive; that is, a pair of assaults on the provincial capitals Cartago and Puerto Limón. Arana had written to him to express his concern that the revolution had seemed to lose its "rhythm." "Remember," he warned, "the revolution that does not move forward, is lost."[59] But Figueres knew that he was winning; the government forces were ineffectual, and on April 6 Archbishop Víctor Sanabria came to Santa María on a peace mission, proposing a compromise interim president for a year, followed by new elections. Figueres said nothing doing, dramatically emulating his hero Franklin Roosevelt by calling for "unconditional surrender."[60]

On April 10 Figueres personally led one column of the two-pronged offensive, code-named the "Magnolia Plan," consisting of a surprise attack upon Cartago, the nation's second city. He began "the phantom march" that night, assembling six hundred men at El Jardín, just below El Empalme. He descended from his mountain stronghold undetected, passing through the enemy line, traveling at night and helped by ground fog, traversing the back country single file on footpaths and ox trails, and entering the sleeping city at 6 A.M. on April 12. Cartago was an Oppositionist town, and the welcome was enthusiastic; only the small garrison holed up in the military barracks offered a half-hearted resistance. Of more concern were the troops up on the ridge. Finding out that they had been outsmarted, they advanced toward Cartago, but the Empalme Battalion (Marshall and Rivas Montes) met them a few miles out of town at El Tejar and, in "one of the bloodiest and most tragic battles of the entire civil war,"[61] crushed the government will totally. One objective had fallen.

Synchronized with "Magnolia," Figueres set into motion the "Pink Carnation Plan" ("Plan Clavel"), an airborne assault on Puerto Limón. Figueres needed the Caribbean port in order to open a sea route for supplies, claiming that a ship was already waiting in Cuba to bring in weapons and materiel too bulky for his planes.[62] Limón was connected with Cartago by the Northern Railway, the "jungle train" built by the banana entrepreneur Minor C. Keith in the 1870s. On April 8 two DC-3s carrying sixty-five men under the command of Horacio Ornes and Ludwig "Vico" Starke, another *tico* man of action of German nationality, took off from San Isidro and flew first to Altamira, far to the north in the San Carlos Plains. This was a diversion, but it was also for the purpose of picking up Chico Orlich and his men to bring them to San Isidro for "Magnolia." After doing this the planes returned to Altamira to continue with the Ornes-Starke group for the attack on Limón on April 11. "Pink Carnation" was a complete success also.

Figueres designated the force carrying out the operation the "Caribbean Legion" ("Legión Caribe"),[63] the first group to be identified by that term. He explained that he had adopted the practice of giving "each group or front a name in order to honor the brave men involved."[64] This original group, he affirmed, was made up entirely of *ticos*, except for Ornes and Marcos Ortega, a Honduran, but he lost control of the name to events. Jerry Hannifin, a *Time* magazine correspondent, picked up on it, writing inaccurately that Limón had been taken by "a group of *caribeanos*," which he "baptized" the Caribbean Legion.[65] Having a romantic sound, "Caribbean Legion" quickly became part of the vocabulary of the antidictatorial struggle in the Caribbean; at the suggestion of Ornes, and in order to distinguish their group from rival factions, Rodríquez and Ramírez adopted the name informally. But Figueres resented its implication, describing the Legion as a "phantom" used by dictators and reactionaries "to disfigure and condemn our noble effort."[66]

The Government Surrenders

In mid-April 1948, however, that "noble effort" was enjoying nothing but success. With the fall of Cartago and Limón, President Picado placed San José under the protection of the foreign diplomatic corps on April 12 and requested the diplomats to mediate the government's surrender. Figueres appointed Padre Benjamin Núñez, an activist priest and head of the "Rerum Novarum" labor union, as his chief negotiator to travel to the Mexican embassy in the capital for the peace talks. There, Núñez learned that Picado and Calderón were not the main problem; Mora and his labor brigades, which were far more formidable than the Costa Rican Army, were out of control and threatening to raise a "Madrid-style" defense of San José, to engage in house-to-house fighting.[67] In order to meet this emergency, Núñez arranged a late night meeting on April 15 between Figueres and Mora at Ochomogo, a hilltop site between Cartago and San José, in "no-man's land." Striving to appease Mora, Figueres guaranteed that he would preserve labor's gains of the "eight years."[68]

Though the so-called "Pact of Ochomogo" cleared the way for Núñez to resume the talks, they were disrupted again almost immediately. Calderón's brother Francisco had traveled to Managua to encourage Nicaragua to intervene in the government's behalf (Somoza had gotten wind of Arévalo's intervention), but U.S. Ambassador Nathaniel Davis, a member of the diplomatic team of mediators, weighed in, condemning the maneuver and demanding that Picado repudiate it.[69] The final obstacle had been removed, and Núñez signed the "Pact of the Mexican Embassy" on April 19, permitting Picado to surrender without humiliation by transferring the executive power to an interim president, who in turn agreed to deliver the reins of government to Figueres (Figueres had abandoned his "unconditional surrender" bravado).[70] The Army of National Liberation entered San José unmolested on April 24, giving the Picadista-Calderonista forces time to empty the arsenals and government ministries of guns, typewriters, files, and furniture and truck it all north to Nicaragua.[71]

The Realities of Victory

In the victory parade on April 28 the exile revolutionary leaders occupied a prominent place in the line of march, giving substance to the existence of the Caribbean Legion and growing its myth. Figueres had provided the generalship and grand strategy, and Costa Ricans did the fighting. But everyone was saying that a millionaire Dominican general bankrolled the war, sending a steady stream of arms and supplies that made victory possible, and that his legionnaires furnished the leadership and training to transform *tico* farmers into soldiers.[72] The General came to San José expecting to exercise his position as commander in chief of the allied armies under the terms of the Caribbean Pact. Figueres needed to set him straight, but first he had Otilio Ulate nipping at his heels.

Much to his chagrin, Figueres learned that the legitimacy of his struggle rested upon the upholding of Ulate's election. "We fought to create the Second Republic," remarked Daniel Oduber, "but the people fought for their vote."[73] Figueres was impulsive and strong-willed, but he was no dictator. As head of the Founding Junta of the Second Republic, he made a pact with Ulate on May 1 whereby, recognizing Ulate as president-elect, the junta was empowered to govern for eighteen months (with a possible six-month extension) for the purpose of holding elections for a constituent assembly and the drafting of a new constitution. Before reaching this agreement with Ulate, Figueres was already having second thoughts about the Caribbean Pact, as noted, but now his situation was even weaker with reference to fulfilling the rash promises he had made.

For Rodríguez, Costa Rica was a stop on the way back to the Dominican Republic; for Figueres, it was the end of the line. But they had a deal. The sticking point was Rodríguez's insistence on being supreme commander. There was no way that Don Pepe could or would fulfill this part of the bargain. Costa Rica had lost two thousand lives in the War of National Liberation, and Figueres could not ask the nation to sacrifice more under any circumstances. And how much of an excuse would Somoza need to send a reinforced Calderón back across the frontier? Figueres was grateful to Rodríguez for his aid and he still needed his guns because Picado and Calderón had looted the arsenals before fleeing north, but he regarded this assistance as "lend-lease," for which he was prepared to make restitution. Even so, he explained the lodging of the General in an "elegant villa" and the maintenance of Ramírez and his legionnaires in the Second Artillery Barracks downtown as humanitarian gestures toward "the displaced persons of the New World."[74] Horacio Ornes sensed that Figueres was going to renege, and he complained angrily to Arévalo, who acted to salvage what he could.

Arévalo wrote to Figueres on May 27, expressing the view that there were "defects" in the Caribbean Pact but that "they could be corrected with intelligence and a little bit of diplomacy." The pact was written, he observed, "in moments of inexperience and some of its clauses were drafted under the personal influence of the principal author, the General." Arévalo stated that the business of a "Supreme Committee" and "General Staff" was Rodríguez's doing and implied that it need not be taken too seriously. Nonetheless, he appealed to Figueres's honor to avoid the "tremendous political error" of pulling out of the pact, signed "with an oath of loyalty and discipline . . . until the fall of the last dictator." He suggested the signing in San José of a new agreement, "complementary to the first, in order to perfect it and adapt it to the new situation."[75] Figueres had gotten what he wanted; he was free to assist the exile revolutionary movement as much or as little as he pleased.

The complementary agreement eventually drafted and signed concurrently in Guatemala City and San José on September 21, 1948, was a rhetorical statement of "aims and principles of the Caribbean Liberation Movement." It lacked any mechanism for implementation, describing the movement as "essentially democratic and Americanist, opposed, therefore, to any extremist political-economic system, either of the left or of the right." In its strongest affirmation the movement proposed to fight by every means of its ability—"particularly by means of arms, considering this means the only decisive way"—against the "cruel" regimes of Nicaragua, the Dominican Republic, and Honduras. But the agreement did not create a central committee or allied command for purposes of the armed struggle. After the liberation of the enslaved lands, the revolutionary governments agreed to undertake reforms to ensure the stability of democratic institutions and the elimination of causes of poverty. Committed to human rights and freedoms, the movement pledged to sponsor "the formation" of such organs as may be necessary for that purpose.[76] Though it borrowed some of the highfalutin language of the Caribbean Pact, particularly with reference to inter-American treaties and hemispheric solidarity, only the shell was left.

In the meantime, with the approval of Figueres, the various parties to the Caribbean Pact had established headquarters in San José and begun preparations for a possible invasion of Nicaragua.

On to Managua

While Figueres worked to extricate himself from his fealty to Rodríguez, he remained dependent upon the General for his weapons. As a result, Figueres promised to return to Rodríguez twice as many guns as he had brought to Costa Rica and agreed to pay the expenses and provide quarters for the Caribbean Legion as custodians of the arsenal. Furthermore, he did indeed conspire in the preparation of an armed movement on Costa Rican soil against Somoza of Nicaragua. "Yes, I admit it," Figueres wrote almost forty years later. "I was an accomplice and a comrade, besides. And why? I know how to honor my word. Moreover, I sympathize with the freedom of all peoples."[77] He stationed the Caribbean Legion in the Second Artillery Barracks in San José and appropriated 167,177 *colones* for its care and feeding, usually in allotments of 10,475 *colones* spread out over an eight-month period beginning at the end of April 1948.[78] (In 1948, ₡ 5.67 = $1.00.) Evidence indicates that the Caribbean Legion in San José consisted of approximately thirty exile revolutionary officers and that it guarded Rodríguez's weapons and supervised military training for rebuilding the Costa Rican armed forces and possibly for exile revolutionary recruits at a drill ground and target range established at Ochomogo.[79] The trainees were bussed to the site in the morning and returned to San José in the late afternoon.

Despite the modest size of his command, Ramírez had big plans for the future. He prepared large wall charts, dated July 29, 1948, depicting the table of organization of the Liberation Army of the Caribbean (*Ejército de Liberación del Caribe*), using the formal title, not the sobriquet Caribbean Legion. Unfortunately the chart for the ground forces is not available, but those for the air forces and naval forces were preserved and are reproduced herein (see Figs. 2 and 3). Though these are paper forces that did not exist then, nor in such form at any time in the future, they provide some under-

EJERCITO DE LIBERACION DEL CARIBE
ORGANIZACION DE LAS FUERZAS DEL AIRE

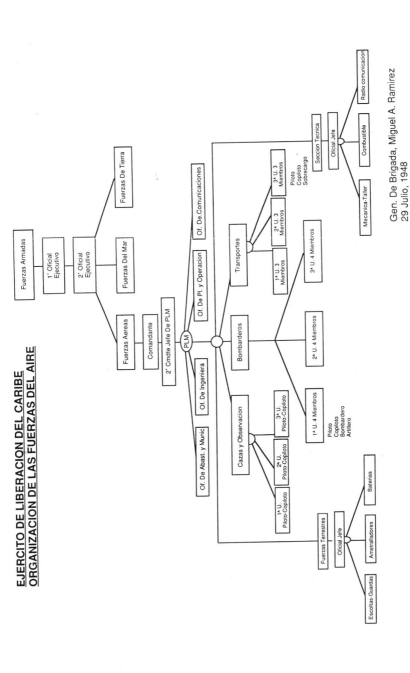

Gen. De Brigada, Miguel A. Ramirez
29 Julio, 1948

Fig. 2. Reproduction of wall chart depicting the organization of the air forces of the Liberation Army of the Caribbean. Prepared by Brigadier General Miguel A. Ramírez, July 29, 1948.

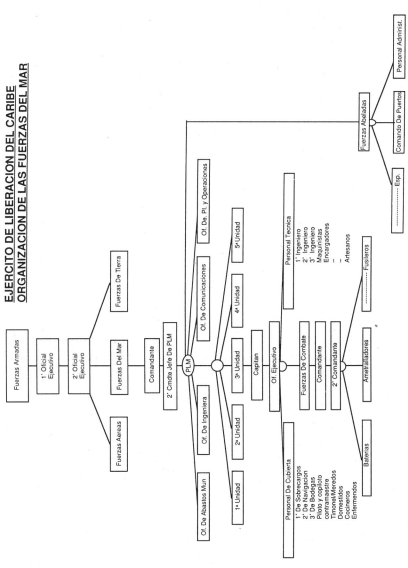

Fig. 3. Reproduction of wall chart depicting the organization of the naval forces of the Liberation Army of the Caribbean. Prepared by Brigadier General Miguel A. Ramírez, July 29, 1948.

standing of the myth and reality of the Caribbean Legion. The air forces, for example, included the staff; nine aircraft classified as pursuit and observation, bomber, and transport, with crews; and ground and technical support personnel, with arms and equipment. The naval forces apparently called for a larger number of personnel, encompassing a fleet of five vessels. One can only imagine the chart for the ground forces.

While Ramírez dreamed, Figueres picked Argüello to lead the liberation of Nicaragua. The Figueres-Argüello relationship went back to 1942, and they had plotted the antidictatorial struggle long before Rodríguez entered the scene. Following his victory, Figueres appointed Argüello as secretary general of the presidency and chief of the presidential guard. In this capacity Argüello reformed the presidential guard, cleaned up its barracks and parade ground, and improved the security of the presidential house (*Casa Presidencial*). But by achieving this largely with Nicaraguan personnel, he incurred the enmity of Army Chief of Staff Frank Marshall, Minister of Public Security Edgar Cardona, and Minister of Government and Police Fernando Valverde Vega, all of whom he in turn accused of atrocities and plunder in connection with mopping up operations after the War of National Liberation.[80] As a result of these confrontations, Argüello asserted that "the military leaders of the Second Republic . . . were out to get Nicaraguans."[81]

Facing a minicrisis in his government and unwilling to abandon yet another group of exiles who had aided him, Figueres killed two birds with one stone. In order to get Argüello out of town, Figueres installed him on a finca at Río Conejo, in the mountains near La Lucha, for the purpose of organizing an armed revolution against Somoza. Argüello opened his camp around the middle of June, first with twenty-six men, but the force eventually reached two hundred, for which Figueres put up 244,500 *colones* over a six-month period.[82] Argüello named his command the "Rafaela Herrera Company," which, he affirmed, was completely separate from, and "had nothing in common with," the Caribbean Legion. The Legion, he charged, "made a brave show marching and countermarching around the patio of [their] barracks, making sure that they drew their salaries, and in the late afternoons annoying the girls. . . . At night they got drunk and raised hell."[83] Apparently a lot of carousing went on, on all sides. Alberto Bayo, a Spanish Republican instructor who later trained Fidel Castro in guerrilla tactics, described Argüello's camp as similarly disorganized and undisciplined, run by a drunk.[84] Figueres later said that he "lost enthusiasm" for Argüello's operation because of his drinking.[85]

Life in the Camps

Certain information about Argüello's activities and those of the Caribbean Legion appears in statements by defectors from the respective camps. Manuel Valle Urbina, a former lieutenant in the Nicaraguan National Guard, told investigating officials in Managua on October 8, 1948, that he left Nicaragua on May 22 to join the "revolution" being prepared in Costa Rica. Starting out in Jinotega, he traveled by way of Estelí and Choluteca (Honduras) to Guatemala, where Raúl Arana put him up in the Pensión Alzamora with about twenty others (all Nicaraguans) until Argüello Jr. flew them to San José on June 6. In Costa Rica, according to Valle Urbina, a split developed among the ex-Guardia officers, the majority going with Colonel Manuel Gómez, the ranking officer, to the Caribbean Legion, but Valle, along with Guillermo and Augusto Cuadra, Federico Cabrera, Julio Tapia, Wladimir Barquero, and Julio García Mongalo, chose to stick with Argüello.[86]

Valle declared that he was at the Río Conejo camp from around June 15, when there were about twenty-six men present, until he withdrew on August 13, when the number had risen to ninety-three. Life in the camp, according to Valle, consisted of instruction in "handling rifles, automatic weapons, and open and closed order drills" and of repeated visits by Figueres and members of the Founding Junta, such as Alberto Martén and Daniel Oduber. Valle himself became disillusioned with the alleged influence of foreign—particularly Spanish—officers, who, he said, had a plan to infiltrate Nicaragua that was "a copy" of one they had for Spain: "They only had to change the names; where it said Spain, they inserted Nicaragua, and where it said Franquista, they substituted Somocista. I didn't see the plan, but they told me that it consisted of spreading terror, that is, a *communist* plan."[87] Titillating his inquisitors further, Valle described Argüello and his brothers as "alcoholic degenerates" who would ruin Nicaragua if they ever came to power, "in which case it would be better to leave it as it is." He affirmed that they had organized a junta of government comprised of Argüello Sr., president; Gustavo Manzanares; and Edelberto Torres, secretary.[88]

This same lineup was confirmed by Octavio Arana Jiménez, yet another defector and ex-Guardia lieutenant who gave his testimony to Nicaraguan officials in Managua on October 9, 1948.[89] Arana declared that "los Chendos" (the nickname of the Argüellos, padre and hijo) enjoyed the full confidence of Figueres and hence the group at Río Conejo was also known generally as "Los Puros" (akin to "The Untouchables").[90] Arana left Rivas on June 7 and entered Costa Rica at La Cruz a few days later, for the purpose, he said, of joining the revolutionary movement. Reaching San José, the "Chendos" would not take him in, suspecting him of being a spy, since no one vouched for him, nor did he come by way of the apparent established channel through Guatemala. But Manuel Gómez invited him to join the Caribbean Legion, offering him "food, lodging, and fifty *colones* a week." He was given the rank of major and assigned as an instructor at the Ochomogo camp, "primarily in closed order drill and for the courses in reconnaissance and patrols."[91] In describing the layout of the camp, particularly the target range, Arana testified that the U.S. military attaché in Costa Rica visited on one occasion.[92]

Lobbying for U.S. Support

The U.S. military attaché in San José at the time was Lieutenant Colonel James K. Hughes, who was the target of a campaign to win U.S. support for the antidictatorial movement in the Caribbean. In an unsigned "Memorandum for Colonel Hughes" in the fall of 1948, which bore the unmistakable influence of Dominican political exiles, the leaders of the Caribbean Liberation Movement (Arévalo, Figueres, and Rodríguez) proclaimed their revolutionary intentions but disclaimed any communist tendencies. The leaders expressed their "veneration" for Franklin Roosevelt and the Good Neighbor policy but lamented that FDR's policy of seeking an end to "injustice, poverty, and slavery" in the Caribbean was being thwarted by certain U.S. diplomats in collaboration with the tyrants Trujillo, Somoza, and Carías Andino.[93] Showing an acute sense of what was going on in Washington, they named specifically Joseph Davies, Homer Cummings, Henry Norweb, and Avra Warren, expressing particular concern that Warren, the former pro-Trujillo U.S. ambassador to the Dominican Republic (1943–44) and then U.S. ambassador in Lima, might be promoted to assistant secretary of state for inter-American affairs.[94]

At the same time they knew who their friends were: "In the opinion and judgment of the most responsible men of the Caribbean region—intellectuals, doctrinaire politicians, and liberal revolutionaries—Mr. Ellis O. Briggs, among the North American diplomats who recognize our problems, is the one who best understands the principles and nature of the new relationship that Franklin D. Roosevelt initiated with our peoples."[95] And there were others, they said, who were "worthy of mention," including Charles

Hauch, an educator and History Ph.D. then serving in the State Department; Nathaniel P. Davis, the U.S. ambassador to Costa Rica; Colonel Hughes himself, "a hero of the late war who enjoys our highest respect and esteem"; and Allan Stewart and George Barriman, officials of the U.S. embassy in Cuba. These were the North Americans, "guided by ideals of justice and freedom," whom the "genuinely democratic forces" of the Caribbean were counting on to counteract Rafael Trujillo's "powerful lobby" in Washington, "which also served the purposes of Somoza and Carías Andino."[96] Arana testified that he did not know the nature of the report that the "American colonel" made about his visit to Ochomogo, but there is reason to believe it was friendly.

Cuba Still an Ally

Arana also claimed, as did Valle in his deposition, that Carlos Prío Socarrás, the president-elect of Cuba, had promised to turn over to Rodríguez and the Caribbean Legion the remaining arms in Cuba seized in the Cayo Confites affair.[97] They added that Argüello Sr., whom Figueres had appointed as his representative to Prío's upcoming inauguration (October 10, 1948), had secured this pledge.

As president-elect, Prío traveled to Guatemala, Venezuela, and Costa Rica, and, without question, Caribbean conspiratorial matters were strongly on his mind. The U.S. embassy in Guatemala speculated that Prío's upcoming visit, August 20–25, was "more than a good-will visit," basing this largely on Juan Bosch's arrival there on August 4 as an "advance agent" and the indications that "he came at least partly on Caribbean Legion business."[98] The guess was good; following the visit, the embassy reported that Prío and Arévalo had denounced "tropical dictatorships" and noted furthermore the "conspicuous presence" of Ramírez, Eufemio Fernández, Argüello Jr., Francisco Morazán, and "others known to be involved in the Caribbean Legion."[99] "The prime purpose" of Prío's visit, the embassy asserted, was to let Arévalo know "just how far" he was willing to go in supporting the overthrow of Trujillo, Carías, and Somoza "and to enter into some form of agreement for the coordination of their activities."[100]

Prío traveled next to Venezuela, where the Rómulos—Betancourt and Gallegos—were barely hanging on, for more Caribbean conspiratorial business, and then on to Costa Rica. Bosch showed up in San José on September 2, again as Prío's "advance agent," with the American embassy breath-lessly reporting: "Possibility exists Nicaraguan Conservatives—Dominicans forcibly holding Figueres to commitment. They have even hinted assassina-tion Argüello hijo."[101] The part about wanting to do in Argüello was insight-ful—rival exile leaders deplored Figueres's insistence that "Chendo" lead the Nicaraguan liberation movement—but that about demanding that Figueres comply with his pledges does not square with his claim that Rodríguez on his own initative had let him off the hook just days before.

Writing in 1987, Figueres reproduced the text of a note, dated August 24, 1948, in which Rodríguez, in his capacity as "Supreme Chief of the Libera-tion Army of the Caribbean," "relieved" Figueres of his commitment of "last December" because of the "difficult situation presently burdening Costa Rica."[102] Nor does this square with the September 21 statement of the Carib-bean Liberation Movement. In any case, the evidence is that Figueres was an unreliable ally, meaning that by the end of the summer of 1948 Arévalo and Rodríguez had grown tired of waiting for him to act.

General Colindres Tries Again

Arana Jiménez, in his testimony before Nicaraguan officials, referred to the death of the Sandinista Colindres in a clash with the Nicaraguan Guardia on October 2. He related that Arévalo planned to assist an uprising in Nicara-gua by airlifting arms and ammunition to Colindres and that one of the planes in the operation was piloted by "Captain Cilfa [*sic*], Dominican, a naturalized North American. . . . These planes made two trips, on consecu-tive days, but since they did not encounter the prearranged signals on the landing field, they did not land and returned to their base in Guatemala."[103] This account corroborates the tale that Nicolás Silfa told in his memoir, *Guerra, traición, y exilio,* published in 1980.

Silfa described how the Costa Rica operation was going sour in the sum-mer of 1948. The combined forces of the Rafaela Herrera Company (Río Conejo, "Los Puros") and the Caribbean Legion barely exceeded two hun-dred, and when talk developed about forming a single Nicaraguan Libera-tion Army, Figueres insisted that Argüello be made commander in chief, with Ramírez as chief of staff. Carlos Pasos, Gustavo Manzanares, and An-tonio Velásquez, among other Nicaraguan exile leaders, did not like the arrangement but went along as "the only way" to maintain Don Pepe's support, planning to dump Argüello once their situation improved.[104] For his part, Rodríguez, who had been shuttling back and forth between Guatemala and San José, decided to remain in Guatemala, not fully appeased by Arévalo's efforts to smooth things over.[105] Silfa stayed with him.

Though Rodríguez's position in Costa Rica was diminished by Figueres, he remained in effect Arévalo's covert action chief, enabling him to regain influence over exile revolutionary activities. The American embassy in Guatemala reported in September that Arévalo's "principal supporters at home"—organized labor and the leftist political parties—did not like the "rightist" Figueres, or Prío, the latter because of "his present antagonism toward communist labor leaders in Cuba," and predicted that if Arévalo persisted "in forming such distasteful alliances, he may eventually find himself and his country involved in undertakings [outside] his borders which have little or no popular support at home."[106] Rodríguez helped Arévalo overcome this problem by providing him with the means to conceal his international intrigues; when revolutionary exiles contacted the President, his usual reaction was, "go see General Rodríguez."[107]

One of those sent to see Rodríguez was the old Sandinista general Colindres, whom Rodríguez (with Arévalo's connivance) pledged to supply with weapons. Rodríguez gave Silfa, the wild man who nearly blew up part of Manhattan in December 1946, the mission almost two years later of playing secret agent in the mountains of Nicaragua. Silfa told that he drove with Colindres and Colonel Reglas Raudales ("Reglita") to Nicaragua to check out the landing strip to be used in flying arms to the guerrilla forces in Nueva Segovia. Returning to Guatemala by car, Silfa then made two flights from Los Cipresales Airport to the airfield in the Segovia region but did not land either time, precisely as Arana testified because the "three white sheets," the signal to land, were not in place.[108] Silfa maintained that Jacobo Arbenz helped plan and facilitate these clandestine flights. Shortly after the unsuccessful second flight, Colindres was killed (October 2) in Nicaragua in a skirmish with Somocista forces.[109]

Somoza Aroused

On the heels of this clash at the beginning of October, and armed with the "confessions" of ex-Guardia lieutenants Arana and Valle, Somoza denounced Arévalo, Betancourt, Figueres, and Prío for plotting an armed action by "a legion of bandits" against Nicaragua.[110] Rodríguez's note to Figueres on August 24 notwithstanding, Silfa claimed that Somoza's angry charges forced the Caribbean Legion to get out of Costa Rica once and for all.[111] The *New York Times* published a report dated October 26 that the Legion "had just been moved to Guatemala."[112] And a month later Figueres publicly announced the "demobilization" of the Caribbean Legion, thanking Ramírez for his past service to Costa Rica and for acting now "to ease" international tensions.[113] More concretely, the Founding Junta issued four checks to General Rodríguez on October 5, 1948, totalling $125,000, as compensation for the arms lost or destroyed in the War of National Liberation.[114] It requested him not to move the weapons still in his possession since the government had been unable to purchase others and in view of "the imminent threat of an invasion."[115] The junta had authorized $250,000 for the purchase of arms to replace those of Rodríguez, and Daniel Oduber made two arms-shopping trips to Canada and the United States in May and July, without success.[116]

These developments made no reference to "Los Puros" at Río Conejo. Argüello accused Figueres of betraying him, but Figueres kept faith with him longer than anyone else. Don Pepe blamed Argüello's own incompetence for his failure to get things done; though he conceded that the infighting among the various groups hampered his efforts. "They competed for everything," Figueres wrote. "The leadership of the movement, priority of actions, control of the arms, and even for my favor. Their conduct was not always proper, causing resentment on the part of the civilian population."[117] This was a common charge, stated repeatedly at a later date. Considering that Figueres was in full control of Río Conejo, it appears that he was content to let matters slide. Clearly, the steam had gone out of the movement.

But Somoza was not one to ignore even a paper threat. In possession of statements by deserters from both the Caribbean Legion and Río Conejo, he knew the nature of the exile opposition, and his intelligence chiefs compiled an extensive "enemies list" (see Appendix A). He collected further testimony about the Río Conejo camp on November 3 from Guillermo Segundo Trejos Aguilar, a Nicaraguan student who had trained there between June 26 and August 4. Trejos was an unhappy soul who seemed to spend most of his time malingering, for which he was repeatedly disciplined. He confirmed that Río Conejo was the property of Figueres and that the purpose of the movement was to overthrow Somoza; the detachment at Río Conejo wanted to replace Somoza with Argüello, hijo, he related, whereas the Caribbean Legion favored Gustavo Manzanares.[118] In response to a question about the plans for invading Nicaragua, Trejos Aguilar declared, "some will enter by way of las Segovias, others via Los Chiles [Costa Rica], and also Rivas, by land and by air. . . . General Carlos Rivera Delgadillo told us: patience, boys, everything is ready, we are only waiting for the right moment for the invasion of Nicaragua."[119] Such expressions convinced Somoza that Costa Rica was no longer the trouble-free neighbor it had been and that Figueres was the cause. Don Pepe had been poking his stick in the viper's den too long. At the same time, inconsistent with his risky behavior, Figueres abolished the Costa Rican Army on December 1, 1948.

Somoza Precipitates a Crisis

On the morning of December 9, 100 to 150 men proceeding from Nicaragua attacked and occupied the Costa Rican border town of La Cruz, routing the fourteen customs guards on duty there. In the next two days additional armed groups of Costa Rican exiles, followers of Rafael Angel Calderón Guardia, seized the undefended neighboring hamlets of Puerto Soley, El Amo, and Murcielago.[120] The Nicaraguan Guardia assisted the rebels to the border, but once in Costa Rica they were on their own, and they penetrated no farther than Santa Rosa in the remote northwest corner of the country.[121] Without an army Don Pepe might have asked the Caribbean Legion or Los Puros for help in repelling the invaders—Somoza was hoping he might, because such action would give him an excuse to intervene—but Figueres did not take the bait and instead invoked the Inter-American Treaty of Reciprocal Assistance (the Rio Treaty), sending a note to the president of the Council of the Organization of American States on December 11.

The OAS Council met in extraordinary session on December 12 to hear Costa Rica's complaint and Nicaragua's rebuttal. It resolved to solicit more information and reconvene on December 14, appealing to Figueres and Somoza to cooperate in the meantime for the maintenance of peace.[122] By his action Figueres had essentially stopped the invasion from becoming serious, but he also submitted his government to the authority and censure of the inter-American juridical process. Either way, the Caribbean Legion was the loser. On December 14 the OAS Council convoked a Meeting of Consultation but, acting under the provisions of the Rio Treaty, constituted itself as the Provisional Organ of Consultation and appointed a committee to make an on-site investigation. It charged the committee with investigating Costa Rica's accusation that Nicaragua had helped armed rebels to invade its territory and with examining Nicaragua's concerns about the "antecedents" of the affair, meaning the activities of the Caribbean Legion in Guatemala and Costa Rica.[123]

The Investigating Committee, comprised of Luis Quintanilla (Mexico) as president, and José María Bello (Brazil), Silvio Villegas (Colombia), and Paul C. Daniels (United States) as members, arrived in San José on December 17. During a four-day stay it interviewed Calderonista prisoners of war captured at Santa Rosa on December 10 and General Ramírez, "leader of the Caribbean Legion," who was "accompanied by" Dr. Virgilio Mainardi, Dr. Andrés Alvarado Puerto, Major Francisco Sánchez, and Colonel Jorge Rivas Montes.[124] The committee raised the possibility of a meeting between Figueres and Somoza, but Figueres refused on "historic and political grounds" and on the basis of "personal feelings."[125] The committee then flew to Managua on December 20, where it interviewed, among others, former President Picado and the defectors Valle Urbina and Arana Jiménez.

Argüello and Ramírez had suspected that Arana Jiménez was a spy, but he denied it vehemently. In fact, while he was still in Costa Rica, he demanded an investigation of such accusations (on September 7), which he claimed were undermining the efforts and "steady progress of our Legion."[126] The Nicaraguan Foreign Ministry gave the Investigating Committee a *copy* of this "request for an investigation" on its official stationery, reproducing the letterhead "General Headquarters of the Caribbean Legion, San José, Costa Rica."[127] This is a rare item, if genuine (see Fig. 4).

The committee returned to Washington on December 23 and prepared its conclusions for presentation to the Provisional Organ of Consultation (OAS Council) the following day. It confirmed Costa Rica's charges that the Calderonista invasion originated in Nicaragua and that the Nicaraguan government did not take adequate measures to prevent it from happening. The committee reported that once the rebel force entered Costa Rica, Nicaragua cut off further assistance, and that it discovered no evidence that Nicaraguan armed forces themselves violated Costa Rican territory, though it "had the impression" that Nicaraguan military elements provided "technical assistance" to the rebels before they crossed over.[128] On the other hand, it affirmed as "undeniable" that the Caribbean Legion enjoyed the "material and moral support" of the Costa Rican government in its determination "to overthrow certain Governments, among them the present Nicaraguan re-

MINISTERIO
DE
RELACIONES EXTERIORES

REPÚBLICA DE NICARAGUA

<u>C O P I A</u>

CUARTEL GENERAL DE LA LEGION CARIBE
San José   Costa Rica

7 de Septiembre 1948

De los   : Tenientes Manuel Ag. Alfaro C., y Octavio Arana.
Al   : Oficial Comandante.

Asunto   : INVESTIGACION, solicitud de.

1.- Por conducto del Teniente Antonio Orúe, hemos sido informados que el señor
Angel Argüello, tiene en su poder correspondencia o documentos llegados de Nicaragua, en los cuales se nos sindica como "Espías" ó agentes al servicio del régimen
de Somoza.- Como tal aseveración, nos coloca en una situación sumamente delica-
da, con detrimento de nuestra dignidad personal y de nuestro honor militar, de
la manera más enérgica rechazamos tan vil calumnia y al mismo tiempo solicitamos
se sirva Ud., levantar una investigación personalmente ó por medio de una Junta
de Oficiales para que investigue inmediatamente la veracidad de tal cargo.

2.- Como militantes activos y desinteresados de la causa de los pueblos del Caribe, estamos ajenos a ciertas torpes maquinaciones de carácter político y per -
sonal, que algunos elementos úrden con el propósito de malograr el buen éxito
hasta ahora logrado por nuestra Legión del Caribe en todos los aspectos del
movimiento de liberación. No sería pues extraño, que la información aludida
formara parte de un vasto plan de desintegración, que se han propuesto tales
elementos, para sabotear los esfuerzos y los sacrificios hechos hasta la fecha,
para destruir poco a poco al personal militar nicaragüense y con ello, la bue-
na marcha de nuestra Legión. Es por tal motivo que requerimos cuanto antes la
investigación solicitada, a fin de desenmascarar de una vez a los verdaderos
saboteadores que esgrimen como arma de combate la calumnia y la mentira.-

3.- Rogámosle encarecidamente se sirva acusarnos recibo por endoso.

(Fdo.) Manuel Agustín Alfaro   (Fdo.)   Octavio Arana J.
        Teniente Inf. AM de N.   Teniente Inf. AM de N.

Fig. 4. Copy of Octavio Arana Jiménez's request for an investigation of charges of
espionage against him; submitted to the OAS Investigating Committee by the government of Nicaragua.

gime."[129] In view of its findings the Investigating Committee submitted a
resolution to the Provisional Organ of Consultation, which the latter approved the same day.

The December 24 resolution enjoined the governments of Costa Rica and
Nicaragua "to abstain immediately from any hostile actions between them."

It chastised Nicaragua for failing to restrain the Calderonista forces and advised Costa Rica that it "could and should" remove from its territory armed groups "conspiring against Nicaragua and other American Republics." It called upon both nations to observe the principles of nonintervention and inter-American solidarity.[130] In order to implement its resolution the OAS Council acting provisionally as the Organ of Consultation resolved to create an Inter-American Commission of Military Experts to oversee the steps taken by Nicaragua to fulfill its treaty obligations (particularly the Havana Convention on the Rights and Duties of States in the Event of Civil Strife), meaning the muzzling of Calderón, and by Costa Rica to expel armed conspiratorial elements, meaning the Caribbean Legion.

Prisoners of War Provide Insights

According to statements by *tico* recruits and volunteers who fell into the hands of the Nicaraguan Guardia, the withdrawal of the Caribbean Legion was well under way before the Military Commission arrived in San José on December 30. To explain: during the Investigating Committee's on-site inspection, Costa Rica retook the four towns occupied by Calderonista forces, but no sooner had the committee departed than rebel forces raided Puerto Soley again on December 25, torching the town and carrying off thirty-nine "prisoners of war."[131] The prisoners were taken to Nicaragua, where the Guardia accepted them in a "humanitarian gesture" (to save them from being shot) and transported them to Managua, where they were interrogated, "voluntarily and in accordance with international law."[132]

One might argue that the capture of prisoners for intelligence purposes was the reason for the raid. In any event the nature of the questions themselves revealed a determination on the part of the Guardia officers to expose the Caribbean Legion. Though they concluded that the Caribbean Legion indeed existed and was stationed in the Artillery Barracks in San José under the command of the Dominican General Ramírez, the information collected was probably disappointing.

The *ticos* were volunteers who responded to Figueres's call on December 11 to come to the defense of the nation. As a group they volunteered between December 11 and 15 and received from four to ten days training before being sent to the front. They were aware generally of the Caribbean Legion but could provide few details, other than identifying from photos legionnaires such as Ramírez, Jorge Rivas, Adolfo Báez Bone, Manuel Gómez, José María Tercero, Francisco Morazán, and "El Indio" Sánchez; only one had ever heard of "Los Puros" or "Los Chendos." Captain Eladio Alvárez Urbina, the commander of the force captured in Puerto Soley, related that he was a member of the Caribbean Legion, but of the *criollo* Legion, made up of Costa Ricans, that captured Puerto Limón in April and had since disbanded. The only foreigner in that Caribbean Legion, he stated, was the Dominican Horacio Ornes, "who left Costa Rica more than six months ago."[133] Concerning the other "so-called" Caribbean Legion, he knew "absolutely nothing," except "that of the foreign officers who had been in my country, none remain."[134]

This detail was confirmed by others, who testified that because of the presence of the Investigating Committee in Costa Rica, Captain "Vico" Starke disarmed the "Legion" (comprised of as few as seven or eight men in one statement and as many as twenty or twenty-five in another) and on December 14 removed it from the Bella Vista Fortress, where the *tico* volunteers were training.[135] According to Alvaro Castro Herrera (one of the POWs), besides wishing to escape embarrassment the Caribbean Legion had been disarmed "because this was our fight and the Costa Rican people would not approve of foreigners meddling in our affairs."[136]

There was general negative comment about the behavior of the Caribbean Legion, which gave Somoza something of propaganda value. José Ramón Villalobos Jiménez described the legionnaires as "lazy bums, lying around doing nothing,"[137] and José Manuel Solís Vargas complained that they were "getting a lot of money that ought to be spent on us."[138] "We never had much contact with them," Claudio Malavasi Mora declared, "because they were loud and boisterous, and that kind of people disgust Costa Ricans."[139] They all agreed that the legionnaires were rude, ridiculing and laughing at them during their training. That was the real reason, they insisted, why Captain Starke became angry and took away their guns and threw them out of the Bella Vista Fortress.[140] These sentiments may have contributed to the portrayal in some quarters of the Caribbean Legion as a band of irresponsible adventurers, but it is not clear that the group of vagabonds described were the same persons identified in photographs. Nor is it clear what they were doing in Bella Vista, when all accounts placed the Caribbean Legion in the Second Artillery Barracks, on the other side of town.

Somoza Achieves His Purpose

It may be that Figueres wanted the Caribbean Legion out of sight, especially while the Investigating Committee was in San José (though Ramírez met with it), but he had not counted on the appointment of a watchdog committee. When the Military Commission reached Costa Rica, it picked up the trail of the Caribbean Legion. On January 21, 1949, it reported to the Provisional Organ of Consultation that the "principal leaders of the so-called Caribbean Legion still remain in Costa Rica, especially San José." And, furthermore, that the Calderonista rebels in northern Costa Rica were "still receiving aid from Nicaraguan territory."[141]

Aware that the council was considering the possibility of a pact of friendship between Costa Rica and Nicaragua, the Military Experts recommended that the agreement include a guarantee on Nicaragua's part to close the frontier "to the passage of Costa Rican rebels and supplies for same" and a pledge by Costa Rica "to take effective and immediate measures for control and absolute vigilance over the leaders of groups conspiring to overthrow the Nicaraguan Government."[142] In accordance with the recommendations of the Military Commission, which also urged that the parties reiterate adherence to the Havana Convention and the Resolution of December 24, 1948, the OAS Council appointed a drafting committee on January 25 to prepare a pact of friendship for the signatures of Costa Rica and Nicaragua.

In the meantime Figueres invited his erstwhile allies to leave Costa Rica. He suggested to Argüello that he "take a vacation in Cuba or Mexico for a couple of months," giving time for "the air to clear."[143] In truth, they never reconciled. Ramírez and his staff also took the hint, being provided with passage money and a form of severance pay; that is, "initial expenses in their new places of residence."[144] Bowing to criticism within his own party, however, Figueres expelled only high-profile activists and revolutionaries. Out of a sense of gratitude and respecting the right of asylum, Costa Rica did not force "the majority" of those whom Nicaragua had listed as "threats to the peace" to leave the country.[145] The Military Commission was satisfied, nonetheless, that these persons "were not engaged in political-revolutionary activities" and concluded in its final report on February 17 that "at the present time militarily organized groups of nationals or foreigners do not exist on Costa Rican territory."[146] Considering that the rebel forces did not exceed two hundred men and that Costa Rica had no army to speak of, the Military Commission concluded that "the nature of the problem and its solution lie essentially in the political field and not in the military."[147]

The Legion Moves On

Acting in that spirit, the OAS Council proceeded with the conclusion of a Pact of Friendship between Costa Rica and Nicaragua on February 21. Under the terms of the pact and in reference to the recent events, the parties pledged no hard feelings for the statements they had made about each other and promised to prevent a repeat of their behavior in the future, respecting the principles of nonintervention and hemispheric solidarity, as well as faithful compliance with inter-American treaties. In the event of a dispute in the future, the parties agreed to employ the procedures for pacific settlement provided by the Rio Treaty and the OAS Charter. They agreed further to adhere to the Havana Convention, especially with reference to effective measures for controlling their frontiers and preventing the use of their territory by revolutionary groups hostile to either party.[148] With the signing of this agreement by Costa Rica and Nicaragua, the OAS Council considered its work done and canceled the call for a Meeting of Consultation.

The OAS had saved Figueres from defeat, but it put him out of the revolution business for awhile. He learned the bitter lesson that in a juridical sense the OAS made no distinction between democrats and dictators, nor was it troubled by Spruille Braden's complaint that the principle of nonintervention ought not be a shield for dictators. By pushing a handful of armed men across the border in a low-risk operation, Somoza had removed a nuisance and a potentially dangerous situation. The Caribbean Legion initially enjoyed success in Costa Rica and ultimately notoriety. The OAS ordered its dissolution, but the U.S. Central Intelligence Agency estimated, as of March 1949, that that had not happened and, in fact, expected the Caribbean Legion to rise again "as a vigorous and significant force in Central American-Caribbean intergovernmental relationships."[149] Juancito Rodríguez was not licked yet, and he had an arsenal of guns and money to purchase more.

1949

Luperón

New Plan/New Hope

Even before Anastasio Somoza's action hastened the withdrawal of the Caribbean Legion from Costa Rica, Juan Rodríguez had shifted his base of operations to Guatemala and his focus away from Nicaragua to the Dominican Republic. The inability and reluctance of José Figueres to fulfill his pledges was a contributing factor, but in addition the Legion commanders "developed a greater respect for the loyalty of the Nicaraguan *Guardia Nacional* to its chief, Somoza."[1] If they could not count on significant defections on the part of the Guardia, they realized they did not have the firepower to overcome Tacho alone, so the sense was to back off. After its setback in Costa Rica, the Legion was described as "quiescent,"[2] reduced to some fifty or sixty men.[3] But Rodríguez possessed "an indomitable will and unquenchable thirst for revenge," meaning that, with the Nicaragua invasion off, he was ready to take his turn in preparing an invasion of the Dominican Republic.[4] Juan José Arévalo apparently approved.

Although Arévalo's antidictatorial stance was linked to his goal of Central American federation, his support of Rodríguez's project to overthrow Trujillo, though outside the isthmian region, was no less intense. It began with the purchase in December 1948 of twenty-five Reising submachine guns from the Harrington and Richardson Arms Company of Worcester, Massachusetts, by the Ministry of Defense of Guatemala (meaning Jacobo Arbenz was privy to the affair). Fifteen of these guns ended up in the hands of

Trujillo, taken from the group that invaded the Dominican Republic the following June (see Fig. 5). Although Rodríguez's relations with Figueres had cooled, the General was much influenced by the strategy that Figueres used in winning the War of National Liberation. Instead of the grand-scale Cayo Confites invasion plan, he envisioned airlifting a small expeditionary force to the Dominican Republic, with enough guns and ammunition to arm and train volunteers on the spot. This plan tended to mesh with one that a group of Dominican exiles in Puerto Rico had been working on also.

Tulio Arvelo, who was last seen being led from the *Berta* at gunpoint, did not follow Rodríguez to Guatemala after Cayo Confites but took up residence in Puerto Rico, working as a reporter for the *Diario de Puerto Rico,* Luis Muñoz Marín's paper. There, he and other Dominican exiles continued to meet and plot against Trujillo. The elements in Puerto Rico tended to have more contact with family and friends in Santo Domingo and came up with the idea that maybe they could start a revolt within the country if only they could smuggle in enough arms. "Drawing on the experience of Cayo Confites," Arvelo explained, "we decided on a change of tactics and instead of sending armed men we would send arms, delivering them to a group organized within Dominican territory called the Internal Front. Once armed, the men would begin the rebellion."[5] They developed this scheme in secret correspondence, writing in invisible ink between the lines of ordinary letters to friends and relatives back home. In order to carry out this plan, they decided to request the use of the Cayo Confites arms still in Cuba.

For this purpose Arvelo traveled to Havana in February 1949, using the excuse that he was covering the Inaugural Caribbean World Series of baseball set to begin play on February 20. He stayed at the Hotel San Luis, still the haven for exile revolutionaries (in fact, Rómulo Betancourt was there then, having been ousted from Venezuela in a coup), contacting Cruz Alonso, Juan Bosch, and especially Eufemio Fernández, the chief of secret police and President Carlos Prío's top bodyguard. They all showed interest in the plan but wanted more information about the strength and determination of the Internal Front and the number and kinds of ships needed for delivering the arms. Arvelo favored transferring the weapons on the high seas to local craft that could take them ashore without arousing suspicion.[6]

Making a second trip with the additional data requested, Arvelo seemed to make no headway, and Cruz Alonso introduced him to Antonio Román Durán, who was on a similar mission for Rodríguez. Román Durán was a Spanish Republican refugee who came to the Dominican Republic in 1937

CONFIDENTIAL

MEMORANDUM

March 1, 1950

Subject: Origin of certain sub-machine guns
           captured by Dominican authorities
           from the PBY destroyed at Luperon

The Dominican Government in a statement of
January 30, 1950 delivered to the Investigating Committee
of the provisional organ of consultation of the
Organization of American States lists the serial numbers
of twenty-five Reising sub-machine guns, caliber 45,
model 50, manufactured by the Harrington and Richardson
Arms Company of Worcester, Massachusetts, which were
captured from the PBY destroyed at Luperon on June 19,
1949.   The serial numbers of fifteen of these submachine guns are identical with those of fifteen of a
group of such guns approved for export by the Department
of State on December 17, 1948 from the Harrington and
Richardson Arms Company to the Ministry of Defense of
Guatemala.

The serial numbers of the sub-machine guns
captured at Luperon which correspond to those approved
for export to the Ministry of Defense of Guatemala are
the following:

110877	111224
110917	113195
111331	113389
112401	113663
113086	112278
110767	111944
	110408
110527	109028

CONFIDENTIAL

Fig. 5.   Document prepared by Charles Hauch of the U.S. State Department for the
OAS Investigating Committee verifying that fifteen submachine guns captured at
Luperón were originally approved for export from the United States to the Ministry
of Defense of Guatemala.

and whom Trujillo accused of bringing communism to the island.[7] He was not having any luck either and suggested to Arvelo that he go to see Rodríguez in Guatemala; he would arrange passage. Rodríguez followed up, cabling him to come to Guatemala "as soon as possible."[8]

Rodríguez told Arvelo, as Arvelo recalled it, that he was not surprised the Cubans were giving him the runaround and that he could "expect nothing" from them. He blamed the Cubans for the Cayo Confites debacle and said he wanted nothing to do with them, nor with the Dominican crowd there. He stressed repeatedly that his experiences with the Cubans and the Dominicans in Havana "had been very painful."[9] He did not trust any of them, with the exception of Cruz Alonso, Eufemio Fernández, Cotubanamá Henríquez, Prío, and Bosch (the lone Dominican).[10] He hastened to add that the exiles in Puerto Rico were "trustworthy" and that he was anxious to work with them and make use of their contacts in the homeland, but that he "did not like" their plan of relying solely on the Internal Front "because within Santo Domingo and owing to the prevailing situation nobody knew who was a friend or who was an enemy."[11]

But he did like the idea of raising the bulk of the fighting force on Dominican soil. Rodríguez proposed that, instead of only sending in the arms, the Puerto Rico plan be combined with his plan whereby he would fly in with a cadre of veteran officers, distribute the arms to the recruits of the Internal Front, and take military command of the uprising. In addition, the operation differed from Cayo Confites "in that it was not a true invasion that would confront Trujillo's army immediately."[12] Arvelo agreed to the proposal—his main purpose being to fight against the "tyrant"—and agreed also to serve as liaison between Guatemala and Puerto Rico. He communicated this to his confidants in Puerto Rico in cipher and received their approval as well.[13] Arvelo eventually discovered that something else was different from Cayo Confites. When the expeditionary force entered its final phase of preparations in June, it assembled in an encampment near the San José Air Force Base on the Pacific, where it trained with career instructors of the Guatemalan Army, slept in barracks, ate in the mess hall, and had showers and privies.[14]

Setting the Operation in Motion

In the meantime Rodríguez was busy procuring aircraft for the operation. His son José Horacio and Alberto Bayo carried out the mission in Mexico and the United States, though Jacobo Fernández Alverdi, another Spanish refugee, replaced Bayo in May, when things bogged down. Spanish Republican refugees appeared quite prominent in this latest phase of exile revolutionary activity; in addition to Bayo, Fernández Alverdi, and Román Durán, there were Daniel Martín, Ignacio González, and Antonio and Gregorio Osuna. Martín and González were combat veterans of the Spanish Civil War and the Osuna brothers served in the French underground in World War II.[15] Working through Alfredo del Valle of RAMSA (Rutas Aéreas Mexicanas, S.A.) and Marion Findley of Houston, Texas, José Horacio and Fernández Alverdi managed to acquire seven aircraft: a C-46 Curtiss Commando; two Douglas C-47s; two PBY Catalina seaplanes; a Lockheed Hudson; and an Avro Anson V.[16] They also hired pilots and crews for the planes, but because they could not raise a sufficient number, the Lockheed and Avro Anson had to be left behind in Mexico.[17]

As in most clandestine operations, true patriots get mixed up with hustlers of one kind or another. In Guatemala, Arévalo, Arbenz, and Air Force Colonel Francisco Cosenza cooperated completely, but the situations in Mexico and the United States were different. José Horacio and Fernández Alverdi, in dealing with Del Valle, dealt with someone whom Mexican authorities believed was a contrabandist and who was notorious as a deadbeat.[18] Mexican officials became suspicious when Fernández Alverdi purchased the C-46 (Mexican registry XB-HUV) and C-47 (Mexican registry XA-HOS) from Del Valle on May 2 and 4, respectively, "it being notorious that he did not have that kind of money," and they decided to put a "special watch" on the planes in question.[19] Customs officials went over these planes thoroughly before they left Mexico City for Oaxaca on May 18 but lost track of them after that and advised all airports in the southeast of the Republic to be on the lookout for them.[20] The planes had skipped the country, flying to the San José Air Force Base in Guatemala.

While arranging for the planes, Rodríguez sent Arvelo to Cuba on a related mission in April. He instructed him to secure a fueling stop in Cuba for the air armada on its way from Guatemala to the Dominican Republic and to invite Eufemio Fernández to join the invasion force. He was to contact Cruz Alonso and Cotubanamá Henríquez, Prío's brother-in-law, but to avoid all Dominicans, except Bosch.[21] The bad experience of Cayo Confites was one reason, Rodríguez admitted, but also he had all the people he needed and he did not want to feed the rumor mill. For this reason Arvelo did not stay in the Hotel San Luis, but his mission did not go well in any event. He met with Bosch, who told him that "the questions of the Dominican revolution [could] not be resolved by one man." Bosch insisted that they would have to be thrashed out "in a meeting of *notables*."[22] Arvelo realized then and there that his mission was "a complete failure."[23] Bosch could hold the fueling stop hostage until he got his meeting, despite whatever influence Fernández and Cotú Henríquez might exert.

In his depression Arvelo violated his instructions and visited the Hotel San Luis, where he bumped into his childhood friend and fellow *cayoconfitero* Federico Horacio ("Gugú") Henríquez Vásquez. He tried to be evasive, but Gugú knew something was up and made him promise to speak to Rodríguez on his behalf. "It was the farthest thing from both our minds," Arvelo rued in hindsight, "that with that promise the doors were opened to his death scarcely two months later."[24] Gugú Henríquez was Cotú's cousin and had served in the U.S. Navy in the Pacific in World War II.

In Guatemala, Rodríguez said that of course Gugú could join them, but concerning the failure of Arvelo's mission, he was philosophical: "I have always said you cannot count on that bunch in Cuba for anything."[25] Rodríguez paid dearly for ignoring the politics of the affair but pushed ahead as commander in chief of the Liberation Army (Caribbean Legion). Conferring with his chiefs, they agreed upon Cozumel Island as a possible alternative for a fueling stop and entrusted their agent in Mexico, the former law school dean José A. Bonilla Atiles, to make the necessary arrangements. He apparently succeeded in this task, though the details are sketchy, and whatever understanding he achieved ultimately came undone. Horacio Ornes said Bonilla did it "through friends influential in Mexican politics but not officially" and that there were specific conditions tied to the permission to land.[26] It is possible that these "influential friends" included Vicente Lombardo Toledano and the Latin American Workers Confederation (CTAL).[27]

By the end of May the plan for the airborne invasion of the Dominican Republic had taken shape. The expeditionary force proposed to come in three groups, landing in distinct places on the island. Using the largest plane, the C-46 (XB-HUV), Rodríguez, with Eufemio Fernández as his battle chief, would land with thirty-six men in the central zone, the La Vega region, where he expected the people to rally around him once his presence became known; Miguel Angel Ramírez and Jorge Rivas Montes, in the C-47 (XA-HOS), would land in the southern zone with twenty-five men, in the vicinity of San Juan de la Maguana, which was Ramírez's hometown; and Horacio Ornes, with twelve men and a crew of three, would descend on the Bay of Luperón in the north, the Puerto Plata region, in a Catalina seaplane.[28] Each group was transporting large quantities of arms and ammunition, counting on the Internal Front to commit acts of sabotage and "to swell its ranks."[29] Félix García Carrasco, serving as a courier from Puerto Rico, announced that the Internal Front was ready.[30] It is difficult to believe that grown men would contemplate such a foolhardy venture, but Trujillo had been in power for nineteen years and they were apparently ready to try anything.

By Air, Land, and Sea

Trujillo had gotten wind of the movement, and his intelligence service reported that it involved a great deal more than an airborne invasion by approximately eighty men (when one adds in the air crews) carrying extra weapons to arm the underground. He had been ranting about the Caribbean Legion all year, reviling it as a "core of Marxism" under the protection of the "Communist degenerate" Arévalo,[31] but his concerns became serious as a result of information from agents and sources that he believed to be highly reliable. An official of "another" government "friendly to the Dominican Republic" informed Trujillo on May 16 that during March and April "large quantities of arms and ammunition" had been shipped from Guatemala and Mexico to the Cuban port of Baracoa, at the eastern tip of the island, and from thence to the Haitian port of Port-de-Paix. These weapons, according to the informant, had been acquired "by the filibusters of the Caribbean Legion" for the purpose of attacking the Dominican Republic. He added, "I am informed, furthermore, that Dr. Eufemio Fernández Ortega, Chief of the Secret Service of the Presidential Palace of Cuba, along with Sr. Cruz Alonso, the owner of the Hotel San Luis of Havana, have been giving their most determined cooperation and assistance to the members of the Legion that presently reside in Cuba."[32]

The report further identified a person by the name of Pichirilo, a Dominican national, as the captain of the vessel transporting the weapons from Cuba to Port-de-Paix. Writing thirty years later, Nicolás Silfa related that on June 18, 1949, Ramón Emilio Jiménez Pichirilo was the captain of a ship anchored in a port in eastern Cuba with three hundred men on board awaiting an additional contingent of five hundred men in order to reinforce the expeditionaries being airlifted from Guatemala.[33] He affirmed that Juan Bosch was in charge of the force and that Prío had arranged the vessel for his use.[34] Angel Miolán claimed that he was among the five hundred men who had assembled at that time at Bosch's home in Havana, "rifles on shoulders," waiting for the signal to set sail for the Dominican Republic.[35]

There were in fact two ships allegedly of Guatemalan origin involved in this movement, the *Alicia* and the *Patricia,* owned by the Indo-American Maritime Company, of which Cruz Alonso was the president and one of three stockholders.[36] The company was formed on June 11, 1949, giving the vessels a very thin cover of Cuban ownership at a very late date (in reference to the events a week later), and they were sold (resold?) to the Guatemalan ambassador in Cuba the following September 26.[37] The *Patricia* was described as a small gunboat; both vessels had a range of five hundred miles and could carry a cargo of sixty-three net tons.[38]

The final alarming aspect of the intelligence report placed Rolando Masferrer (the "tiger" of Cayo Confites) at that moment "in a strategic point on Haitian territory close to the Dominican frontier." Tying this to the clandestine shipment of arms to Haiti, the Dominican government was convinced that Masferrer was in Haiti plotting an invasion of the Dominican Republic.[39] In fact, the evidence is strong that what came to be known as the Luperón raid of June 18–19, 1949, would have been an air, land, and sea attack if everything had gone right: by air from Guatemala; by sea from Cuba; and by land from Haiti. But even as a combined operation it did not appear to be a coordinated effort, rather a piggybacking onto whatever Rodríguez might get started. Arévalo and Prío probably had the full picture but apparently stayed out of it; certainly they did not support Bosch's demand for a political understanding before proceeding.

Agitated by the reports from his spies, some of whom would be killed if discovered,[40] Trujillo sent a cable to President Prío to protest the activities of Eufemio Fernández and Cotubanamá Henríquez. He charged that "in combination with the Arévalo Government of Guatemala, they are leading a surprise invasion against my Government and they have offered military vessels, airplanes, and airports."[41] Prío replied with a handwritten memo in which he stated, "the information is not true in regard to Eufemio Fernández and Cotú. Guatemala could be [planning] something with regard to Nicaragua."[42] On the margin of the note he penned a vertical scrawl, "*Imposible cooperación de Cotú y Eufemio.*" Given Eufemio's deep involvement in the movement and his close relationship with Prío, it is likely that the Cuban president was engaging in a deception; in any case, commenting on the note later, Dominican officials pointed out the lie: the attack "was not against a Central American country, it was against the Dominican Republic."[43]

The Revolutionary Manifesto

By the second week in June, Rodríguez was set to go and he primarily was calling the shots. Bosch did not get his meeting of *notables* but apparently agreed to take part anyway. Much to Arvelo's surprise, he showed up in Guatemala for a last-minute briefing.[44] If Bosch had gained any concessions for himself or the struggling Dominican Revolutionary party, they did not appear in the operation's only public document, a "Manifesto" for distribution in the homeland, exhorting the Dominican people to rise up and join the liberation movement.

Though the Spaniard Román Durán was the manifesto's author, Rodríguez, Ramírez, and Ornes were its signatories, inscribing "on behalf of the Provisional Junta of Government and the Liberation Army" (no reference to the Caribbean Legion). They signed as Commander in Chief of the Liberation Army, Chief of Staff, and Chief of Operations, respectively. The junta of government, "to assume power temporarily," but not identified specifically, promised freedom of speech and assembly; agrarian reform; workers' rights, including a labor code and social security; the elimination of illiteracy; respect for private property; equal and honest administration of justice; an army and police worthy of a free and democratic people; it also pledged to stand beside authentically democratic regimes in the international arena, to honor freely contracted international commitments, and to convoke free elections once the country returned to normal.[45] Despite the revolutionary rhetoric a la mode, the General was acting like an old-style caudillo, largely ignoring the Dominican exile activists in Havana. The CIA noted in its estimate in March that "the Legion" had no "clearly defined ideology" and warned of the possibility that it might create only more of the same in the Caribbean.[46]

The Luckless Warriors

D-day was set for June 18. Rodríguez and Ramírez assembled their groups at the San José base in order to board the transports, and Ornes gathered his men on the Caribbean side at Lake Izabal prepared to lift off in the seaplane as soon as the main party passed over and circled twice as the signal to begin. Ramírez said the planes were "of the first quality,"[47] but Arvelo wrote that the condition of the C-46, for one, "left much to be desired," citing a defective altimeter in particular.[48] But if the planes were bad, the pilots were worse. Just three hours before H-hour, the mercenary pilots Ralph Wells and Bob Hosford—North Americans—and Pablo Herrera and Arturo Camacho—Mexicans—took off in their C-47 and Catalina, respectively, and headed for Mexico. José López Henríquez, the Mexican pilot of the C-47 (XA-HOS), had to be stopped at gunpoint from joining the mutiny.[49] Only José María del Castillo Altamirano, Mario Treviño Baxter, José Cardona, and Julián Valderrama Ibarra, the Mexican crew of the C-46, remained loyal.

Eufemio Fernández suggested postponing the expedition, but Rodríguez insisted on going forward and apparently arranged substitute aircraft without delay. If these were the two Guatemalan Air Force C-47s (T-1 and T-2) that indeed accompanied the expedition as cargo planes, the speed with which this came about is amazing, and it is a mystery as to where they were going to deliver the weapons. It boggles the mind to think that active duty pilots were going to fly aircraft with official Guatemala markings as part of a filibustering expedition to the heart of the Dominican Republic.

Nonetheless, at four in the afternoon of June 18, the expedition took off from the San José base in four planes and flew across Guatemala, circling Lake Izabal on the other side to signal Ornes to follow them, and proceeded past Belize and Yucatán. The tiny air fleet encountered fierce storms over the Caribbean, causing the C-46 with its faulty instruments to lose its way and land on the beach at El Cuyo, on the north shore of Yucatán. The three C-47s, though tossed around, reached Isla Cozumel as intended.[50] But the plans went awry. Mexican authorities immediately seized all four aircraft, impounding the cargo and detaining the occupants (almost the complete Caribbean Legion; see Appendix B).

Foiled Again

The action of the Mexican authorities squashed the expedition just that fast, but why? There was a tendency to hold Bonilla Atiles responsible for some kind of foul-up. Ornes blamed Ramírez, saying he disregarded every one of Bonilla's careful instructions.[51] Silfa spoke darkly of betrayal, claiming that Trujillo's gold was again a factor. He noted that Trujillo was close to former Mexican President Manuel Avila Camacho (1940–46) and closer still to his brother General Maximino Avila Camacho, whom Silfa described as "a crook and a Petán."[52] Miolán also accepted the betrayal theory but cast Francisco

Arana in the role of Genovevo Pérez Dámera in this latest drama.[53] The ambush slaying of Arana only a month later—and after Trujillo had broadcast a warning to him over *La Voz Dominicana*—fueled speculation that the Caribbean Legion killed him out of revenge. But the scholar Piero Gleijeses has proven that the death of Arana stemmed from internal politics; that is, Arana had strong-armed Arévalo and died resisting arrest when the President and Arbenz determined he needed to be disciplined.[54] It is true that Arana was killed while on a mission to seize some of Rodríguez's rifles, but that was more a circumstance than a factor in his demise. Debunking the revenge angle further, Miguel Feliú Arzeno, one of the expeditionaries, identified Colonel Arana, in particular, as a Guatemalan officer he judged to be *simpático*.[55]

In reality, the expedition may have failed because of circumstances unrelated to its purpose. As previously stated, two of the aircraft had left Mexico illegally in May, they were suspected of being used for smuggling operations, and all airports in southeast Mexico had been given their registries (XB-HUV and XA-HOS) and told to be on the lookout for them. Though Bonilla, Arévalo, or someone acting for them may have paid bribes to arrange the fueling stop, they were unaware that these particular planes were on a watch list, which created an entirely unforeseen situation when they landed at Cozumel and El Cuyo. This circumstance caused some awkwardness for the Guatemalan Air Force transports, but they were released in about forty-eight hours and permitted to return to Guatemala.

The presence of the Guatemalan planes, nonetheless, could not be denied, much to the embarrassment of the Guatemalan government. Though the planes were permitted to fly home, the names of their pilots, Gustavo Girón and René Valenzuela, appeared on the roster of detainees (see Appendix B). In a very clumsy effort by Guatemala to cover its tracks, the Guatemalan military attaché in Mexico addressed a note to the Mexican Ministry of National Defense, dated June 20, 1949, in which he requested landing permits for two Guatemalan Air Force C-47 transports, T-1 and T-2, at Cozumel or Mérida (the planes had been moved to Mérida, where they had been seen by tourists and other travelers) "possibly on the 21st of this month."[56] The attaché further apologized for the short notice but explained that he had not gone to his office on either Saturday (the eighteenth) or Sunday (the nineteenth), implying that the request had been there over the weekend (along with the C-47s).

If the episode had ended with the fiasco in Yucatán there would have been only red faces and recriminations, but it took on a more serious aspect because Ornes made it to the Dominican Republic.

The Luperón Raid

After the planes circled Lake Izabal, Ornes tried five times in vain to take off. The Catalina was overloaded and the wind conditions were poor, so the pilot had to give up when darkness fell. The following morning, after jettisoning some cargo, and after a few more tries, the seaplane finally lifted off and began its flight to the Dominican Republic.[57] Ornes and his group had no idea as to the fate of the others the night before, nor did they encounter any storms. The flight path took the plane out over the Caribbean past the Swan Islands, Jamaica, the north coast of Haiti, and onto the Bay of Luperón on Santo Domingo's north coast. The flight was smooth, and the adventurers tuned in a small portable radio to *La Voz de Santo Domingo,* hoping to pick up news about the invasion that surely was well under way. Instead, they heard the lilting sounds of Agustín Lara's "Granada," and small talk by the station announcer. How come? Well, suggested José Rolando Martínez Bonilla, "even if the government was falling, Trujillo would play popular music on the radio, so that the people would not know what was happening." Besides, he reasoned, the landings were in the interior and "the tactic was to avoid immediate contact with the enemy."[58] Everyone figured he was right, unaware that there had been no invasion yet. They were the only ones coming.

By whatever name—the Liberation Army or Caribbean Legion—the men on the Catalina were representative of the exile revolutionary movement. There were eight Dominicans: Ornes, Arvelo, Gugú Henríquez, José Rolando Martínez Bonilla, Miguel A. Feliú Arzeno, Hugo Kundhardt, Salvador Reyes Valdés, and Manuel Calderón Salcedo; three Nicaraguans: Alejandro Selva, Alberto Ramírez, and José Félix Córdova; and a Costa Rican, Alfonso Leyton. Six of the Dominicans had been at Cayo Confites (Ornes, Arvelo, Gugú, Martínez, Feliú, and Calderón); Gugú and Kundhardt were World War II veterans; Ornes and the *tico* Leyton took part in the seizure of Puerto Limón in 1948; and all three Nicaraguans were former Guardia officers, one of whom, Córdova, flew with Silfa in September 1948 in the vain effort to bring arms to Sandinista General Colindres. The crew of the Catalina were soldiers of fortune, U.S. citizens from Miami: John W. Chewning (pilot), Habet Joseph Maroot (copilot), and George Raymond Scruggs (mechanic-engineer).

They had been in the air almost eleven hours when Arvelo made reference to a neatly tied package, which appeared to contain books. Ornes told him it was a "manifesto" informing the Dominican people that their "hour of liberation was at hand" and calling upon students, workers, professionals, and the armed forces to join the liberating movement. Arvelo had not read it before. He was going home to destroy the tyrant; he let the chiefs fill in the details.[59] Ornes told the men for the first time that their destination was the Bay of Luperón, and at about 7:15 in the evening the seaplane touched its waters and taxied toward the small wooden pier of the village.

The Luperón raid was not an earth-shaking event, serving mainly as a convenient label for the Caribbean Legion's last effort to overthrow Trujillo. But for those who were there, it was a once-in-a-lifetime happening. It was Sunday evening, a band concert was in progress, and it was the first time that a seaplane had touched down there. The villagers flocked to the shoreline and crowded the pier, casting lines to the Catalina and volunteering to help the visitors unload their cargo of arms and ammunition. They held up their identity cards and shouted "vivas" for Trujillo. It was Gugú who "broke the spell," changing the mood: "This is an invasion. Down with Trujillo. Viva Horacio Vásquez."[60] There was panic—a "stampede"—some jumped off the pier into the water, not able to escape fast enough. The fiesta was over; the invaders could now get on with the serious business.

The invasion did not go well. Ornes, in command of the action team, headed for the plaza, his mission to occupy the seat of authority (the town had one policeman) and seize the telegraph office. A comedy of errors ensued. As they approached the town's center, a sniper's bullet struck and wounded Leyton; at that instant they sighted the band musicians coming down the street and, because of their uniforms and brass instruments, mistook them for a troop of soldiers and opened fire and hurled grenades. Thus alerted, someone at the electric plant cut the power and the place went dark; in the confusion Kundhardt and Ramírez shot each other, Ramírez wounded fatally.[61] Arvelo, who remained on the dock unloading the weapons, realized that things were going badly when the wounded and dead were brought in, but was startled when Ornes returned with his diminished column and proclaimed: "It's failed, we're going to Santiago de Cuba."[62] In despair, he added that the "other planes" had not arrived and that they were unable to seize the telegraph, meaning that reinforcements were probably on the way and that they would not have time to make contact with the Internal Front (supposedly at Duvergé [*sic*], some 30 kilometers away). "Besides, we have had three casualties already, among them the two wounded. If we make it to a hospital in time, we could save their lives."[63] No one argued; they scrambled on board the plane, but misfortune piled on.

The Catalina did not make it out of the bay. It became stuck on a sand bar, and the desperate men returned to the shore, leaving the wounded and dead on board in the care of Reyes Valdés, who was a University of Havana medical student. They watched in horror as the Coast Guard cutter GC-9 entered the bay and machine-gunned the seaplane, causing it to explode, incinerating its occupants, the living and the dead.[64] The survivors lit out now to the west on foot. They had no plan but hoped to reach Haiti (about 130 kilometers away), terrorized now by the thought of capture. But the Americans lagged behind, hoping that they might be spared as "crazy gringos," and the Nicaraguan Selva "decided to cast his lot with them," possibly to act as an interpreter.[65] Trujillo did not spare them; once overtaken they were executed on the spot as an object lesson for other "crazy gringos."[66]

The remaining seven managed to elude pursuers until the morning of June 22. They were unfamiliar with the region; only Kundhardt was a native of those parts and he was dead. Beset with hunger and thirst and having to carry a fever-ridden Ornes on a litter, they did not get very far before Antonio Imbert, the governor of Puerto Plata Province (and future assassin of Trujillo), caught up with them. The athletic Gugú Henríquez and Calderón Salcedo at the head of the column managed to escape but were never seen again alive. Gugú's cousin Cotú Henríquez later charged that Gugú and Calderón were executed after being captured, citing discrepancies in the offical accounts: in one, Gugú was killed on the morning of the twenty-third, "trying to cross the frontier into Haiti"; in another, he was killed in the evening of the twenty-third at a place called El Caño "in the same commune of Luperón."[67]

Barely two weeks before (June 11), Gugú had written his father from somewhere in Texas, telling his family not to worry, that he was well and seeing new places. He gave no return address, since "we are" on the go and he did not know where they would be stopping. Apparently he had left Havana in a hurry, leaving behind "almost all [his] clothes."[68] It was the letter of a vibrant young man, fully expecting to return home again. But too much went wrong, and he was not among the five that survived (Ornes, Arvelo, Feliú, Martínez Bonilla, and Córdoba Boniche; see Fig. 6).

The Luperón Five

The prisoners, expecting the worst, did not fare badly. There was no rack or thumbscrews. Arvelo reasoned that Trujillo had decided to use them as tools in a propaganda campaign against his enemies on the international front.[69] Ornes related that Trujillo interrogated him personally in a calm, "almost friendly" manner, interested mainly in the degree of involvement of such prominent figures as Arévalo, Prío, and Figueres.[70] He had expected to

Fig. 6.   The survivors and weapons of Luperón after their capture in the Dominican Republic, June 1949. L. to r.: Horacio Julio Ornes, Miguel Feliú Arzeno, José Rolando Martínez Bonilla, José Félix Córdoba Boniche, and Tulio Arvelo.

be tortured in order to extract information about the Internal Front, but Trujillo hardly raised the issue, nor did other officials who questioned him next.

The reason for this lack of interest was that the Internal Front had already been compromised and smashed. A Trujillo spy, Antonio Jorge Estévez, had penetrated the Internal Front of Puerto Plata and identified its leaders as Fernando Spignolio and Fernando Suárez. Though the spy did not learn the exact time and place of the invasion, once the shooting started Trujillo's troops moved against the two leaders, killing them in a firefight and going on a rampage, liquidating two hundred persons in Puerto Plata Province alone.[71] After Luperón, Estévez attempted to continue his charade, traveling to Puerto Rico and Cuba with the story that the Internal Front was still intact and wanted to establish new contacts; Eufemio Fernández had him killed.[72]

Though Ornes and his fellow captives "confessed" to the essential features of the Luperón attack, they insisted that they did not reveal anything Trujillo did not know already. "We did not wish to be *quijotes,*" Arvelo explained, "much less martyrs for no purpose."[73] Nonetheless, "Of this I am certain," he declared, "no one within our country suffered the slightest harm because of our statements."[74] The only stressful time during the interrogations involved Trujillo's firm belief that another plane—a Grumman seaplane that served as Arévalo's personal plane—had flown escort for the Catalina. Ornes and the others denied the assertion, but the Dominican government would not drop it, and it was repeated in subsequent official protests.

Nonetheless, Trujillo got what he wanted: "evidence" that he was "the victim of international communism personified by the rulers of Cuba, Guatemala, and Costa Rica."[75] In order to achieve the maximum effect, he moved the prisoners to the Ozama Fortress and ordered a showcase trial on August 8. After a day in the Palace of Justice, consisting of testimony by villagers from Luperón and statements by the accused, the trial judge found the filibusters guilty "of crimes against the public peace and the stability of the State" and sentenced them to thirty years at hard labor.[76] Trujillo brought no charge of murder against Ornes and his men, even though he acknowledged one death on his side—that of a policeman. He blamed that killing on the North American crew of the Catalina, probably in an effort to blunt the protest of the U.S. embassy over their executions. Feliú, the actual shooter, already in a tight spot, let the charge stand, as did witnesses terrified of contradicting the tyrant.[77]

As a result of the capture and interrogation of the Luperón invaders, Trujillo had a strong case against Arévalo and the government of Guatemala. Ornes had stated in open court: "More or less four days before arriving on Dominican soil, Lake Izabal, in Guatemala, and the airplane that brought us here were placed at my disposition. Then, on Friday, June 16, I flew in another of the expedition's planes, a C-46, to Puerto Barrios, Guatemala, where I left with the men, the arms, and the gasoline for the seaplane, and we went up the lake to El Estor."[78] Going on to describe the preparations and takeoff, Ornes left little doubt that Guatemalan officials had aided him every step of the way. On this basis Trujillo charged that Guatemala in concert with Costa Rica and Cuba (the Figueres-Arévalo-Prío axis) had breached the peace of the Americas, and he acted to invoke the Rio Treaty requiring a Meeting of Consultation. But the United States moved to head him off.

The United States Proposes a Study

Instead of invoking the Rio Treaty by which one or more states specifically is accused of armed aggression or a threat to the peace, the United States proposed that the Inter-American Peace Committee (IAPC) study the problem of unrest in the Caribbean in general and make recommendations, including, if necessary, the convoking of a Meeting of Consultation.[79] By seeking a no-fault solution the United States hoped to get rid of the Caribbean Legion without appearing to defend Trujillo. Working in its favor was the argument that too frequent use of the Rio Treaty might diminish its effectiveness, as well as the fact that a number of states would not support an action that appeared to take Trujillo's side in a dispute with Arévalo and other liberal presidents.[80] On August 4, following the initiative of Ambassador Paul C. Daniels of the United States, Enrique V. Corominas, the acting president of the IAPC, addressed a circular letter to the American governments inviting them to provide information and suggestions on "the situation prevailing in the Caribbean political areas."[81]

Predictably, the Dominican Republic responded first on August 15 with a lengthy fourteen-page brief. It did not limit its complaint to the Luperón affair but gave a reprise of revolutionary activity in the Caribbean in recent years, beginning with Betancourt's seizure of power in Venezuela in 1945. It continued with Cayo Confites, criticizing the Cuban government for failing to confiscate the movement's weapons. If it had done so, the brief observed, events might have been different, but instead the arms were transferred to Guatemala, then to Costa Rica, back to Guatemala, and on to Luperón.[82] They were the thread linking the region's subversive activity, constituting a "patrimony sui generis."[83] And Horacio Ornes was living proof, having shouldered these weapons in Cayo Confites, Puerto Limón, Lago Izabal, and Luperón.[84]

The Dominican statement presented the events of Luperón in detail. It had the essential features exact, from the acquisition of aircraft in Mexico, to the use of the San José base and Lake Izabal, to the participation of the Guatemalan C-47s, T-1 and T-2. But it did not stop there. The Dominican government charged that the Caribbean Legion was not finished and was regrouping, citing a statement by Eufemio Fernández on July 9 that the Luperón failure did not matter: "We are prepared to lose all the battles that may be necessary."[85] It claimed that the Caribbean Legion continued to pay the monthly salary of the crew of the C-46 (XB-HUV), keeping them on standby for "the new movement being planned."[86] It referred further to the strange activities of Eufemio Fernández, who, in the aftermath of Arana's assassination (July 18), flew to Guatemala to help suppress a revolt by Arana's supporters. Acting outside the normal bounds of international behavior, he returned to Havana with a number of the would-be *golpistas* in tow and turned them over to Erundino Vilela Peña, the interim chief of the Secret Police of Cuba, who took them to the Hotel San Luis, "where they remained under guard for some time."[87]

The Dominican government had the facts but could not resist hyperbolizing: "The imperialistic interventionism that is disturbing the peace of the Caribbean zone persists in its criminal acts against the institutions of the Dominican Republic and those of other states in the region, and continues in its determination to impose by force the ideology that is inspiring all this revolutionary activity."[88] Given its conviction that its enemies continued to plot and that it had been the victim of aggression, the Dominican Republic reserved its right to invoke the Rio Treaty, notwithstanding its response to the IAPC's request for information.[89]

The United States was next to respond to the IAPC's request. Its memorandum acknowledged that there was "a deeper significance" to the political unrest in the Caribbean area since World War II than that reported in the sensational accounts of exile revolutionary activity but believed that that truth did not justify the "violation by established governments of their international obligations" but only made matters worse.[90] The United States reviewed the steps it had taken to prevent the use of its territory for revolutionary activity directed against another state and its actions against persons in violation of U.S. neutrality and export control laws. It cited the 1947 convictions of Edward Browder and Karl Eisenhardt for arms theft in connection with Trujillo's plot against the Betancourt government, and the indictment and trial of Manolo Castro, Miguel Angel Ramírez, and Hollis Smith for gunrunning in the matter of Cayo Confites.[91] The United States argued that each state needed to determine if its laws and enforcement machinery were adequate "to insure compliance with international obligations" and suggested further that the IAPC might review the 1928 Havana Convention for the purpose of bringing it up to date in view of new and unforeseen circumstances. It praised as a "valuable precedent" the actions of the OAS Council acting as the Provisional Organ of Consultation in the case of Costa Rica and Nicaragua, specifically the Resolution of December 24, 1948, that resulted in improved relations through adherence to the principles and rules of nonintervention and solidarity.[92] This meant, of course, the disbandment of groups like the Caribbean Legion.

On August 26 the Cuban government addressed the IAPC. It did not treat unrest in the Caribbean in a specific sense but as "a consequence of a reflection of political, social, and economic phenomena of a universal nature, within an historical process whose influence America cannot escape."[93] Though the parties of the democratic left had declared economic opportunity and social justice as the purpose of democratic government, Cuba stood virtually alone in this exchange in raising economic and social issues as underlying factors in the antidictatorial struggle. In extremely florid language Cuba lectured about the attributes of a democratic state and affirmed that "the exercise of democracy, consecrated in the inter-American system, is the only sure means of peaceful coexistence." Within the verbiage it had a message: as long as there are dictators, there will be no peace; as long as the inter-American system shields tyrants, it will lack respect. "Non-intervention is an American principle. At the same time, democracy is the basic principle of the American States, and the Bogotá Charter stipulated that 'the solidarity of the American States, and the high aims which are sought through it require the political organization of those States on the basis of the effective exercise of representative democracy.' "[94] Cuba was saying essentially that the inter-American system could not work if it treated the symptoms (exile revolutionary activity) and ignored the illness (dictatorial government).

The Costa Rican government echoed these sentiments, only in a more direct manner. Costa Rica had not responded to the IAPC's circular, but upon reading portions of the Dominican government's statement in the *New York Times,* charging Costa Rica with harboring "an international brigade . . . to plot against the Dominican Government," Costa Rican Ambassador Mario A. Esquivel angrily rebuked the IAPC for its intervention. "If the Four Freedoms existed in all parts of the Caribbean," he said in a television interview, "there would be no need for a study by the Peace Committee."[95] However, because the *Times* had editorialized about "lawless intervention" in the Caribbean and suggested that it was time for "the ghosts of the soldiers of fortune" to join those of the buccaneers of the past, Esquivel made a response of sorts in a letter to the editor, protesting what he regarded as a "slur" on the Caribbean's exiles, whom he described as "sincere patriots" fighting for the restoration of democracy in their homelands.[96]

Fourteen (Foregone) Conclusions

Taking these and other reports and suggestions under advisement, the IAPC issued "Fourteen Conclusions" on September 14, 1949, summarizing the "various principles and standards" necessary for the maintenance of peace and security in the Western Hemisphere. The document reflected heavily the influence of the U.S. position, trivializing the powerful reasons for conflict in the Caribbean by giving primacy to the principle of nonintervention.

It began by citing the absolute position of the Buenos Aires Protocol of 1936: "No State or group of States has the right to intervene, directly or indirectly, for any reason whatever, in the internal or external affairs of any other State." It referred next to the Havana Convention of 1928, with its stern warning to states to prevent the use of their territory for the preparation of armed expeditions against neighboring states. In order to emphasize the message further, it counseled consideration of the Resolution of December 24, 1948—what might be called the "get the Caribbean Legion resolution"—wherein Costa Rica and Nicaragua were told to "rid" their territories "of groups of nationals or foreigners, organized on a military basis with the deliberate purpose of conspiring against the security of other sister Republics."[97]

Touching upon other principles defining good behavior, the committee advised states to avoid "systematic and hostile propaganda" against other countries of the hemisphere and to maintain "close and cordial diplomatic

relations" as an effective means of strengthening inter-American cooperation.[98] After setting forth a clear code of conduct—constituting the first
seven conclusions—the committee cited the inter-American agreements establishing the "exercise of democracy" as "a common denominator of
American political life."[99] But it set no standards of conduct in this regard,
or measures that the American States might take in concert to promote
democracy.

The "Fourteen Conclusions" were a pious hope that political unrest in
the Caribbean would diminish if revolutionary exiles were denied a base of
operations. The IAPC bowed to U.S. influence, establishing a code of conduct that recognized the sovereign equality of states, regardless of their
form of government. It gave a passing nod to the position of Costa Rica and
Cuba, among others, that inter-American solidarity rested on the effective
exercise of representative democracy. But it paid no heed at all to Cuba's
list of criteria for determining that a nation's political system truly reflected
the popular will and respected the freedom and rights of its people, nor did
it make any serious reference to economic and social issues.

The main concern of the United States was the Soviet Union, and it did
not want anybody making waves in the Caribbean that might expand the
Cold War there. Upon signing the "Fourteen Conclusions," Ambassador
Daniels declared that "emphasis is properly laid" on the principle of nonintervention, observing that "only careful and scrupulous adherence to the
rule of law in our inter-American relations . . . will achieve that high mea-
sure of solidarity and mutual confidence on which our future economic,
social, and cultural progress depends."[100] Secretary of State Dean Acheson
was more forceful, giving little quarter: "Aggression or plotting against any
nation of this Hemisphere is of concern to us. [We] shall use our strongest
efforts . . . to oppose it and to defend the peace of the Hemisphere."[101]
President Harry Truman tried to have it both ways; reiterating America's
commitment to the principle of nonintervention, he told the OAS ambassadors in a speech on October 12, "At the same time, we are definitely
committed to the proposition that our solidarity and high aims are fostered
by the exercise of representative democracy in the American states."[102]

Down but Not Out

The revolutionary exiles of the Caribbean might have grasped at this straw,
but the dynamics of world affairs had turned against them. Juan and José

Horacio Rodríguez, Ramírez, and Rivas Montes returned to Cuba and moved into the Hotel San Luis.[103] "We are romantics devoted to the cause of liberty," Ramírez told a Cuban journalist.[104] *Bohemia,* Cuba's most popular magazine of the day, published two interviews with General Ramírez in August in which it described the Caribbean Legion as the "democratic bulwark of America" and traced its action in the Caribbean. Ramírez commented sadly, "Up to a certain point, the international organizations, with their conventions and pacts, have supported the tyrannies of our countries." He could not understand, he said, "why in these treaties, like the Pact of Bogotá, they acknowledge and concede the same rights to the regimes of Trujillo, Somoza, and Carías as they acknowledge for the rest of the democratic states."[105] Although his spirits appeared down, he insisted that they would persevere, that they would not give up the struggle until "Santo Domingo, Honduras, and Nicaragua were restored to their place among democratic nations."[106] It would be more difficult now, not only because of the U.S. attitude but because Rodríguez's guns were scattered all over the Caribbean: in Cuba, Guatemala, Mexico, and the Dominican Republic.

1950

The OAS Puts on the Lid

Continuing Unrest

It was obvious from the beginning that the "Fourteen Conclusions" of the Inter-American Peace Committee were not going to end the conflict in the Caribbean: they relied upon the good will of the parties where there was none. The political exiles of the Caribbean and their allies had no will to obey a set of standards that denied them the opportunity to do what they believed was necessary and right. And Trujillo was determined to end the threat to his regime from abroad, especially now that he had his enemies on the run. There was tremendous frustration in the Caribbean; the exiles, whose hopes had been raised by Braden, Briggs, and Butler, were now reduced to the status of "malcontents" and "adventurers."[1] A vicious cycle developed; as the United States endeavored to keep the Cold War out of the Caribbean, it tended to view any challenge to the existing order in Cold War terms.

U.S. policy in the Caribbean emboldened Trujillo. Though the United States continued to hold him at arms length, as it did in using the IAPC instead of the Rio Treaty to defuse the Luperón crisis, Trujillo knew that he could be a great deal more aggressive than before. If Luperón had showed the Caribbean Legion to be inept, it also demonstrated the boldness and daring of the exile revolutionary movement and the risks the Caribbean's democratic governments were willing to take on its behalf. Accordingly, at the first inkling of renewed exile conspiratorial activity Trujillo began to develop countermeasures.

Among the earliest clues Trujillo received that the exiles were back at it again were reports about the activities of Enrique Cotubanamá ("Cotú") Henríquez. Nicolás Silfa maintained that after Luperón a large number of Dominican exiles were "disheartened" and "almost resigned" to Trujillo's continued control over their homeland.[2] But apparently Cotú Henríquez was not among them. When asked by a State Department officer in January 1950, who were the principal Dominican exile leaders, Cotú responded: Juan Rodríguez, Miguel Angel Ramírez, Juan Bosch, Angel Morales, "*y yo.*"[3] He allegedly reactivated the anti-Trujillo movement using the facilities of the Cuban Red Cross as cover (his brother, Rodolfo, was president of the organization). Cotú Henríquez was also a medical doctor, along with being a congressional deputy from Oriente Province, head of the Cuban Farmers' Union, and President Carlos Prío Socarrás's brother-in-law.

The allegations that the Cuban Red Cross was the front for an exile military buildup came to light on October 11, 1949, in the newspaper column "Pasquín" written by Luis Ortega Suárez and printed in *Prensa Libre* of Havana. Ortega charged that the Cuban Red Cross was engaged in "certain activities of an international character," which he cryptically described as "taking an active part in Caribbean politics."[4] The source of the allegation was José Caminero, one of a number of Red Cross officials whom Rodolfo had fired and who, in turn, brought charges of misuse of funds by the Henríquez brothers — "*botellas*" — and the use of Red Cross facilities for clandestine operations. Caminero charged specifically that Cotú was building an airfield at L'Amelie in a mountainous region of Oriente to use as a staging area for an invasion of the Dominican Republic.[5] Cotú retorted that L'Amelie was nothing more than an air-strip being constructed by the Red Cross for use in emergencies and to evacuate injured and sick people from a region where overland travel was extremely difficult.[6] He believed that Caminero and Ortega were agents of Trujillo.[7]

Acting as a catalyst for these developments was the death of Federico Henríquez ("Gugú") at Luperón. The Henríquez family grieved his loss, and Cotú and Rodolfo, using the channels of the Cuban Red Cross, aggressively probed the circumstances of his death and implied that he was executed after being taken prisoner. Despite official (though conflicting) announcements of Gugú's death on July 23, Cotú and Rodolfo possessed a cable from the Dominican Red Cross, dated July 25, that did not include Gugú or his companion Manuel Calderón Salcedo on either the list of captives or casualties.[8] When the death was confirmed, the Cuban Red Cross tried to claim the body either for transfer to Cuba or for burial in the family tomb in Santo Domingo, but Dominican authorities would not produce his remains.[9] Not even the intervention of the U.S. embassy helped; Gugú Henríquez was a World War II U.S. Navy veteran. Because of the bitter controversy raised by this tragic circumstance, Trujillo targeted the Cuban Red Cross as a hostile organization.

The L'Amelie Affair

Héctor Incháustegui Cabral, the Dominican chargé in Havana, took seriously the "obligation of being well informed." He carefully followed the movements of Rodolfo Henríquez, "not only . . . to the countries which seem to form a front against our Government," as he related in his reports, "but also to the United States where I learned that he was negotiating the purchase of various aircraft and a small, but fast, boat."[10] Over time he developed a strong suspicion that the Cuban Red Cross under Rodolfo and Cotú Henríquez was engaged in something other than humanitarian services. Instead of ambulances they bought "jeeps" and "comandos" (command cars) in the United States, "the least appropriate of any for the transport of the injured and the sick."[11] They even tried to acquire a Catalina seaplane, but their sister, Cuba's first lady, a member of one of the Red Cross governing boards, refused to okay it, observing, "What the Red Cross needs are small planes and not a warplane like that."[12] This episode only made Incháustegui probe deeper.

He reported that during the last months of 1949 Rodolfo concentrated greater power in his own hands, removing a large number of persons from the organization's general assembly and minor positions as well, "filling these vacancies, little by little," Incháustegui asserted, "with Cayo Confites veterans."[13] If the Dominican chargé had it right, it was a repeat performance of the Cayo Confites affair, with Rodolfo Henríquez and the Cuban Red Cross now playing the roles of José Alemán and the Ministry of Education. And he had further evidence of a rerun, reporting that the Red Cross had leased the Anacra airfield, next to Rancho Boyeros, and had commenced pilot training.[14] This was "precisely" one of the fields "used for the recruiting and training of the revolutionaries of Cayo Confites."[15] As the clincher, Incháustegui informed his government that the Cuban Red Cross was planning to construct an airfield at L'Amelie, near Guantánamo, in order to enable "a small group of planes to take off for the Dominican Republic and bomb the residence of the Honorable President Trujillo and his family."[16]

Trujillo had other sources of information that added spice to this plot supposedly being concocted in the waning months of 1949. One of these sources was Paul Giacometti, a twenty-three-year-old Dominican (in January 1950) who had resided in Haiti for over three years as an agent of the Dominican government and who, according to his own claim, had infiltrated a group called "Caribbean Democratic Action" (ADC, *Acción Democrática del Caribe*).[17] Giacometti told a fantastic tale implicating high Haitian officials in the developing L'Amelie affair and asserting that Haiti was to be the "springboard" for an invasion of the Dominican Republic.[18]

He claimed that the principal revolutionary leaders of the Caribbean— Juan Rodríguez, Miguel Angel Ramírez, Juan Bosch, Cotubanamá Henríquez, and Eufemio Fernández—had mapped out a Dominican invasion plan in collaboration with high-level Haitian leaders such as Colonel Paul Magloire, chief of the guard of the National Palace; Love Leger, the presidential secretary; and Jean Brierre, the under secretary of tourism, who was "one of the principal secret agents of Haiti abroad."[19] Under the cover of "Good Will" or "Special" missions on behalf of the Cuban Red Cross, Giacometti related, Cotú Henríquez; Dr. Humberto Olguín, the editor of the Cuban Red Cross *Boletín*; and Dr. Filiberto Ramírez Corría, Director of the Carlos Finlay Institute, traveled repeatedly to Port-au-Prince for the "exclusive" purpose of organizing an invasion of the Dominican Republic.[20] For their general headquarters they used the "Hotel des Caraibes," on the road from Port-au-Prince to Pétionville, administered by the widow Señora Destouches, the mistress of Cotubanamá Henríquez.[21]

In the course of these "missions," Giacometti reported, the conspirators elaborated a "bold and diabolical plan" to assassinate Trujillo. They planned to carry out an air raid at noon against the "Estancia Ramfis," where, according to their calculations, Trujillo and his family would be lunching and resting.[22] They intended originally to launch the attack from Haitian territory but "for unknown reasons" changed it to Cuba, where Caribbean Democratic Action agreed to provide the facilities and aircraft. As part of this operation the conspirators planned to stockpile a large quantity of weapons on the island of Tortuga, ready to arm an invading force proceeding from Haiti.[23]

Giacometti maintained that ADC and "Free Dominicans" (*Dominicanos Libres*) had become more influential in Cuba than the Caribbean Legion, though Rodríguez and Ramírez were still prime movers and were in direct contact and collaboration with these groups. In fact, he said, "both" ADC and the Caribbean Legion "planned and carried out the assassination of General Arana of Guatemala with the consent of President Juan José Arévalo of Guatemala."[24] Rómulo Betancourt allegedly headed ADC, supported by Cotú Henríquez ("representing" President Prío), Aureliano Sánchez Arango (the minister of education), Alejandro Fidel Valdés (the ADC secretary), Olguín, and Ramírez Corría. Bosch was the head of the Free Dominicans (as well as the PRD).[25]

Giacometti's allegations are hard to accept with a straight face, but if Trujillo smiled, he nonetheless took them seriously, especially since they tended to confirm the reports of his intelligence services.[26] The activities of Cotú Henríquez, especially, stood out in the accumulated evidence, establishing a link between L'Amelie and Haiti. Trujillo focused on one incident in particular; Henríquez supposedly met with a group of Haitian military officers in the Rex Theater in Port-au-Prince and claimed that he had Haiti's support in his plans to overthrow Trujillo.[27] Henríquez himself said that his lecture was open to the public and that his audience was made up of all sorts of people, not just military officers, but admitted that in certain remarks his patriotism got the best of him.[28]

Trujillo believed that his enemies were getting ready to pounce again and, even if they were not, he figured it was time for a showdown with Cuba and Haiti. Appearing before the National Congress on December 12, 1949, Trujillo reviewed the events of Luperón and affirmed that the same revolutionary elements were preparing new aggressions with the support of foreign governments. He requested the authority to declare war on any country that permitted the "concentration of militarily organized forces" for the purpose of invading the Dominican Republic. On December 26 the National Congress completed the charade, conferring war-making powers upon President Trujillo.[29] Armed with the authority to make war on his enemies at his discretion, Trujillo needed an act of provocation to make his threat real. And if one did not occur, he would manufacture it.

A Bizarre Plot Uncovered

The general belief was that Trujillo took the extraordinary step of seeking war-making powers in order to prod the OAS to get Cuba to cease its support of the Caribbean Legion in accordance with the "Fourteen Conclusions." In reality he was exploiting the L'Amelie and Cuban Red Cross flaps to justify a plan of his own to invade Haiti and achieve the ouster of President Dumarsais Estimé. Whereas during 1949 attention was focused on the activities of Dominican exiles and their allies in Guatemala, Costa Rica, and Cuba, similar intrigues were occurring between the Dominican Republic and Haiti. Trujillo, who complained that Cuba and Guatemala tolerated and protected exile conspiracies against his regime, acted in precisely the same manner, assisting Haitian exiles against the government of Estimé. His principal agent was Colonel Astrel Roland, who had turned against Estimé after being denied a high government office.

In Ciudad Trujillo, Roland began radio broadcasts over *La Voz Dominicana* in January 1949, inciting the Haitian people to revolt and using "indescribably vulgar" language.[30] The Haitian government complained before the OAS and sought to convoke the Organ of Consultation, charging the Dominican Republic with "moral aggression."[31] The OAS Council, reluctant to employ the Rio Treaty, encouraged the parties to talk it through one-on-one; when that did not work, it referred the matter to the IAPC. An agreement of sorts was reached in June whereby the parties promised to refrain from activities "that have as their objective the disturbance of the domestic peace of either of the two."[32] But the radio broadcasts and other offenses continued off and on throughout the year, with Roland's activities assuming a more sinister nature in November.

Roland's handler was Anselmo Paulino, a Trujillo henchman who served his master in various high-level posts over time but who specialized in Haitian affairs.[33] These two fashioned a particularly bizarre scheme as a diversion to enable Roland to cross into Haiti at the head of an armed band. They planned to create panic and confusion in Port-au-Prince by assassinating certain Haitian officials and by torching the Dominican embassy, killing Rafael Oscar de Moya, the first secretary of the embassy; Sebastián Rodríguez Lora, the chargé d'affaires; and their entire families.[34] Putting this plan into motion, Roland passed money and weapons, including two submachine guns, to John Dupuy, a confederate in the Haitian capital. But Haitian police, suspicious of Dupuy's activities, killed him in a shootout on December 19, when they came to search his house. As these events were occurring the Dominican Congress debated Trujillo's request for war-making powers. Nicolás Silfa claimed that Roland was not to be alone on the border, asserting that Trujillo had massed five thousand troops there, ready to take advantage of the "provocative" act.[35]

Completing the comic opera nature of this episode, De Moya and Rodríguez Lora discovered the plans targeting them for murder and decided to spend Christmas in New York. However, before departing on December 26, Rodríguez Lora called on Haitian Foreign Secretary Vilfort Beauvoir and told him the whole story. Putting two and two together—the granting of war-making powers to Trujillo and the planned massacre of the Dominican diplomats—Haiti addressed a note to the OAS Council on January 3, 1950, requesting an "immediate convoking" of the Organ of Consultation in accordance with the Rio Treaty. "Once the pretext was created," the Haitian note observed, "the Republic of Haiti could be invaded and a new international crime could thus be committed."[36]

Denials and Countercharges

The Dominican government, of course, denied everything. Paulino hastened to New York to get the terrified diplomats to change their story. On January 6, Joaquín E. Salazar, the Dominican ambassador to the OAS, addressed Council President Luis Quintanilla, describing the Haitian note in such terms as "absurd," "fantastic," and "novelistic."[37] He affirmed that De Moya and Rodríguez Lora had denounced "categorically" the statements attributed to them. The powers granted to President Trujillo "to exercise the legitimate right of self-defense," Salazar declared, were not directed against Haiti but stemmed from "the present state of anarchy and permanent threat of aggression predominating in the Caribbean."[38]

Salazar ran through the entire litany of alleged wrongs against the Dominican Republic in recent years, that is, the Dominican version of many of the events described in this book. He recounted the sacking of the Dominican Legation in Caracas and the rupture of relations in October 1945 on the occasion of Betancourt's coming to power. He spoke of Cayo Confites and "the training and equipping of some 1,600 men of various nationalities . . . for the sole purpose of invading the Dominican Republic," adding that President Grau San Martín "has confessed his active participation" according to an interview published in *Bohemia* on June 26, 1949. He complained that the governments of Guatemala in 1947 and Costa Rica in 1948 also broke off diplomatic relations with the Dominican Republic. He referred finally to the Luperón invasion, "organized and prepared on Guatemalan territory with the proven cooperation of President Arévalo and other officials of his Government."[39]

As a result of the "scandalous" activities of the Caribbean Legion and the "tragic results" of Luperón, Salazar observed, the United States requested the Inter-American Peace Committee "to study the grave situation existing in the Caribbean area." After a thorough study of all aspects of the problem, he continued, the committee issued its "points of view," setting forth non-intervention and reciprocity as the golden rules of conduct among the American nations. But to no avail; scarcely four months after Luperón, "new warlike preparations began in Cuba," this time "more powerful" than ever and "with the aid of the Cuban Red Cross."[40] These were the circumstances, Salazar explained, that "required" President Trujillo to solicit special powers for the exercise of the legitimate right of self-defense. He concluded: Haiti has it all wrong; it is the Dominican Republic whose territory and sovereignty "have been and continue to be" threatened. Denouncing Cuba, Guatemala, and Haiti, the Dominican representative requested the Council of the OAS to convoke the Organ of Consultation "immediately."[41]

The Caribbean Crisis, 1950

On January 6, in accordance with the petitions of Haiti and the Dominican Republic, the OAS Council resolved to convoke the Organ of Consultation. Pending the fixing of a time and place for the meeting, the council constituted itself as the Provisional Organ of Consultation and appointed an Investigating Committee to make on-site studies of the facts and antecedents of the Haitian and Dominican complaints.[42] In truth, there would be no Meeting of Consultation. The Rio Treaty allowed the council to act at its level without bothering the American foreign ministers, but Trujillo had still managed to activate the heavy machinery of the OAS in his aim to eliminate the threat to his regime from abroad.

Council President Quintanilla designated OAS Ambassadors Guillermo Gutiérrez (Bolivia), Eduardo Zuleta Angel (Colombia), Alfonso Moscoso (Ecuador), Paul C. Daniels (United States), and José Mora (Uruguay) to serve on the committee, and the committee elected Mora as its president. Serving Daniels as advisers were State Department officers Charles Hauch and Hobart Spalding, who did a great deal of the leg work for the committee. Hauch, it will be recalled, had been cited as a friend by the Caribbean

Liberation Movement in September 1948. The committee organized itself and received its charge from the council on January 11; it worked in Washington until January 22; then traveled to Haiti, the Dominican Republic, Cuba, and Guatemala; it returned to Washington on February 15, where it prepared its report for submission to the council on March 13, 1950. Actually, the committee submitted two reports. Although it investigated the Haitian and Dominican appeals simultaneously, it rendered separate reports on the issues raised by Haiti (Case "A") and those by the Dominican Republic (Case "B"), to which it attached a single set of conclusions and a series of five draft resolutions.

The Investigating Committee on the Road

Washington

Among its activities in Washington the committee met in private with Dominican Ambassadors Salazar and Arturo Despradel on January 17 and 18. The Dominicans endeavored frantically to persuade the committee of the connection between Cotubanamá Henríquez and the Haitian government for the purpose of invading the Dominican Republic. But they had a hard time proving it because this charge, as well as much of what the Dominican government allegedly knew about its enemies' intentions, was the product of espionage. The envoys said that the information came from "friendly sources and confidential sources, often from nationals of the countries where the reports [were] produced and often from officials of other governments, whose identity the Dominican Government [could not] reveal."[43]

Pleading with the committee to have faith in their assertions, they related that repeatedly the reports of these clandestine sources "about previous events have been confirmed by the fact that the events indeed occurred." Displaying an intelligence report dated May 16, 1949, describing an exile plot to invade the Dominican Republic, Despradel declared, "and on the 19th of June, 32 days later, the attack took place [Luperón]."[44] These same sources, Despradel continued, told us that Rolando Masferrer was on the Haitian-Dominican frontier on June 19, 1949. "It is logical to relate that report with the fact that they were shipping arms to Haiti. It is logical to relate it with the fact that the Cuban press reported that Masferrer had gone to Haiti. . . . And so, we are not writing fiction, we are not making up a story. We are presenting facts proceeding from sources . . . whose reports have been shown to be true by the events themselves."[45]

For this reason, Salazar interjected, the Dominican government "did not have the slightest doubt" about the accuracy of a report from these same sources that in the week before November 29, 1949, "one of the international leaders of the interventionism that we suffer" met with Haitian presidential confidants Love Leger and Jean Brierre in Port-au-Prince and received confirmation of their pledge "to continue offering Haitian territory in support of the [revolutionary] movement."[46] According to Salazar, the permission to use Haiti as a springboard "had already been requested by Humberto Olguín, by Cotubanamá Henríquez, and by somebody else, officially in the name of the Government of Cuba, and it was granted."[47] But in response to questioning by Ambassador Daniels, Despradel said it was impossible to provide documentary evidence. If Cuba were to discover the source of our information, he explained, "it would inevitably cost that person his life."[48]

The Dominican envoys had presented a stark lesson in Caribbean intrigue and had given the committee much to consider. The facts about Cayo Confites and Luperón were easier to ascertain—much had already been exposed—but finding the truth about L'Amelie and the Haitian connection was more challenging. At the same time the Dominican government was less cooperative with reference to De Moya and Rodríguez Lora, the diplomats who had abandoned their mission in Haiti and fled to New York. De Moya refused the committee's invitation to come to Washington for an interview, remaining in New York, saying, "he was not disposed to appear before the Committee."[49] Rodríguez Lora, who in the meantime had accepted the position of minister counselor in the Dominican embassy in Washington (but without returning home), did appear before the committee on January 18 and 19. He insisted that he did not say the things that Haitian Foreign Minister Vilfort Beauvoir "attributed to him," but he refused adamantly to confront the Haitian Foreign Minister in the presence of the committee, even though Beauvoir traveled to Washington for that express purpose.[50] The Dominican performance in Washington was a wash.

Haiti

In Haiti the committee interviewed a score of officials from President Estimé and Colonel Magloire to Leger and Brierre and Major Marcaisse Prosper, the chief of police, who displayed the weapons confiscated in the

Dupuy shooting. Judging from the committee's report, it concentrated its efforts on the charges contained in Haiti's note and virtually ignored those of the Dominican Republic that Haiti was in league with Cotubanamá Henríquez and other exile revolutionaries. It spent most of its time investigating the nature of the radio broadcasts of Astrel Roland and the Dupuy-Roland plot of November–December 1949.[51] The Haitian case was greatly strengthened by the behavior of the Dominican diplomats De Moya and Rodríguez Lora.

Santo Domingo

In Santo Domingo, from January 27 to February 2, the committee had the opportunity to interview the survivors of the Luperón affair. Among them, José Rolando Martínez Bonilla and Manuel Feliú Arzeno talked openly about the collaboration of Cuba, Costa Rica, and Guatemala in the Cayo Confites and Luperón episodes. They admitted to Charles Hauch, who visited them in their jail cells and took notes, that Juan Rodríguez indeed acquired the guns for Cayo Confites in Argentina, with Cruz Alonso as his agent, and that José Figueres, after using them in Costa Rica, returned them to Rodríguez for the Luperón invasion.[52] They stated that there were no Cuban military officers active in Cayo Confites but that Guatemalan army officers in Guatemala helped them prepare for Luperón, naming specifically "Major Sardi and Colonel Arana."[53] Martínez told Hauch that the North American crew of the Catalina had been hired for the job and that the Catalina flew to Luperón alone, without an escort. This latter point refuted Trujillo's repeated insistence that Arévalo's presidential plane, a Grumman seaplane, had accompanied the Catalina to Luperón.[54]

But if Martínez denied this aspect of the Luperón operation, Feliú Arzeno confirmed other details of greater significance. He testified that the Catalina's mission was to secure the Luperón beachhead in anticipation of reinforcements arriving from Cuba. "Up to a thousand men were to come from Cuba," he affirmed, "Cubans and Dominicans."[55] And he named Eufemio Fernández among them (overlooking the fact that Fernández had been interned in Yucatán). He complained, however, that Juan Rodríguez had "deceived them" because "they had no popular support in Luperón."[56] Responding to a question about Lombardo Toledano's role in the operation, Feliú said that "he did not know" but added, "the planes should not have landed in Cozumel."[57] He concluded by telling Hauch that he had been treated well as a prisoner. The committee also interviewed Julio Horacio

Ornes, but its records contain no transcript or notes of his testimony. The committee did not interview Tulio Arvelo, who could not figure out why.[58]

After the visit of the Investigating Committee, the Luperón prisoners feared for their lives. They reasoned that their usefulness to Trujillo for propaganda purposes was over and that the brutal tyrant would now extract his vengence. Perhaps committee president José Mora saw the situation in the same light because he personally asked Trujillo to free the men. Trujillo agreed; he did not have much choice but thought at least he might persuade the OAS ambassadors of his "nobleness and magnaminity."[59] Toward this end he had the Investigating Committee inspect the weapons captured at Luperón, and Hauch subsequently determined that they included fifteen submachine guns acquired in the United States by the Guatemalan Ministry of Defense (see Fig. 5). The Luperón survivors were granted amnesty and released on February 25, and shortly thereafter each went his own way, getting out of the country. The OAS committee could take credit.

Cuba

Going next to Havana, the contrast with Ciudad Trujillo had to be startling even for seasoned travelers like the ambassadors of the Investigating Committee. Though they interviewed the usual lineup of civilian and military authorities, they were beset with communications and petitions from all sorts of people and groups giving their version of Caribbean affairs. The most moving statement was that of the top Dominican exile leaders. Their letter to committee president Mora, dated January 16, 1950, was signed by Angel Morales, Juan Rodríguez, Miguel A. Ramírez, Leovigildo Cuello, José Horacio Rodríguez, and Félix Servio Ducoudray, the members of the executive committee of the General Union for the Establishment of Democracy in the Dominican Republic, and by Juan Bosch, Romano Pérez Cabral, Angel Miolán, Buenaventura Sánchez, Virgilio Mainardi Reyna, Alexis Liz, and Juan I. Jiménez Grullón, serving as the executive committee of the PRD in Exile.[60]

The document had impact because the Dominicans described the loneliness of exile with much emotion. "We have spent long years separated from our parents, our brothers and sisters, our children, our friends and from the places which are part of our best feelings and earliest memories. . . . When a mother, a son or daughter, or a brother or sister dies, we learn about it if someone passing through our country sees the notice and has the kindness to send it to us."[61] And the exiles concentrated on two principal points:

they were the victims, not the cause, of the situation in the Caribbean; and they alone were responsible for the armed attacks against Trujillo.

The Dominican exiles resented deeply the implication in the "Fourteen Conclusions" of the IAPC that they were to blame for "the situation prevailing in the Caribbean." "We have gone into exile in order to save our lives," they stated, pointing out that the Trujillo regime violated the fundamental principle of American solidarity requiring "the effective exercise of representative democracy." The exiles affirmed that they had resorted to violence only to assert their legitimate right to live in their homeland. The OAS Charter, they reminded the committee, provides that "every person has the right to establish his residence in the territory of the State of which he is a citizen." Trujillo has tried to "confuse" public opinion, they charged, by circulating the false story "that the attacks of which he has been the object on our part—the Dominicans opposed to his system of terror—have been the work of foreign governments."[62]

Thus, Trujillo's charges that Costa Rica, Cuba, Guatemala, Haiti, and Venezuela had, at one time or another, committed acts of aggression against the Dominican Republic, the exiles declared, were merely a "smokescreen" to justify his massive arms buildup and assumption of war-making powers. The democratic countries of the Caribbean view "an implacable dictator armed to the teeth" with contempt, they conceded, but "the Dominican Government has converted that passive hostility into fantasies of aggression, in order, as we have already said, to justify the maintenance of a war machine that is the instrument for oppressing and exploiting its people." The struggle was among Dominicans, they emphasized, and the way to achieve peace in the Caribbean, they counseled, was to restore "the exercise of democracy and of human rights." "Peace in the Caribbean," the exiles addressed Mora, "will take immediate effect as soon as there cease to be exiles," and that will occur "when we are able to exercise the rights proclaimed in our own national Constitution," precisely those reaffirmed in the OAS Charter under the principle—and they repeated it again for the nth time—"The solidarity of the American States . . . require the political organization of those States on the basis of the effective exercise of representative democracy."[63]

In addition to this moving letter, the committee heard from Cotubanamá Henríquez, who drew up a petition and gathered the signatures of a galaxy of political activists in Havana, many of them members of the Lyceo Lawn Tennis Club (see Appendix C). The petition condemned the dictatorships of Santo Domingo, Nicaragua, and Venezuela as the true disturbers of the peace in the Caribbean and called upon the OAS to end this situation by approving two resolutions: first, that in America democratic governments ought not to coexist with dictatorial governments; and second, that a Court of Inter-American Justice be created with the authority to review cases of an "internal order" where there is a threat to the democratic system and to the guarantee of human rights in violation of inter-American treaties.[64]

The petition further requested the OAS to notify the dictatorial governments of the Caribbean that "they exercised power illegally" and to require them to hold free elections under the supervision of inter-American electoral commissions. In the event that any dictatorial government refused to comply, the petitioners proposed that the inter-American system sever all diplomatic and consular ties with the outlaw regime, impose an economic blockade, and respect the right of the enslaved peoples to oppose the regime "by any means of resistance necessary, including armed rebellion."[65] Clearly Cotú Henríquez and his colleagues were not going to let the principle of nonintervention stand in the way of ridding the hemisphere of dictators.

While the committee met with many of the same persons whose names appeared on Henríquez's petition, Ambassador Moscoso of Ecuador and Hobart Spalding made an aerial reconnaissance of the L'Amelie site on February 9. They returned with photos that revealed only a rudimentary air strip in the mountainous region of southeastern Cuba. Those who examined the photos concluded that the airfield might serve the purposes of the Cuban Red Cross for relief flights by small planes but that "it could not be used, in any case, for purposes of a military invasion of the Dominican Republic."[66] The Investigating Committee tended to minimize the Red Cross flap, but it actually may have been the Caribbean Legion's "last olé."

Coincidental with the committee's departure from Havana on February 10, the Cuban government delivered a copy of a document certifying that Eufemio Fernández Ortega had resigned as chief of the National Secret Police on April 1, 1948,[67] over a year before the events of Luperón. Despite Cuba's effort to dissociate itself from Fernández's activities, it was widely known that he continued to serve President Prío in special capacities, even if undercover.

Guatemala

The committee proceeded to Guatemala where it found Arévalo's large handprints all over the Luperón affair. His nickname, "El Elefante," seemed appropriate in this case. The committee showed particular interest in the whereabouts of the Guatemalan C-47s, T-1 and T-2, in June 1949 and had questions about the vessels *Alicia* and *Patricia*, which were in Cuban waters at the time of Luperón and which were subsequently purchased by the Guatemalan government in September 1949. Despite clear evidence to the contrary, the Guatemalan government would not admit that their planes had landed by design in Yucatán on June 18. It claimed that the aircraft T-1 was on a flight to Houston, when weather forced it to land in Mexico, but Hauch checked it out and reported "that no Guatemalan military aircraft had requested clearance to land at or near Houston in June, and no such aircraft landed at any airport in the Houston area during that month."[68]

The committee did secure from the Mexican government the back-dated copies of Guatemala's request for landing permits for the military aircraft T-1 and T-2 at Cozumel or Mérida, "possibly on the 21st [June]."[69] The Mexican government also turned over to the committee the complete list of persons detained in Mérida, El Cuyo, and Cozumel in connection with the Luperón affair (see Appendix B). But the Guatemalans were less forthcoming, admitting only that the government had indeed acquired the *Alicia* and *Patricia*, renamed the the *Pedro de Alvarado* and *Tecún Umán*, respectively, and put them into service as patrol craft.[70] The committee had also requested information about "the suicide of Captain Rosales" on August 20, 1949, the second in command of the San José Air Force Base, but there is no response to this query among the committee's records or any reference to the matter in its report.[71]

The committee sought information about the deportation of certain Guatemalan army officers in the aftermath of the assassination of Arana and the subsequent barracks revolt. There is no evidence that the death of Rosales was linked to these events, but the committee, in addressing a note to Colonel Arbenz, displayed a similar quandary about the movements of Eufemio Fernández, who took the Guatemalan officers into custody and flew them to Havana. The committee asked Arbenz for a list of the deportees, the details of their travel, the names of those who accompanied them (Francisco Morazán was one), and the arrangments for their lodging in Cuba.[72] This was a strange affair, revealing a highly unusual relationship between Prío and Arévalo and providing an additional inkling of the nature of the Luperón operation. The Caribbean legionnaires Morazán, Jorge Rivas Montes, and Francisco "El Indio" Sánchez were active in suppressing the Aranista revolt, and the committee interviewed them on February 11.

The Findings of the Investigating Committee

After twenty-four days on the road, including a one-day stopover in Mexico, the Investigating Committee returned to Washington to complete its work. As noted, it prepared two reports. Case "A" dealt with Haiti's request and Case "B" with that of the Dominican Republic. There were no surprises in either report; the fact that the democratic and dictatorial states had been meddling in each other's affairs was well-established. The question was, would the OAS impose a Fourteen Conclusions-type peace, tilting heavily in favor of the principle of nonintervention, or would it address the fundamental problem of military dictatorship in the Caribbean and recommend something radical like the propositions in Cotú Henríquez's Lawn Tennis Club petition? Its course was predictable.

In Case "A", the Investigating Committee criticized the Dominican Republic for failing to take adequate measures to prevent the inflammatory and provocative broadcasts of Astrel Roland against the government of Dumarsais Estimé. It concluded further that certain Dominican officials aided and abetted the Dupuy-Roland plot of November–December 1949, accusing Anselmo Paulino specifically of orchestrating the entire affair.[73] The conduct of the Dominican diplomats De Moya and Rodríguez Lora, in particular, persuaded the committee that the Haitian government had an airtight case against Trujillo.

Case "B" was a more complex matter, involving six Caribbean countries and the Cayo Confites, Luperón, and L'Amelie affairs. Concerning Cayo Confites, the Investigating Committee agreed that the concentration of men and arms was too big and too public to escape the notice of the Cuban government and that, indeed, high civilian and military authorities had cooperated, including President Grau and especially José Alemán and Manolo Castro.[74] Furthermore, the committee confirmed that the Cuban government failed to control the Cayo Confites armaments after the expedition collapsed.[75]

Regarding the Luperón affair, the committee followed the trail of Juan Rodríguez's guns from Cayo Confites to Guatemala to Costa Rica and back to Guatemala. The investigators wrote that it was "obvious" Guatemalan authorities "expedited and permitted" the organization of the expedition and that Eufemio Fernández, Juan Rodríguez, Miguel Angel Ramírez, and Francisco Morazán, "among others," enjoyed "privileges and facilities" for the purposes of the Luperón invasion.[76] Moreover, the committee stated flatly that the Guatemalan military air transports T-1 and T-2 accompanied the invasion squadron on June 18 and landed at Cozumel.[77] It also cited Arbenz's submachine guns captured in Luperón.

With reference to the L'Amelie affair and the alleged role of the Cuban Red Cross, the committee acknowledged that there was some smoke but doubted there was much fire. José Caminero and Luis Ortega Suárez, the two persons who said the Cuban Red Cross was intervening in Caribbean political affairs, failed to back up their charges when the committee visited Cuba. Caminero hedged on his story, and Ortega failed to show up for his interview with the committee.[78] The committee expressed concern that the Henríquez brothers had a monopoly of control over the Cuban Red Cross and had filled many of its positions with Caribbean Legion types, but, in accordance with its own aerial reconnaissance, gave little credence to the idea that L'Amelie was an invasion base.[79] The ambassadors noted that the Cuban Red Cross had invited the Dominican Red Cross to join with it in a petition before the International Red Cross for an investigation of the charges of the Dominican government, and they thought it was a good idea.[80] They tended to put L'Amelie in the rumor or fantasy category, but there were strong feelings and real elements that made anything possible.

The Investigating Committee was not unmindful of this circumstance. In assessing the "current situation" as part of its report, it observed that the factors that caused Cayo Confites and Luperón "continued and persisted."[81] The committee cited the mix of determined political exiles, sympathetic national leaders, unchecked trafficking in arms, and professional revolutionaries. "All this leads to the conclusion," the committee affirmed, "that if the so-called Caribbean Legion does not exist, . . . there is a band of elements that constitutes a subversive force, less organized and systematic than the hypothetical Legion, but more dangerous and more disposed to cause grave confrontational situations."[82] Within this aggregate, the committee pointed out, there were patriots and mercenaries, but in no case—and here it revealed its fundamental position—might one justify violating the principle of nonintervention. It quickly added that in condemning intervention it did not shut off "legitimate channels of evolution and change."[83] It was now clear where the report was heading.

Reviewing its findings, the committee concluded that certain "general considerations" applied. The committee endorsed the concept that a Caribbean Legion-type movement existed and that it had assumed the character of "revolutionary professionalism," exploiting the legitimate interests of "sincere and idealistic" persons. It was a clever ploy: showing sympathy for the genuine patriots while discrediting the movement because a few adventurers were mixed in. As a solution it recommended strengthening the 1928 Havana Convention in order to control the "illegitimate" activities of political exiles and prevent the "illegal" traffic in arms.[84] At the same time it recognized the lack of adequate measures for promoting the principle of representative democracy, in accordance with Article 5(d) of the OAS Charter. And it suggested that the OAS order a study of the means to overcome this shortcoming, though in doing so it referred to Article 15, specifically the principle of nonintervention.[85] Thus, more obfuscation.

Recognizing the fact that the problems in the Caribbean continued to persist, the committee proposed the creation of a special committee to monitor compliance with the resolutions of the Organ of Consultation.[86] To its credit, among the problems, it included the large arms buildup by certain governments of the Caribbean region, respectfully paying heed to the letter of the Dominican exile leaders and administering a slap to Trujillo and other dictators whose armed forces exceeded the requirements of national defense. It admonished Trujillo a second time; without mentioning his war-making powers, the committee pointed out the existence of mechanisms for collective defense and for the pacific settlement of disputes. It declared that any state that threatened war without exhausting all reasonable opportunities for peaceful solution violated "the essential norms of inter-American coexistence."[87]

The OAS "Resolves" the Problem

In submitting its report on March 13, 1950, the Investigating Committee proposed five resolutions for action by the council of the OAS acting provisionally as the Organ of Consultation. The council approved these resolutions on the eighth of April. The resolutions fixed responsibility for the events that had been disturbing the peace of the Caribbean since 1947 and proposed measures that the affected governments might take to prevent the events from happening again. The resolutions did not totally ignore the human factors that were basic to the disturbances, but they adhered strictly to the juridical position that OAS action was limited to relations among nations. Under the circumstances the Caribbean exiles were left out in the cold.

The first resolution, after criticizing the Trujillo regime for intervening in Haiti, called upon the Dominican government to restrain its officials from assisting subversive movements against other governments. It suggested that the governments of the Dominican Republic and Haiti enter into bilateral negotiations to reaffirm their commitments under the 1928 Havana Convention and it requested the governments to take steps to avoid hostile propaganda against each other. It expressed the desirability that the two nations restore and maintain normal diplomatic relations.[88]

Resolution II contained the heart of the OAS action. It stated in unusually blunt terms that Cuba was responsible for Cayo Confites in 1947 and that Guatemala bore a similar responsibility for Luperón in 1949. But it did not excuse the Dominican Republic, maintaining that certain of its actions were "contrary to the norms of American coexistence." Having settled that, it called upon the governments of Cuba and Guatemala to prevent the formation on their territory of armed groups "with the deliberate purpose of conspiring against the security of other countries," and asked Cuba, Guatemala, Haiti, and the Dominican Republic to respect without reservation the principle of nonintervention. It requested the governments of Cuba and Guatemala to seize any weapons in possession of revolutionary elements and to prevent the illegal traffic of arms. It asked the governments of Cuba, Guatemala, Haiti, and the Dominican Republic to refrain from "systematic and hostile propaganda" against each other. The council reaffirmed support for the September 14, 1949, "Conclusions" of the IAPC and expressed its "fervent desire" that Cuba, Guatemala, Haiti, and the Dominican Republic, "once the present problems were resolved," would find the means to reestablish normal and positive relations.[89] Arévalo and Prío had their faults, but they did not kill people as Trujillo did; the OAS jeopardized its effectiveness by treating them all equally in this way.

In accordance with the recommendation of the Investigating Committee, the council resolved to create a Special Commission on the Caribbean charged with overseeing compliance with resolutions I and II. The OAS had put on the lid and it wanted to make certain that it stayed closed. The Special Commission was comprised of the same members that made up the Investigating Committee and it rendered three reports: June 30, 1950; October 31, 1950; and May 14, 1951.[90] By the time of the third report, the Special Commission gave Cuba and Guatemala high marks for good conduct, and the troubles between Trujillo and Estimé had been resolved with the establishment of the Magloire dictatorship in Haiti.

In resolutions IV and V, the OAS Council addressed the perplexing problem of "harmonizing" the principles of nonintervention and the effective exercise of representative democracy. But the council was not serious. In the former resolution it discussed the "confusion" between the two in philosophical terms, and in the latter it ordered a series of studies for the purposes of recommending, first, ways to promote democracy in America without violating the principle of nonintervention; second, means to strengthen the 1928 Havana Convention to eliminate interventionist activity; and, third, guidelines for the handling of cases of diplomatic asylum, exiles, and political refugees. It referred these studies to the Juridical Department of the Pan American Union, the Inter-American Council of Jurists, and the Inter-American Juridical Committee. The study on the promotion of representative democracy was pigeonholed; the other studies emerged years later, with results of little consequence, to wit: an unratified additional protocol to the 1928 Havana Convention and two conventions dealing with diplomatic and territorial asylum.[91] Nonetheless, at the time, the OAS Council was satisfied with its work and it canceled the call for a Meeting of Consultation.

Taps for the Legion

OAS Resolution II proved to be unusually effective because of the convergence of circumstances involving the operational failures of the Caribbean Legion and the general decline in the fortunes of democratic government in the region. The Dominican exiles were beaten and there was little they could do about it. They did not know it, but they were sentenced to another eleven years of exile, during which Trujillo pillaged their homeland. After Luperón, the Dominican exiles tended to abandon conspiratorial and filibustering activities, adopting more conventional political strategies, reorganizing the PRD and using it as a vehicle to marshal international public opinion in defense of democracy and freedom. Silfa spent the 1950s in New York leading protest demonstrations every time Trujillo came to town.

The PRD in Exile wrote to Ambassador Mora on March 31, 1950, after portions of the Investigating Committee's report appeared in the Havana press. Mainardi Reyna, Miolán, Alexis Liz, and Buenaventura Sánchez, who signed the document, generally praised Mora for his "energy and political courage" but noted that Trujillo's pledge of amnesty was a sham, "proof of this is the fact that many Dominican citizens have had to go into exile even now."[92] They further dissented with the idea that certain governments had aided and protected their revolutionary activities. "The truth is that the only aid we have received is that which, through solidarity and the sharing of ideals, the free peoples of America have bestowed upon us."[93] Even to the bitter end they maintained that the fight was among Dominicans.

Filibustering activity did not cease after 1950, but it was more sporadic and had fewer sympathizers than previously. In its third report, dated May 14, 1951, the Special Commission on the Caribbean confirmed that the governments of Cuba and Guatemala were complying with Resolution II, "not to permit armed movements on their territories contrary to the principle of nonintervention nor the illegal traffic in arms."[94] In addition to the new hard-line position of the United States against instability in the Caribbean, the opportunity for exile revolutionary activity declined because the number of democratic governments continued to shrink. Costa Rica, Mexico, and Puerto Rico were just about the only places refugees from tyranny could go, though Trujillo's thugs hunted them down wherever they fled, even in the United States. By the middle of the decade José Figueres was one of the last democratic presidents in the region. He aided remnants of the Caribbean Legion from Guatemala in a failed plot to assassinate Anastasio Somoza García in April 1954, which claimed the lives of Rivas Montes and José Félix Córdoba Boniche (one of the Luperón five). On the other hand, there were armed exile movements on the right: the CIA and Carlos Castillo Armas (an Aranista), using Honduras as a springboard, overthrew Jacobo Arbenz in Guatemala in 1954; and Somoza, seeking his revenge, supported another Calderonista invasion of Costa Rica against Figueres in 1955.

In the only successful filibustering expedition of the 1950s Fidel Castro invaded Cuba from Mexico in December 1956. After overthrowing Fulgencio Batista on New Year's Day 1959, he became the new patron of exile revolutionary movements and sponsored armed expeditions against Panama, Nicaragua, and the Dominican Republic. In the disastrous invasions of Constanza, Estero Hondo, and Maimón in the Dominican Republic in June 1959, the legionnaire José Horacio Rodríguez Vásquez was killed.

On November 20, 1960, in Barquisimeto, Venezuela, General Juan Rodríguez García put his gun to his head and ended his life.

The Legion in Perspective

The fate of the Caribbean Legion serves as a metaphor for the collapse of the democratic surge in the Caribbean and Latin America in the post-World War II era. What began as a time of optimism for overcoming ignorance and poverty through democratic government ended up reinforcing authoritarian rule and crushing the expectations of the popular classes. Latin America experienced a "political cycle" in the 1940s, described as "the sudden eruption of new democratic forces toward mid-decade and the gradual fading of those forces at the end of the decade."[95] The ups and downs of the Caribbean Legion were in perfect symmetry with this cycle. Setting aside its performance and concentrating on its purpose, the Legion was strong in 1946–47, when its democratic sponsors were viable, and had declined by 1949–50, when its allies were weakened. Though local conditions in the Caribbean and Latin America accounted for certain variables, the defining factors of the cycle were external in nature. Democratic fortunes were high in the aftermath of World War II and had fallen with the start of the Cold War. Stated another way, since the United States, the hegemonic power in the region, was a major player in both World War II and the Cold War, its policies largely determined the rules of the game and strongly influenced the time frames that Ruth Berins Collier has labeled as "political opening and reformist initiatives (1944–1946)" and "collapse of reformist initiatives and political closing (from 1946 to 1947 on)."[96]

This is evident in the manner that U.S. policy affected the Caribbean Legion. Spruille Braden's prointerventionist stance in support of democracy clearly encouraged the revolutionary exiles of the Caribbean. The Braden Corollary gave the green light to Cayo Confites, even though U.S. policy was already changing. One does not dispute Francesca Miller's observation that following the Rio Conference "the attention of the Inter-American diplomatic community shifted from social and economic reform to opposition to communism."[97] The Rio Conference also corresponded with the creation of the Central Intelligence Agency which shortly thereafter began to function as a "Cold War department" as revealed in the December 17, 1947, National Security Council Directive authorizing "covert psychological operations."[98]

At a time when the United States was concerned about the "growth of nationalism" in the former colonial areas of the "Near and Far East" and was convinced that the Soviet Union was "effectively exploiting the colonial issue and the economic nationalism of the underdeveloped areas as a means of dividing the non-Soviet world,"[99] the U.S. sensitivity to related issues in the Caribbean and Latin America was manifest. Thus, the Cold War intruded into Caribbean affairs, what the United States viewed as a problem of unrest. Wishing neither to appear to disavow the democratic governments nor to embrace the region's strongmen, the United States resorted to a strict noninterventionist position as exemplified by the "Fourteen Conclusions" of September 14, 1949, and the OAS resolutions of April 8, 1950. In effect, in order to eliminate the Caribbean Legion, it abandoned its commitment to the promotion of the effective exercise of representative democracy in the hemisphere.

It is apparent that history would have been very different if the United States had helped rather than hindered the struggle of the democratic revolutionaries against the dictators of the Caribbean. At least that was the thinking in the early 1960s, when U.S. policy makers decided that instead of arming dictators they could fight communism more effectively by eliminating the poverty and injustice on which it bred. Reflecting this position, the United States completely reversed its policy again with reference to the principle of nonintervention. John C. Dreier, who served as the U.S. ambassador to the OAS from 1951 to 1952 and as director of the State Department's Office of Regional Political Affairs (1952–60), noted in 1962 that the Rio Treaty "was not intended to provide international protection for arbitrary tyrants, so that they could with impunity violate the most fundamental human rights and outrage the conscience of mankind."[100] In referring to a filibustering expedition in 1959 against the sons of Anastasio Somoza in Nicaragua, he stated, "no one had thought that [the Rio Treaty] would be used to protect an authoritarian government from a popular uprising just because such an uprising, by force of circumstance, had to start in a neighboring country."[101]

This policy, if followed ten years earlier, might have averted such eventualities as the Cuban Revolution, though much still would have depended upon the success of the democratic governments in resolving economic and social problems. In this regard there is a "Catch-22"; if these governments had been too aggressive in carrying out social democratic programs, it is just as likely that there would have been more episodes like that in Guatemala in 1954; that is, more examples of covert intervention by the CIA.

History has a way of being a product of the times. In 1950 the United States placed a premium on stability, preferring obsequious tyrants to nationalistic democrats perceived as "soft" on communism. The policy was wrong-headed, but in the Cold War atmosphere of the 1950s and given the zealous anti-Communist policy of John Foster Dulles, one is hard-pressed to imagine what the correct one would have produced. The *Auténticos* failed miserably in Cuba, and Jacobo Arbenz fared no better in Guatemala, but if the Caribbean Legion had succeeded, one is intrigued by the thought of a

President Juan Bosch or Juan Rodríguez in the Dominican Republic in 1952. In any case, sooner rather than later, the Caribbean would have been a great deal better off without Fulgencio Batista, Marcos Pérez Jiménez, Anastasio Somoza, and Rafael Trujillo. The Caribbean Legion represents possibly a missed opportunity in the post-World War II era for the development of societies dedicated to the ideals of the Four Freedoms in a region where the United States had the best chance to make a difference. The Legion was capable of failing on its own, but, if unimpeded, its leaders had the spirit to keep coming back. As Eufemio Fernández declared after Luperón, "We are prepared to lose all the battles that may be necessary."

Appendixes

Appendix A

Anastasio Somoza's enemies list, allegedly constituting the Caribbean Legion, January 9, 1949.

Lista de Nicaragüenses y extranjeros que viven en San José de Costa Rica y que constantemente se mueven a las Repúblicas de Guatamala, El Salvador, Cuba y Méjico procurando como alterar la Paz y tranquilidad de Nicaragua. Todos o su mayor parte, componen la LEGION DEL CARIBE.

NICARAGÜENSES QUE HAN SIDO MILITARES:

Señor	Manuel Gómez F.	Coronel
"	Federico Cabrera	Capitán
"	Gustavo Zavala	Capitán
"	Edmundo Vargas Vásquez	Capitán (Piloto)
"	Rafael Ch. Praslin	Teniente
"	Augusto Cuadra	Teniente
"	Guillermo Cuadra	Teniente
"	Abraham Mendoza	Teniente
"	Agustín Alfaro	Teniente
"	Mario Alfaro	Teniente
"	Adolfo Báez Bone	Teniente
"	Joaquín Cortés	Teniente
"	Nicolas Sequeira	Teniente
"	Antonio Orue R.	Teniente
"	José María Tercero D.	Teniente
"	Julio Alonso	Teniente
"	Julio Tapia	Teniente
"	Alejandro Selva	Teniente
"	Abelardo Cuadra	Teniente

"	Alberto Ramírez	Teniente
"	Wladimir Barquero	Teniente
"	Adolfo Vélez H.	Teniente
"	Amadeo Baena L.	Teniente
	NICARAGÜENSES CIVILES PERO CON RANGO:	
"	Emiliano Chamorro	General
"	Carlos Pasos	General
"	Carlos Castro Wasmer	General
"	Roberto Hurtado	General
"	Carlos Rivera Delgadillo	General
"	Adan Vélez	General
"	Antonio Velásquez	General
"	Alejandro Cárdenas	
"	Ramon Raudales	
"	Carlos Reyes Llánez	
"	Octavio Pasos Montiel	
"	Rosendo Argüello	
"	Rosendo Argüello h.	
"	Eduardo Conrado Vado	
"	Eduardo Jarquin Báez	
"	Felipe Argüello Bolaños	
"	Carlos Castillo Ibarra	
"	Juan José Mesa	
"	Ricardo Orúe Reyes	
"	Gustavo Manzanares	
"	Mariano Fiallos Gil	
"	Ronaldo Delgadillo	
"	Rodolfo Correa	
"	Leonte Pallais Tiffer	
"	Horacio Fernández R.	
"	Edmundo Delgado	
"	José León Montes	
"	José Antonio Montes	
"	Toribio Tijerino	
"	Indalecio Bravo Silva	
"	Julio García Mongalo	
"	Juan Martínez Reyes	(Ex.-Gn. Teniente)
"	Enrique Molina	
"	José Tapia V.	
"	Luis H. Morales	
"	Bismarck Flores	
"	Guillermo Quezada	
"	Octaviano Morazán	
"	Octavio Caldera	
"	Arsenio Alvárez	

"   Alejandro Lacayo C.
"   Hildebrando Miranda
"   Federico Solórzano Montiel
"   Gonzalo Rivas Novoa
"   Alejandro Cuadra
"   Raúl Montalván
"   Miguel Angel Argüello
"   Manuel Ignacio Argüello
"   César Cárter Cantarero
"   Alberto Noguera Gómez
"   Dolores Morales h.
"   Mariano Morales
"   Víctor Hurtado
"   Carlos A. Prado
"   Virgilio Vega Fornos
"   Eddie Escobar
"   Guillermo Borge
"   Nemesio Ordóñez
"   José Simón Delgado
"   Rodolfo Argüello
"   José Durán
"   Armando Urbina Vásquez
"   Carlos Urbina
"   Francisco Castillo
"   Jacobo Jáen
"   Clemente Cuadra
"   Juan Francisco Fonseca Rivas
"   José Félix Córdoba
"   Alejandro Benavides
"   Eduardo Hurtado
"   Mexsicale Castillo
"   Gilberto Bello
"   Florencio Martínez
"   Domingo Ramíres
"   Adam Argeñal
"   Melecio Benavides
"   David Marenco
"   Hermógenes Pineda
"   Antonio Valle
"   Herman Mairena
"   José María Pavón
"   Mario Morales
"   Ernesto Morales
"   Aníbal Tórres Nascimento
"   Arnoldo Muñez

"	Luis Mairena	
"	Juan Rivera	
"	Vicente Corrales	
"	Raúl Viduarre Barrios	
"	Arturo Téllez	
"	Guillermo Ruiz	
	HONDUREÑOS:	
"	Jorge Rivas	Coronel
"	Herman Aguiluz	Coroneles
"	Presentación Ortega	Coronel
"	Alfredo Inextroza	Coronel
"	Mario Soussa	Mayor
"	Francisco Sánchez	Mayor
"	Paco Morazán	Mayor
"	Alfredo Mejía Lara	Mayor
"	Eberto Ramírez	Capitán
"	Jacinto Castro	Capitán
"	José Galeano	Capitán
"	Moisés López	Teniente
"	Pedro Moncada	Teniente
"	Marcos Ortega	Teniente
	DOMINICANOS:	
"	Juan J. Rodríguez	General
"	Miguel A. Ramírez	General
"	Horacio Rodríguez	Mayor
"	Horacio Hornes	Mayor
"	Alejandro Fidel Sánchez	Mayor
"	Julio Castillo Dumas	Mayor
"	Amado Soler	Teniente
"	Británico Guzmán	Capitán
"	J. A. Cilfa	Capitán
	CUBANOS:	
"	Juan Bosch	
"	Pedro Abren	
"	Rafael Bilbao y Hue	
"	Arturo Maxferrer	
"	José Manuel Alemán	
	ESPAÑOLES:	
"	Felipe Laned	
"	Agustín Maurele	
"	H. Robira	
	GUATEMALTECOS:	
"	Federico Mora Peraza	
	SALVADOREÑOS:	
"	Gabriel Castillo	Capitán

ALEMANES:
"   Frank Marshall
"   Bernard Potter
"   Rodolfo Potter
"   Carlos Von Rehnitz
"   Guillermo Von Bergman
"   Agatón Lutez
"   German Lutez

Managua D.N. 9 Enero de 1949

Appendix B

List of persons detained by Mexican authorities in El Cuyo and Cozumel on June 18, 1949. List provided by OAS Ambassador Luis Quintanilla of Mexico at the request of the OAS Investigating Committee, March 2, 1950.

NOMBRE	NACIONALIDAD
Miguel Ramírez Alcántara	Dominicana
Juan Rodriguez García	Dominicana
Jorge Rivas Montes	Hondureña
Juan Varón Gutiérrez	Hondureña
Manuel Gómez	Nicaragüense
Eufemio Fernández	Cubana
Alfredo Mejía Lara	Hondureña (?)
Daniel Martín	Cubana
Antonio Orue Reyes	Nicaragüense
Juan Esteban Luna	Dominicana (?)
José María Tercero	Nicaragüense
Luis Gaboardi Lacayo	Nicaragüense
Gustavo Girón C.	Guatemalteca
René Valenzuela C.	Guatemalteca
Gerardino Mazariegos Z.	Guatemalteca
Mario Alfaro de Alvarado	Nicaragüense
Británico Guzmán	Dominicana
Ignacio González	Cubana
Alberto Manent	Cubana
Sergio del Toro	Dominicana
Jorge Montero Gómez	Costarricense
Luis Morales Palacios	Nicaragüense
Efraín Villamil López	Hondureña
Antonio Luna Fernández	Dominicana (?)
Eduardo Lever Bauman	Mexicana

Factor Méndez A.	Guatemalteca
Jaime Alfaro de Alvarado	Nicaragüense
Miguel Ruiz C.	Nicaragüense
Gregorio Ozuna	Cubana
Antonio Ozuna (a) Roberto Reyes	Cubana
Guillermo Roche V.	Nicaragüense
Noé Cabezas G.	Nicaragüense
Luis Pineda del Sid	Guatemalteca
Guillermo Ruiz Martínez	Nicaragüense
Juan José Ruiz	Nicaragüense
Jorge Mejía R.	Hondureña
Maximiliano López	Hondureña
Rafael Vidal	Cubana
Santiago Ozuna	Cubana
Ramón Rodríguez	Cubana
José Horacio Rodríguez (?)	Dominicana
Frank Knox (a) Earl G. Adams	Norteamericana
Francisco Sánchez	Hondureña
Manuel Nover	Hondureña
Dimas Rodríguez	Hondureña
Amado Soler Fernández	Dominicana
José Marín	Cubana
Joe Marks (a) Marion R. Tinley	Norteamericana
Francisco Ponce de León	Mexicana
José M. del Castillo	Mexicana
José López Enríquez	Mexicana
José Cardona	Mexicana
Julián Balderrama Ibarra	Mexicana
Mario Treviño Baster	Mexicana
Gervasio Adecheguerra G.	Española

Appendix C

Identification of signatories of a petition addressed to the OAS Investigating Committee in Havana on February 7, 1950, condemning the dictatorships of Santo Domingo, Nicaragua, and Venezuela.

IDENTIFICACIONES DE LAS FIRMAS AUTOGRAFAS QUE SUSCRIBEN ESTE DOCU-MENTO ADJUNTO DIRIGIDO A LOS PODERES EJECUTIVOS Y LEGISLATIVOS DE LOS GOBIERNOS DEMOCRATICOS DE AMERICA Y A LOS MIEMBROS DE LA COMI-SION INVESTIGADORA DE LA ORGANIZACION DE ESTADOS AMERICANOS.

Señor doctor *Angel Morales*, jefe civil del Movimiento de Liberación Dominicano, internacionalista.

Señor doctor *Emilio Roig de Leuschering*, eminente historiógrafo y hombre de letras cubano, actual jefe de los Archivos Históricos de la Municipalidad de La Habana.

Señor professor *Raúl Roa*, actual jefe de la Dirección de Cultura del Ministerio de Educación de Cuba y catedrático de la Universidad de La Habana.

Señor doctor *Enrique C. Enríquez*, notable médico y literato, jefe de la Confederación de Campesinos de Cuba.

Señorita *Mariblanca Sabas Alomá*, doctora en pedagogía y ciencias sociales, escritora de renombre internacional y líder femenina del Partido Revolucionario Cubano.

Señor Profesor *Manuel Bisbe*, destacado pedagogo, catedrático de la Facultad de Filosofía y Letras de la Universidad de La Habana y candidato a Alcalde de la ciudad capital.

Señor General *Juan Rodríguez*, jefe militar del Movimiento de Liberación Dominicano.

Señor General *Miguel Angel Ramírez*, segundo jefe del Movimiento de Liberación Dominicano.

Señor *Luis Gómez Wangüemert*, comentarista internacional de la Radiodifusora C.M.Q. de La Habana.

Señorita *Sara Hernández Catá*, vigorosa escritora y comentarista de renombre en Europa y en América.

Señor doctor *Francisco Carone*, abogado y jurista, catedrático de Derecho Penal y Criminología de la Universidad de La Habana.

Señor doctor *Humberto Olguin Hermosilla*, periodista y escritor mexicano.

Señora *Vicentina Atuña*, Vocal de conferencias del Lyceo Lawn Tennis Club de La Habana.

Señor *Francisco Catalán*, escritor guatemalteco y miembro del Partido Acción Revolucionaria de Guatemala.

Señor *José R. Castro*, escritor y periodista hondureño adscrito como agregado de prensa a la Legación de Guatemala en La Habana.

Señor *Cruz Alonso*, hombre de negocios cubano.

Señorita *Conchita Garzón*, Vice-Presidente del Lyceo Lawn Tennis Club.

Señor doctor *Roberto Agramonte*, Director del Departamento de Intercambio Cultural de la Universidad de La Habana.

Señor doctor *Noel Henríquez*, abogado y ex-diplomático dominicano.

Señorita *Rosario Rexach*, secretaria de correspondencia de la directiva del Lyceo Lawn Tennis Club.

Señor professor *Herminio Portel Vilá*, periodista y comentarista, catedrático de la Universidad de La Habana y Director del Instituto Cubano-Norteamericano de La Habana.

Señor profesor *Salvador Massip*, Decano de la Facultad de Filosofía y Letras de la Universidad de La Habana.

Señorita *Angélica Planas*, Secretaria de Actas del Lyceo Lawn Tennis Club.

Señora *Maritza Alonso*, artista y funcionaria de la sección de Cultura del Ministerio de Educación de Cuba.

Señor profesor *Raimundo Lazo*, escritor distinguido y catedrático de la Facultad de Filosofía y Letras de la Universidad de La Habana.

Señora *Gloria Jaime de Domingo*, Presidente del Lyceo Lawn Tennis Club de La Habana.

Señora *Carmita Landestoy*, escritora y educacionista dominicana.

Señor *Alberto Ordóñez Argüello*, escritor y periodista de Nicaragua.

Señor doctor *José Horacio Rodríguez Vázquez*, abogado y ex-catedrático de la Facultad de Economía de la Universidad de Santo Domingo.

Notes

Introduction

1. Edwin Lieuwen, "Post-World War II Political Developments in Latin America," in U.S. Congress, Senate, Committee on Foreign Relations, *United States-Latin American Relations*, 86th Cong., 2d Sess., 1960, Senate Doc. 125, p. 11.

2. Ruth Berins Collier, "Labor Politics and Regime Change: Internal Trajectories versus External Influences," in David Rock, ed., *Latin America in the 1940s: War and Postwar Transitions* (Berkeley and Los Angeles: University of California Press, 1994), pp. 59-60.

3. Robert J. Alexander, *Prophets of the Revolution: Profiles of Latin American Leaders* (New York: The Macmillan Company, 1962), pp. 83-89.

4. *Rómulo Betancourt, interpretación de su doctrina popular y democrática*, editado por SUMA, librería y editorial (Caracas, 1958), p. 147.

5. Quoted in John D. Martz, *Acción Democrática: Evolution of a Modern Political Party in Venezuela* (Princeton: Princeton University Press, 1966), p. 125.

6. Ibid., p. 256.

7. *Betancourt, su doctrina*, p. 127.

8. David Rock, "Introduction," in Rock, ed., *Latin America in the 1940s*, p. 1.

9. Louis A. Pérez Jr., *Cuba: Between Reform and Revolution* (New York: Oxford University Press, 1988), p. 284.

10. Quoted in Martz, *Acción Democrática*, p. 305.

11. Richard N. Adams, "Social Change in Guatemala and U.S. Policy," in Richard N. Adams et al., *Social Change in Latin America Today: Its Implications for United States Policy* (New York: Vintage Books, 1960), p. 233.

12. Ibid., pp. 233-34.

13. Piero Gleijeses, *Shattered Hope: The Guatemalan Revolution and the United States, 1944-1954* (Princeton: Princeton University Press, 1991), p. 34.

14. Ibid., pp. 35-39.

15. Juan José Arévalo, *Istmania; O, la unidad revolucionaria de Centroamérica* (Buenos Aires: Editorial Indoamérica, 1954), pp. 18-19.

16. Thomas L. Karnes, *Tropical Enterprise: The Standard Fruit and Steamship Company in Latin America* (Baton Rouge: Louisiana State University Press, 1978), p. 37.

17. Thomas P. Anderson, *Politics in Central America* (New York: Praeger, 1988), p. 128.

18. Ralph Lee Woodward Jr., *Central America: A Nation Divided* (New York: Oxford University Press, 1985), p. 219.

19. Quoted in Paul Coe Clark Jr., *The United States and Somoza, 1933-1956: A Revisionist Look* (Westport, Conn.: Praeger, 1992), p. 94.

20. Robert D. Crassweller, *Trujillo: The Life and Times of a Caribbean Dictator* (New York: The Macmillan Company, 1966), pp. 57-58.

21. Circular, José Almoina to Dominican Diplomatic Missions, December 28, 1945, Organization of American States, Organ of Consultation, *Situation in the Caribbean, 1950,* documents pertaining to Haiti, Cuba, Guatemala, and the Dominican Republic, Columbus Memorial Library, Washington, D.C. Hereafter cited as OAS/OC (1950), [Country].

22. Bernardo Vega, "Los complots contra Betancourt," in Bernardo Vega, ed., *Los Estados Unidos y Trujillo. Colección de documentos del Departamento de Estado y de las Fuerzas Armadas Norteamericanos. Año 1946,* 2 vols. (Santo Domingo: Fundación Cultural Dominicana, 1982), 1:74-75.

23. "Extracto relativo a Cuba del informe confidencial que sobre la política Dominicana produce el Licenciado José Almoina Mateos, ex-Secretario Particular del Presidente Trujillo," OAS/OC (1950), Cuba.

24. Ibid.

25. Ibid.

26. Ibid.

27. *Betancourt, su doctrina,* p. 107.

28. J. Lloyd Mecham, *A Survey of United States-Latin American Relations* (Boston: Houghton Mifflin Company, 1965), p. 172.

29. Ibid., pp. 172-73.

30. U.S. Central Intelligence Agency, *The Caribbean Legion,* ORE 11-49 (March 17, 1949), papers of Harry S. Truman, President's Secretary File, Harry S. Truman Library, Independence, Missouri, p. 8.

31. Collier, "Labor Politics," p. 65; see also ibid., p. 66 (Figure 2) and p. 72 (Table 12).

32. Rock, "Introduction," p. 3.

33. Ibid., p. 4.

34. Rock, "Acknowledgments," p. xiii.

1946: Mr. Braden Stirs the Pot

1. J. Lloyd Mecham, *A Survey of United States-Latin American Relations* (Boston: Houghton Mifflin Company, 1965), p. 173, and J. Lloyd Mecham, *The United States and Inter-American Security, 1889-1960* (Austin: University of Texas Press, 1961), p. 289.

2. Spruille Braden, *Diplomats and Demagogues: The Memoirs of Spruille Braden* (New Rochelle: Arlington House, 1971), p. 423.

3. U.S. Department of State, *El régimen de Trujillo en la República Dominicana,* Intelligence Research Report, December 31, 1946, in Bernardo Vega, ed., *Los Estados Unidos y Trujillo. Colección de documentos del Departamento de Estado y de las Fuerzas Armadas Norteamericanos. Año 1946,* 2 vols. (Santo Domingo: Fundación Cultural Dominicana, 1982), 1:148-49.

4. Telegram 8458, Allan Dawson (Caracas) to Secretary of State, March 1, 1946, in Vega, ed., *Los Estados Unidos y Trujillo, 1946,* 1:207.

5. Telegram 178, Byrnes to Berle, February 5, 1946, in ibid., 1:155.

6. Ellis Briggs, *Farewell to Foggy Bottom: The Recollections of a Career Diplomat* (New York: David McKay Company, 1964), p. 137.

7. *El régimen de Trujillo,* in Vega, ed., *Los Estados Unidos y Trujillo, 1946,* 2:114.

8. Briggs, *Farewell,* p. 227.

9. Ibid., p. 228.

10. *El régimen de Trujillo,* in Vega, ed., *Los Estados Unidos y Trujillo, 1946,* 2:114-15.

11. Ibid.

12. Memorandum, Byrnes to President Truman, March 12, 1946, in Vega, ed., *Los Estados Unidos y Trujillo, 1946,* 1:220.

13. *El régimen de Trujillo,* in ibid., 2:150.

14. Telegram 682, George F. Scherer to Secretary of State, February 13, 1946, in ibid., 1:183.

15. Telegram 1228, Scherer to Secretary of State, September 4, 1946, in ibid., 1:360.

16. Telegram 311, Butler to Braden, September 21, 1946, in ibid., 1:365.

17. Telegram 148, Butler to Secretary of State, October 30, 1946, in ibid., 1:399.

18. Ibid.

19. Ibid.

20. Ibid., 1:400-401.

21. "Extracts of speech of U.S. Ambassador Butler before the American Chamber of Commerce, Ciudad Trujillo," November 1, 1946, in ibid., 1:406.

22. Telegram 257, Butler to Secretary of State, December 26, 1946, in ibid., 1:468.

23. Telegram 199, Butler to Secretary of State, November 18, 1946, in ibid., 1:421.

24. Telegram 223, Butler to Secretary of State, November 22, 1946, in ibid., 1:424.

25. Ibid., 1:426.

26. Telegram 380, Butler to Secretary of State, December 2, 1946, in ibid., 1:446-47.

27. Memorandum, John C. Dreier to Mr. Barber, December 3, 1946, in ibid., 1:448.

28. Briggs, *Farewell,* p. 186.

29. Telegram 306, Butler to Secretary of State, December 24, 1946, in Vega, ed., *Los Estados Unidos y Trujillo, 1946,* 1:477.

30. Memorandum, Barber to Briggs, January 10, 1946, in ibid., 1:482.

31. Memorandum, Braden to Briggs, January 22, 1946, in ibid., 1:483.

32. *Life,* March 25, 1946.

33. *New York Times,* September 25, 1945.

34. Ibid.

35. Donald Marquand Dozer, *Are We Good Neighbors? Three Decades of Inter-American Relations, 1930-1960* (Gainesville: University of Florida Press, 1959), p. 217.

36. Arthur P. Whitaker, *The United States and Argentina* (Cambridge: Harvard University Press, 1954), p. 148.

37. *Newsweek,* March 25, 1946.

38. David Green, *The Containment of Latin America* (Chicago: Quadrangle Books, 1971), p. 253.

39. *New York Times,* December 24, 1946.

40. Green, *Containment,* p. 253.

41. Ibid., p. 254.

42. J. Lloyd Mecham, *A Survey of United States-Latin American Relations* (Boston: Houghton Mifflin Company, 1965), pp. 280-81.

43. *El régimen de Trujillo,* in Vega, ed., *Los Estados Unidos y Trujillo, 1946,* 2:108.

44. Memorandum, Briggs to Braden, February 7, 1946, in ibid., 1:135.

45. Memorandum, Hauch to Briggs, February 28, 1946, in ibid., 1:186.

46. *El régimen de Trujillo,* in ibid., 2:109.

47. Telegram 682, Scherer to Secretary of State, February 13, 1946, in ibid, 1:182-83.

48. Memorandum, Butler to Braden, August 22, 1946, in ibid., 1:347.

49. Bernardo Vega, "Los cabilderos de Trujillo," in ibid., 1:67.

50. Memorandum, Byrnes to President Truman, March 12, 1946, in ibid., 1:220.

51. Memorandum, Cochran to Braden, January 10, 1946, in ibid., 1:112.

52. Telegram 676, Scherer to Secretary of State, February 12, 1946, in ibid., 1:115-16.

53. Memorandum, Hauch to Briggs and Braden, February 15, 1946, in ibid., 1:191.

54. Memorandum, Cochran to Braden, January 10, 1946, in ibid., 1:111-12.

55. Ibid., p. 112.

56. *El régimen de Trujillo,* in ibid., 2:112.

57. Paul Coe Clark Jr., *The United States and Somoza, 1933-1956: A Revisionist Look* (Westport, Conn.: Praeger, 1992), pp. 117-18.

58. Ibid., 124 n. 34.

59. Memorandum of conversation, participants: Ambassador García Godoy, Braden, and Hauch, March 21, 1946, in Vega, ed., *Los Estados Unidos y Trujillo, 1946,* 1:236.

60. Ibid.

61. Ibid.

62. Telegram 136, Scherer to Secretary of State, April 6, 1946, in ibid., 1:253.

63. Telegram, Byrnes to American embassy (Ciudad Trujillo), in ibid., 1:254.

64. Telegram 1010, Scherer to Secretary of State, June 21, 1946, in ibid., 1:310.

65. Memorandum, Hauch to Newbegin, Cochran, and Briggs, February 28, 1946, in ibid., 1:202 (see editor's note**).

66. Telegram 707, Scherer to Secretary of State, February 23, 1946, in ibid., 1:198.

67. Ibid., p. 199.

68. Memorandum, Hauch to Newbegin, Cochran, Butler, and Briggs, March 15, 1946, in ibid., 1:223.

69. Telegram 716, Scherer to Secretary of State, February 26, 1946, in ibid., 1:201-2.

70. *El régimen de Trujillo,* in ibid., 2:144.

71. Telegram 955, Scherer to Secretary of State, May 29, 1946, in ibid., 1:291.

72. Ibid., p. 292.

73. Memorandum, J. Edgar Hoover (FBI) to Frederick B. Lyon (State), May 21, 1946, in ibid., 1:288-89; Telegram 1176, Scherer to Secretary of State, August 13, 1946, in ibid., 1:344-45.

74. Bernardo Vega, "El acercamiento de Trujillo a los comunistas," in ibid., 1:64.

75. Memorandum, Hauch to Briggs, June 17, 1946, in ibid., 1:301.

76. Vega, "El acercamiento," in ibid., 1:60.

77. Telegram 1176, Scherer to Secretary of State, August 13, 1946, in ibid., 1:346.

78. Telegram 1269, Scherer to Secretary of State, September 18, 1946, in ibid., 1:363; Telegram 46, Butler to Secretary of State, October 4, 1946, in ibid., 1:369.

79. Vega, "El acercamiento," in ibid., 1:63.

80. Ibid.

81. Telegram 129, Butler to Secretary of State, October 26, 1946, in ibid., 1:379.

82. Telegram 240, Butler to Secretary of State, November 30, 1946, in ibid., 1:439-40.

83. Telegram 378, Butler to Secretary of State, November 29, 1946, in ibid., 1:434.

84. Telegram 251, Butler to Secretary of State, December 4, 1946, in ibid., 1:454.

85. Telegram 255, Butler to Secretary of State, December 5, 1946, in ibid., 1:462.

86. Telegram 306, Butler to Secretary of State, December 24, 1946, in ibid., 1:477.

87. Intelligence Report, U.S. Naval Attaché (Havana), January 19, 1946, in ibid., 1:119; *El régimen de Trujillo,* in ibid., 2:149.

88. Memorandum, Braden and Barber to Butler and Briggs, February 6, 1946, in ibid., 1:187-88.

89. Memorandum of conversation, participants: Bonilla Atiles, Ellis O. Briggs, Willard F. Barber, June 14, 1946, in ibid., 1:303.

90. Telegram, Scherer to Secretary of State, February 11, 1946, in ibid., 1:188.

91. Memorandum, Hauch to Barber and Briggs, May 9, 1946, in ibid., 1:278-79.

92. Memorandum, conversation with Angel Morales, October 17, 1946, in ibid., 1:374-75.

93. Telegram 159, Scherer to Secretary of State, November 2, 1946, in ibid., 1:408.

94. Telegram 223, Butler to Secretary of State, November 22, 1946, in ibid., 1:424.

95. Memorandum, Hauch to Barber, Trueblood, Briggs, and Braden, December 10, 1946, in ibid., 1:471.

96. Letter, Bonilla Atiles to Spruille Braden, December 4, 1946, in ibid., 1:460.

97. Telegram 955, Scherer to Secretary of State, May 29, 1946, in ibid., 1:292.

1947: Cayo Confites

1. Nicolás Silfa, *Guerra, traición, y exilio,* 3 vols. (Barcelona: P. Manuel Girona, 1980) 1:209.

2. Angel Miolán, *El perredé, desde mi ángulo,* 2d ed. (Caracas: Avila Arte, 1985), pp. 501-2.

3. Ibid., pp. 516-17.

4. Ibid., p. 99.

5. Ibid., p. 98.

6. Ibid., p. 32.

7. Ibid., p. 44.

8. Ibid., p. 76.

9. Ibid., pp. 87-88.

10. Ibid., p. 88.

11. U.S. Department of State, *El régimen de Trujillo en la República Dominicana,* Intelligence Research Report, December 31, 1946, in Bernardo Vega, ed., *Los Estados Unidos y Trujillo. Colección de documentos del Departamento de Estado y de las Fuerzas Armadas Norteamericanos. Año 1946,* 2 vols. (Santo Domingo: Fundación Cultural Dominicana, 1982), 2:139.

12. Ibid., p. 146.

13. Miolán, *El perredé,* pp. 87-88.

14. Jaime Suchlicki, *University Students and Revolution in Cuba, 1920-1968* (Coral Gables: University of Miami Press, 1969), pp. 51-52.

15. Miolán, *El perredé,* p. 89.

16. Ibid.

17. Ibid., p. 493.

18. Telegram, Allan Dawson to Secretary of State, January 8, 1946, in Vega, ed., *Los Estados Unidos y Trujillo, 1946,* 1:99.

19. Ibid., p. 100.

20. Intelligence Report, U.S. Military Attaché (Venezuela), March 21, 1946, in ibid., 1:242.

21. Intelligence Report, U.S. Military Attaché (Haiti), March 20, 1946, in ibid., 1:231.

22. Telegram, Allan Dawson to Secretary of State, January 8, 1946, in ibid., 1:101.

23. Ibid.

24. Despatch 8458, Dawson to Secretary of State, March 1, 1946, in ibid., 1:209; Miolán, *El perredé,* p. 119.

25. Telegram 131, Dawson to Secretary of State, February 21, 1946, in Vega, ed., *Los Estados Unidos y Trujillo, 1946,* 1:196.

26. Telegram 83, Scherer to Secretary of State, February 25, 1946, in ibid., 1:200.

27. Weekly Analysis, U.S. Military Attaché (Dominican Republic), March 27, 1946, in ibid., 1:247.

28. *El régimen de Trujillo,* in ibid., 2:146.

29. Weekly Analysis, U.S. Military Attaché (Dominican Republic), March 23, 1946, in ibid., 1:245.

30. Memorandum, J. Edgar Hoover (FBI) to Frederick B. Lyon (State), April 9, 1946, in ibid., 1:258.

31. Intelligence Report, U.S. Military Attaché (Haiti), March 20, 1946, in ibid., 1:232.

32. Telegram 83, Scherer to Secretary of State, February 25, 1946, in ibid., 1:200; U.S. Military Attaché (Dominican Republic), March 27, 1946, in ibid., 1:246.

33. Intelligence Report, U.S. Naval Attaché (Havana), January 19, 1946, in ibid., 1:119.

34. Miolán, *El perredé,* pp. 484–85; Silfa, *Guerra* 1:180; Tulio H. Arvelo, *Cayo Confites y Luperón: Memorias de un expedicionario* (Santo Domingo: Universidad Autónoma de Santo Domingo, 1981), p. 24.

35. Intelligence Report, U.S. Air Attaché (Havana), August 15, 1947, in Bernardo Vega, ed., *Los Estados Unidos y Trujillo Colección de documentos del Departamento de Estado y de las Fuerzas Armadas Norteamericanos. Año 1947,* 2 vols. (Santo Domingo: Fundación Cultural Dominicana, 1984), 2:579–80.

36. Background report on Juan Rodríguez García, Dominican Republic, Organization of American States, Organ of Consultation, *Situation in the Caribbean, 1950,* documents pertaining to Haiti, Cuba, Guatemala, and the Dominican Republic, Columbus Memorial Library, Washington, D.C. Hereafter cited as OAS/OC (1950), [Country]. In an effort to discredit Rodríguez the Dominican government provided the OAS Investigating Committee with background data on the general depicting him as a loyal Trujillo supporter and active member of the Dominican party (Trujillo's "official" party).

37. Ibid.

38. Silfa, *Guerra,* 1:177.

39. Miolán, *El perredé,* p. 119.

40. Silfa, *Guerra,* 1:179. This amount is cited by a variety of sources.

41. Ibid. See also Vega, ed., *Los Estados Unidos y Trujillo, 1947,* 2:579–80. José Horacio stated that Trujillo "had ordered his assassination."

42. Despatch 9487, Frank P. Corrigan to Secretary of State, November 21, 1946, in Vega, ed., *Los Estados Unidos y Trujillo, 1946,* 1:423.

43. Despatch 9198, Dawson to Secretary of State, September 6, 1946, in ibid., 1:361; Memorandum of conversation with Angel Morales, October 17, 1946, in ibid., 1:375.

44. Despatch 9198, Dawson to Secretary of State, September 6, 1946, in ibid., 1:361; Despatch 9498, Corrigan to Secretary of State, November 21, 1946, in ibid., 1:422–23; Telegram 378, Butler to Secretary of State, November 29, 1946, in ibid., 1:434–45; Telegram 242, Butler to Secretary of State, November 30, 1946, in ibid., 1:435–39. Trujillo received an intelligence report in November 1946 that contained the key elements of the liberation plan that was to be put into place the following summer.

45. Charles D. Ameringer, *The Democratic Left in Exile: The Antidictatorial Struggle in the Caribbean, 1945-1959* (Coral Gables: University of Miami Press, 1974), p. 61.

46. Miolán, *El perredé,* pp. 484–85.

47. Telegram 242, Butler to Secretary of State, November 30, 1946, in Vega, ed., *Los Estados Unidos y Trujillo, 1946,* 1:439 (see editor's note); Despatch 4615, Lester D. Mallory (Havana) to Secretary of State, December 19, 1947, in Vega, ed., *Los Estados Unidos y Trujillo, 1947,* 1:194 and pp. 197-98. The sources vary in fixing the number of rifles obtained in this way. Miolán, *El perredé,* gives the number as 2,000 on p. 118 but reduces it to 1,000 on p. 443. Silfa, *Guerra,* is likewise uncertain, giving a vague "hundreds" of Mauser rifles and "a large quantity" of Mendoza machine guns, 1:181. Mallory's report (above) is probably closest, placing the figure at 1,500 rifles and 50 machine guns, pp. 194 and 197.

48. Miolán, *El perredé,* p. 119.

49. Editor's note, in Vega, ed., *Los Estados Unidos y Trujillo, 1946,* 1:438.

50. Ibid.

51. Despatch 4434, R. Henry Norweb to Secretary of State, October 17, 1947, in Vega, ed., *Los Estados Unidos y Trujillo, 1947,* 1:175.

52. Silfa, *Guerra,* 1:218 and 233.

53. Ibid., pp. 184–85.

54. Ibid., p. 186.

55. Ibid., p. 187.

56. Ibid., pp. 184–89.

57. Despatch 4615, Mallory to Secretary of State, December 19, 1947, in Vega, ed., *Los Estados Unidos y Trujillo, 1947,* 1:190–91; see also Silfa, *Guerra,* 1:183.

58. Despatch 4615, Mallory to Secretary of State, December 19, 1947, in Vega, ed., *Los Estados Unidos y Trujillo, 1947,* 1:191–93; see also Figure 1.

59. Silfa, *Guerra,* 1:183.

60. Despatch 4615, Mallory to Secretary of State, December 19, 1947, in Vega, ed., *Los Estados Unidos y Trujillo, 1947,* 1:194. Quite likely there were at least another 1,000 rifles obtained from other sources, including Kraggs and Springfields. Hollis Smith claimed he saw 4,000 rifles on board the *Aurora* (mid-September 1947). See "Smith Deposition," April 13, 1948, Nicaragua, Organization of American States, Organ of Consultation, *Situation in the Caribbean, 1949,* documents pertaining to Costa Rica and Nicaragua, Columbus Memorial Library, Washington, D.C. Hereafter cited as OAS/OC (1949), [Country].

61. Despatch 4615, Mallory to Secretary of State, December 19, 1947, in Vega, ed., *Los Estados Unidos y Trujillo, 1947,* 1:194–97; Silfa, *Guerra,* 1:183.

62. Despatch No. 28, Embassy at Havana, January 13, 1948, U.S. Department of State, *Confidential U.S. State Department Central Files: Cuba, 1945–1949,* ed. Michael C. Davis (Frederick, Md.: University Publications of America, 1987). Hereafter cited as *Cuba, 1945–1949.*

63. Ibid.; Despatch 4434, R. Henry Norweb to Secretary of State, October 17, 1947, in Vega, ed., *Los Estados Unidos y Trujillo, 1947,* 1:176; Miolán, *El perredé,* p. 118.

64. Miolán, *El perredé,* p. 48.

65. Ibid., p. 120; Silfa, *Guerra,* 1:182; Despatch 4434, R. Henry Norweb to Secretary of State, October 17, 1947, in Vega, ed., *Los Estados Unidos y Trujillo, 1947,* 1:174.

66. J. L. Wanguemert, "El diario de Cayo Confites," in Vega, ed., *Los Estados Unidos y Trujillo, 1947,* 1:127.

67. Bernardo Vega, "El papel de los veteranos de guerra Norteamericanos en los conflictos del Caribe en 1947," in ibid., 1:111; Despatch 4434, R. Henry Norweb to Secretary of State, October 17, 1947, in ibid., 1:173–74; "Smith Deposition," OAS/OC (1949), Nicaragua.

68. Vega, "El papel de los veteranos," in Vega, ed., *Los Estados Unidos y Trujillo, 1947,* 1:110–11; "Smith Deposition," OAS/OC (1949), Nicaragua.

69. "Smith Deposition," OAS/OC (1949), Nicaragua.

70. Norweb to Secretary of State, April 22, 1946, in *Cuba, 1945–1949.*

71. Despatch 4434, R. Henry Norweb to Secretary of State, October 17, 1947, in Vega, ed., *Los Estados Unidos y Trujillo, 1947,* 1:185.

72. Despatch No. 786, Harold S. Tewell to Secretary of State, September 21, 1948, in *Cuba, 1945–1949.*

73. Ibid.

74. Despatch 4434, R. Henry Norweb to Secretary of State, October 17, 1947, in Vega, ed., *Los Estados Unidos y Trujillo, 1947,* 1:184.

75. Ibid.

76. "Smith Deposition," OAS/OC (1949), Nicaragua.

77. Despatch 4434, R. Henry Norweb to Secretary of State, October 17, 1947, in Vega, ed., *Los Estados Unidos y Trujillo, 1947,* 1:173.

78. Miolán, *El perredé,* pp. 35–37.

79. Despatch 4434, R. Henry Norweb to Secretary of State, October 17, 1947, in Vega, ed., *Los Estados Unidos y Trujillo, 1947,* 1:165.

80. Ibid.

81. There are varying claims about the size of the expeditionary force but from a review

of the sources 1,200 to 1,300 appears to be a good estimate of the number that actually took part. Miolán declared that there were "some 2,000 men" in the force (p. 118), and Smith gave a figure of 1,500 Cubans, 200 to 300 Dominicans, and a sprinkling of "other nationalities"; Arvelo set the number at "some 1,300 men" (p. 55); Silfa was in close agreement, recalling that there were "perhaps" 1,000 Cubans, 300 Dominicans, and the rest (50?) of different nationalities (p. 200). Silfa also related that the force was divided into four battalions, with "more than" 250 men in each (p. 205). In aborting the expedition the Cuban authorities took the revolutionary force into custody, publishing a list of 1,033 persons being held on October 1, 1947, with the caveat that "it was not necessarily a complete list of all the persons making up the expeditionary forces." See Vega, ed., *Los Estados Unidos y Trujillo, 1947,* 1:199–212.

82. "Diario," in ibid., 1:127.

83. Ibid., p. 128.

84. "Statement of Héctor Incháustegui Cabral," OAS/OC (1950), Dominican Republic.

85. Ibid.

86. Cable 19078, Arturo Despradel to Rafael P. González Muñoz, July 23, 1947, in Vega, ed., *Los Estados Unidos y Trujillo, 1947,* 2:473–74.

87. Telegram 139, Marshall to American embassy (Ciudad Trujillo), July 26, 1947, in ibid., 2:482–83.

88. Ibid., p. 483. U.S. citizens Edward Browder and Karl Eisenhardt were eventually tried and convicted for violating U.S. laws (including the theft of twenty-one machine guns from a U.S. arsenal) in connection with the plot to overthrow Betancourt. Browder was sentenced to thirty-six months in prison and Eisenhardt was fined $10,000.

89. Despatch 9960, Corrigan to Secretary of State, March 31, 1947, in Vega, ed., *Los Estados Unidos y Trujillo, 1947,* 1:362; Despatch 9781, Corrigan to Secretary of State, February 21, 1947, in ibid., 1:313.

90. Telegram 418, Butler to Secretary of State, January 29, 1947, in ibid., 1:279.

91. Intelligence Report 4694-M, May 24, 1947, in ibid., 1:408. According to the report Rodríguez and Cruz Alonso claimed to have the backing of President Truman, General Eisenhower, and the Masonic Order.

92. Memorandum of conversation, Jorge García Granados and Spruille Braden, May 24, 1947, in ibid., 1:405.

93. Editor's note, in ibid., 1:405 and 408.

94. Telegram 372, Norweb to Secretary of State, July 17, 1947, in ibid., 1:467–68.

95. Telegram 379, Norweb to Secretary of State, July 19, 1947, in ibid., 1:472.

96. Memorandum, Briggs to the Secretary [of State], July 7, 1947, in ibid., 1:450–51.

97. Bernardo Vega, "Analisis de la política Norteamericana para América Latina y la República Dominicana en 1947," in ibid., 1:92.

98. Memorandum, James H. Wright to Secretary of State, July 17, 1947, in ibid., 2:466–67; Memorandum, Wright to the Secretary [of State], July 29, 1947, in ibid., 2:467.

99. Telegram 399, Norweb to Secretary of State, July 25, 1947, in ibid., 2:478–79.

100. Telegram 363, Marshall to U.S. embassy (Havana), July 26, 1947, in ibid., 2:484–85.

101. Telegram 410, Norweb to Secretary of State, July 28, 1947, in ibid., 2:496–97; see also "Diario," in ibid., 1:132.

102. Miolán, *El perredé,* p. 117.

103. Silfa, *Guerra,* 1:200.

104. Ibid., p. 201.

105. Arvelo, *Cayo Confites y Luperón,* p. 65.

106. "Diario," in Vega, ed., *Los Estados Unidos y Trujillo, 1947,* 1:140–41; see also "Smith Deposition," OAS/OC (1949), Nicaragua.

107. "Diario," in Vega, ed., *Los Estados Unidos y Trujillo, 1947,* 1:142.

108. Silfa, *Guerra,* 1:202.

109. "Smith Deposition," OAS/OC (1949), Nicaragua.

110. Miolán, *El perredé*, p. 120; "Diario," in Vega, ed., *Los Estados Unidos y Trujillo, 1947*, 1:148.

111. Telegram 98, Butler to Secretary of State, May 6, 1947, in ibid., 1:397.

112. Enrique Rodríguez Loeche, "Por qué fracasó la expedición a Santo Domingo," *Bohemia*, August 21, 1949, p. 58.

113. Ramírez File, OAS/OC (1950), Dominican Republic.

114. Arvelo, *Cayo Confites y Luperón*, p. 66.

115. Silfa, *Guerra*, 1:204; Despatch 4434, R. Henry Norweb to Secretary of State, October 17, 1947, in Vega, ed., *Los Estados Unidos y Trujillo, 1947*, 1:178.

116. Silfa, *Guerra*, 1:203; "Diario," in Vega, ed., *Los Estados Unidos y Trujillo, 1947*, 1:144.

117. Silfa, *Guerra*, 1:204; Arvelo, *Cayo Confites y Luperón*, p. 67; Editor's note, in Vega, ed., *Los Estados Unidos y Trujillo, 1947*, 1:179.

118. Silfa, *Guerra*, 1:204-205.

119. Despatch 4434, R. Henry Norweb to Secretary of State, October 17, 1947, in Vega, ed., *Los Estados Unidos y Trujillo, 1947*, 1:178.

120. Arvelo, *Cayo Confites y Luperón*, p. 68.

121. Telegram 469, Norweb to Secretary of State, August 13, 1947, in Vega, ed., *Los Estados Unidos y Trujillo, 1947*, 2:570.

122. General Fausto E. Caamaño to General Genovevo Pérez, July 23, 1947, OAS/OC (1950), Dominican Republic.

123. Telegram 801, Norweb to Secretary of State, August 15, 1947, in *Cuba, 1945-1949*.

124. Telegram 402, Norweb to Secretary of State, July 26, 1947, in Vega, ed., *Los Estados Unidos y Trujillo, 1947*, 2:486.

125. Intelligence Report, U.S. Military Attaché (Havana), August 26, 1947, in ibid., 2:640.

126. Telegram 440, Norweb to Secretary of State, August 5, 1947, in ibid., 2:542-43; Telegram 504, Norweb to Secretary of State, August 25, 1947, in ibid., 2:633.

127. Telegram 411, Norweb to Secretary of State, July 28, 1947, in ibid., 2:498.

128. Despatch 4235, Norweb to Secretary of State, August 4, 1947, in ibid., 2:526-28.

129. Telegram 426, Norweb to Secretary of State, July 31, 1947, in ibid., 2:506.

130. Memorandum, William A. Eddy to Mr. Lovett, August 1, 1947, in ibid., 2:519. On October 16, 1947, Hillenkoetter criticized U.S. intelligence coverage of Cayo Confites, complaining that the United States had no "firsthand" sources and that the coverage was "inadequate and inaccurate" (ibid., pp. 828-31).

131. Memorandum, Marshall to Lovett, August 1, 1947, in *Cuba, 1945-1949*.

132. Intelligence Report, U.S. Military Attaché (Ciudad Trujillo), August 5, 1947, in Vega, ed., *Los Estados Unidos y Trujillo, 1947*, 2:540-41.

133. Intelligence Report No. 4967-M, G-2, Third Army, August 11, 1947, in ibid., 2:562. Bosch identified Fors as Trujillo's agent three days before his death. See Despatch 4240, Norweb to Secretary of State, August 4, 1947, in ibid., 2:535-36.

134. Allegedly, Norweb recommended that the vessel be detained. See Despatch 4255, Norweb to Secretary of State, August 7, 1947, in ibid., 2:549.

135. Ibid.

136. Ibid., pp. 549-50.

137. "Diario," in Vega, ed., *Los Estados Unidos y Trujillo, 1947*, 1:138-39.

138. Interview by author with Angel Miolán, Santo Domingo, July 15, 1992.

139. Despatch 4434, R. Henry Norweb to Secretary of State, October 17, 1947, in Vega, ed., *Los Estados Unidos y Trujillo, 1947*, 1:177.

140. Despatch 4273, Norweb to Secretary of State, August 14, 1947, in ibid., 2:574.

141. Ibid., pp. 575-76.

142. Despatch 4281, Norweb to Secretary of State, August 15, 1947, in ibid., 2:581-82.

143. Telegram 476, Norweb to Secretary of State, August 17, 1947, in ibid., 2:586-87.
144. Telegram 504, Norweb to Secretary of State, August 25, 1947, in ibid., 2:632-33.
145. Arvelo, *Cayo Confites y Luperón*, pp. 73-74.
146. Telegram 500, Norweb to Secretary of State, August 23, 1947, in Vega, ed., *Los Estados Unidos y Trujillo, 1947*, 2:630-31.
147. Despatch 1079, Charles R. Burrows to Secretary of State, August 19, 1947, in ibid., 2:603-604.
148. Despatch 4434, R. Henry Norweb to Secretary of State, October 17, 1947, in ibid., 1:186-87; Telegram 544, Norweb to Secretary of State, September 17, 1947, in ibid., 2:741; Telegram 242, Lovett to American embassy (Caracas), October 1, 1947, in ibid., 2:794-95.
149. Intelligence Report, U.S. Military Attaché (Havana), August 1, 1947, in ibid., 2:515; Despatch 4255, Norweb to Secretary of State, August 7, 1947, in ibid., 2:550.
150. Despatch 4615, Mallory to Secretary of State, December 19, 1947, in ibid., 1:192.
151. Telegram 500, Norweb to Secretary of State, August 23, 1947, in ibid., 2:630-31.
152. Telegram 513, Norweb to Secretary of State, August 28, 1947, in ibid., 2:653-54.
153. Telegram 517, Norweb to Secretary of State, August 29, 1947, in ibid., 2:655.
154. Telegram 406, Lovett to American embassy (Havana), August 15, 1947, in ibid., 2:585.
155. Cablegram, Rafael L. Trujillo to Ramón Grau San Martín, August 20, 1947, in ibid., 2:609-11.
156. Cablegram, Ramón Grau San Martín to Rafael L. Trujillo, August 21, 1947, in ibid., 2:611.
157. Letter, Emilio García Godoy to Miguel Figueroa Miranda [Cuban Chargé], August 23, 1947, OAS/OC (1950), Dominican Republic.
158. Ibid.
159. Memorandum, W. W. Walker, September 12, 1947, in *Cuba, 1945-1949.*
160. Despatch 4434, R. Henry Norweb to Secretary of State, October 17, 1947, in Vega, ed., *Los Estados Unidos y Trujillo, 1947*, 1:191.
161. "Smith Deposition," OAS/OC (1949), Nicaragua.
162. Ibid.; "Diario," in Vega, ed., *Los Estados Unidos y Trujillo, 1947*, 1:145-46.
163. Telegram 523, Norweb to Secretary of State, September 4, 1947, in Vega, ed., *Los Estados Unidos y Trujillo, 1947*, 2:684-85.
164. Intelligence Report, U.S. Air Attaché (Havana), September 12, 1947, in ibid., 2:711.
165. Telegram 251, Burrows to Secretary of State, September 6, 1947, in ibid., 2:696.
166. "Smith Deposition," OAS/OC (1949), Nicaragua.
167. Telegram 251, Burrows to Secretary of State, September 6, 1947, in Vega, ed., *Los Estados Unidos y Trujillo, 1947*, 2:696.
168. Memorandum, Presidential Secretary to Secretary of Foreign Relations [Dominican Republic], September 6, 1947, in ibid., 2:693-94.
169. Memorandum, Presidential Secretary to Secretary of Foreign Relations [Dominican Republic], September 10, 1947, in ibid., 2:702-703.
170. Memorandum, Emilio García Godoy to Presidential Secretary, September 11, 1947, in ibid., 2:704-705.
171. Despatch 4434, R. Henry Norweb to Secretary of State, October 17, 1947, in ibid., 1:184.
172. Memorandum, Emilio García Godoy to President Trujillo, September 13, 1947, in ibid., 2:717-18; Miolán, *El perredé*, pp. 471-72.
173. Telegram 334, McBride to Secretary of State, September 15, 1947, in Vega, ed., *Los Estados Unidos y Trujillo, 1947*, 2:731-32; Letter, Incháustegui to Presidential Secretary, October 2, 1947, in ibid., 2:799; Bernardo Vega, "La supuesta eficiencia de los servicios de inteligencia de Trujillo con relación á Cayo Confites," in ibid., 1:113, 115; Despatch 4434, R. Henry Norweb to Secretary of State, October 17, 1947, in ibid., 1:185.

174. "Diario," in ibid., 1:147.

175. Telegram 506, American embassy (Havana) to Secretary of State, September 17, 1947, in *Cuba, 1945-1949.*

176. Despatch 942, American embassy (Havana) to Secretary of State, November 25, 1949, in ibid.

177. Despatch 4382, American embassy (Havana) to Secretary of State, September 30, 1947, in ibid.

178. Ibid.

179. Ibid.; Telegram 461, Lovett to American embassy (Havana), September 15, 1947, in ibid.; Memorandum of telephone conversation between Norweb and Walker, September 16, 1947, in ibid.

180. Intelligence Report, U.S. Air Attaché (Havana), September 12, 1947, in Vega, ed., *Los Estados Unidos y Trujillo, 1947,* 2:711.

181. Silfa, *Guerra,* 1:211.

182. Ibid.

183. Note, American embassy, Havana, September 9, 1946, in *Cuba, 1945-1949.* In detailing a wave of shootings in Havana the American embassy reported that public order had "broken down" and that the Army may be compelled "to take a direct hand in the performance of the police function." On August 1, 1946, an FBI report stated that Emilio Tró had "killed" secret police detective Julio Abril on July 28, 1946, and was "linked" to the murder of ex-secret police official Desiderio Ferreira on July 19, 1946. Ibid.

184. Despatch 4400, Norweb to Secretary of State, October 3, 1947, in ibid.; Memorandum, Walker to Woodward, October 13, 1947, in ibid.

185. Despatch 4382, Norweb to Secretary of State, September 30, 1947, in ibid.

186. Ibid.

187. Despatch 4400, Norweb to Secretary of State, October 3, 1947, in ibid; see also Memorandum, Dominican Legation, Havana, September 23, 1947, in Vega, ed., *Los Estados Unidos y Trujillo, 1947,* 2:755; Intelligence Report, U.S. Military Attaché (Havana), September 30, 1947, in Vega, ed., *Los Estados Unidos y Trujillo, 1947,* 2:783-84.

188. Despatch 4400, Norweb to Secretary of State, October 3, 1947, in *Cuba, 1945-1949;* Despatch 4421, Norweb to Secretary of State, October 9, 1947, in ibid.; Intelligence Report, U.S. Military Attaché (Havana), September 22, 1947, in Vega, ed., *Los Estados Unidos y Trujillo, 1947,* 2:752-53; Telegram, Norweb to Secretary of State, September 24, 1947, in Vega, ed., *Los Estados Unidos y Trujillo, 1947,* 2:761; "Smith Deposition," OAS/OC (1949), Nicaragua.

189. Telegram 257, Burrows to Secretary of State, September 15, 1947, in Vega, ed., *Los Estados Unidos y Trujillo, 1947,* 2:726-27.

190. Telegram 551, Norweb to Secretary of State, September 22, 1947, in ibid., 2:754-55.

191. "Diario," in ibid., 1:149.

192. Ibid., p. 150.

193. Arvelo, *Cayo Confites y Luperón,* p. 83.

194. "Smith Deposition," OAS/OC (1949), Nicaragua.

195. Ibid.

196. "Diario," in Vega, ed., *Los Estados Unidos y Trujillo, 1947,* 1:154-55.

197. Ibid., p. 156.

198. Ibid.

199. *Washington Post,* October 5, 1947, cited in Vega, ed., *Los Estados Unidos y Trujillo, 1947,* 2:807-8.

200. Arvelo, *Cayo Confites y Luperón,* p. 99.

201. "Smith Deposition," OAS/OC (1949), Nicaragua.

202. *Washington Post,* October 5, 1947, cited in Vega, ed., *Los Estados Unidos y Trujillo,*

1947, 2:807; "Fotografías sobre la expedición de Cayo Confites," in ibid., 1:74, 76, 80; Despatch 28, Norweb to Secretary of State, January 13, 1948, in *Cuba, 1945-1949*.

203. Bernardo Vega, "La estrategia de Trujillo para detener la expedición de Cayo Confites," in Vega, ed., *Los Estados Unidos y Trujillo, 1947*, 1:98; *Time*, October 13, 1947, cited in ibid., 2:821; Miolán, *El perredé*, p. 120.

204. Despatch 4421, Norweb to Secretary of State, October 9, 1947, in *Cuba, 1945-1949*.

205. "Fotografías," in Vega, ed., *Los Estados Unidos y Trujillo, 1947*, 1:74; ibid., 2:807; Despatch 28, Norweb to Secretary of State, January 13, 1948, in *Cuba, 1945-1949*.

206. Organization of American States, *Aplicaciones del Tratado Interamericano de Asistencia Recíproca, 1948-1960*, 3d ed. (Washington, D.C.: Unión Panamericana, 1960), p. 103; Despatch 28, Norweb to Secretary of State, January 13, 1948, in *Cuba, 1945-1949*; "Minutes of Investigating Committee Meeting, January 17, 1950," OAS/OC (1950), Committee File.

207. "Declaración del Comite Central Revolucionario Dominicano," in Vega, ed., *Los Estados Unidos y Trujillo, 1947*, 2:787-89.

208. Silfa, *Guerra*, 1:218.

209. Telegram, Lovett to American embassy, Havana, September 19, 1947, in Vega, ed., *Los Estados Unidos y Trujillo, 1947*, 2:745; Telegram 551, Norweb to Secretary of State, September 22, 1947, in ibid., 2:754.

210. Telegram 557, Norweb to Secretary of State, September 24, 1947, in ibid., 2:762-63; Telegram 242, Lovett to American embassy, Caracas, October 1, 1947, in ibid., 2:794-95.

211. Memorandum, Casey to Norweb, October 6, 1947, in ibid., 2:812-13; "Smith Deposition," OAS/OC (1949), Nicaragua.

212. Memorandum, Casey to Norweb, October 6, 1947, in Vega, ed., *Los Estados Unidos y Trujillo, 1947*, 2:812-13.

213. Despatch 4411, Hutchinson to Secretary of State, October 8, 1947, in ibid., 2:811-14.

214. A State Department memorandum of September 2, 1947, reporting Smith's decision to return to Cuba likewise does not support the spy hypothesis, but one can never be certain in such matters. See Memorandum of conversation between H. B. Smith and William W. Walker, Department of State, September 2, 1947, in ibid., 2:677-78; also, Memorandum, James H. Wright, Department of State, to Rear Admiral Marshall R. Greer, Navy Department, September 18, 1947, in ibid., 2:743-44.

215. "Veteranos," in ibid., 1:111.

216. Airgram 212, Norweb to Secretary of State, February 25, 1948, in *Cuba, 1945-1949*; Despatch 942, Norweb to Secretary of State, November 25, 1949, in ibid.

217. Intelligence Report, U.S. Military Attaché (Havana), October 2, 1947, in Vega, ed., *Los Estados Unidos y Trujillo, 1947*, 2:803-4.

218. Despatch 4434, R. Henry Norweb to Secretary of State, October 17, 1947, in ibid., 1:177.

219. Memorandum of conversation between Sr. Herrera and Mr. Catlett, August 25, 1947, in ibid., 2:634; "press summary," in ibid., 2:778; *Time*, October 13, 1947, cited in ibid., 2:821.

220. Despatch, George H. Butler to Secretary of State, August 26, 1947, in ibid., 2:643.

221. Intelligence Report, U.S. Air Attaché (Havana), August 15, 1947, in ibid., 2:579-81.

1948: Costa Rica

1. Piero Gleijeses, *Shattered Hope: The Guatemalan Revolution and the United States, 1944-1954* (Princeton: Princeton University Press, 1991), p. 108.

2. Ibid.

3. "Memorandum para el Coronel Hughes," in José Figueres, Private Papers, San José, Costa Rica.

4. Nicolás Silfa, *Guerra, traición, y exilio*, 3 vols. (Barcelona: P. Manuel Girona, 1980), 1:244.

5. Ibid., p. 260.

6. Ibid., p. 254.

7. José Figueres Ferrer, *El espíritu del 48* (San José: Editorial Costa Rica, 1987), p. 109.

8. Charles D. Ameringer, *Don Pepe: A Political Biography of José Figueres of Costa Rica* (Albuquerque: University of New Mexico Press, 1978), pp. 7-9.

9. Ibid., pp. 17-21.

10. *By Whom We Were Betrayed . . . And How* [1955], p. 14.

11. Ibid.

12. Ameringer, *Don Pepe*, p. 26.

13. Figueres, *Espíritu*, p. 103.

14. *By Whom We Were Betrayed*, p. 20.

15. Ibid., p. 25; Figueres, *Espíritu*, p. 104.

16. *By Whom We Were Betrayed*, pp. 25-26; Figueres, *Espíritu*, p. 104. This activity was reported in Movimiento Liberación Nacional, *Los pagos de la Guerra de Liberación Nacional* (San José: Editorial Liberación Nacional, 1953), but Figueres has not changed his story much over the years.

17. Figueres, *Espíritu*, pp. 108-9.

18. Ibid.

19. Ibid., pp. 126-27.

20. Ibid., p. 127; *By Whom We Were Betrayed*, pp. 23 and 26-27; Gleijeses, *Shattered Hope*, p. 112.

21. Despatch 447, American embassy, Guatemala, to Secretary of State, September 2, 1948, U.S. Department of State, *Confidential U.S. State Department Central Files: Cuba, 1945-1949*, ed. Michael C. Davis (Frederick, Md.: University Publications of America, 1987); hereafter cited as *Cuba, 1945-1949*. Arévalo later expressed misgivings that he did "the right thing" in aiding Figueres. See *Diario de Costa Rica*, January 31, 1972.

22. *By Whom We Were Betrayed*, pp. 28-30.

23. Ibid., pp. 30-31.

24. Ibid., pp. 30-32; Gleijeses, *Shattered Hope*, states that Arévalo "discreetly refrained" from signing the document but that "his hand was evident in the flowery language that was his trademark" (p. 111).

25. Figueres, *Espíritu*, pp. 128-32 (Spanish version); *By Whom We Were Betrayed*, pp. 33-36 (English version).

26. Ibid.

27. *By Whom We Were Betrayed*, p. 36; Figueres, *Espíritu*, p. 127.

28. Silfa, *Guerra*, 1:245.

29. Figueres, *Espíritu*, p. 132.

30. Silfa, *Guerra*, 1:245.

31. Interview by author with José Figueres, February 17, 1972; Ameringer, *Don Pepe*, p. 42.

32. "Declaración del Señor José Ramón Espinosa Sanders," January 30, 1948, Nicaragua, Organization of American States, Organ of Consultation, *Situation in the Caribbean, 1949*, documents pertaining to Costa Rica and Nicaragua, Columbus Memorial Library, Washington, D.C. Hereafter cited as OAS/OC (1949), [Country].

33. Ibid.

34. Ibid.

35. Ibid.

36. Ibid.

37. Ibid.

38. Ibid.

39. Figueres, *Espíritu*, p. 123; Ameringer, *Don Pepe*, p. 48.

40. Figueres interview, February 17, 1972; interview by author with Frank Marshall, February 27, 1972; in *Espíritu*, published in 1987, Figueres provided a slightly different lineup, i.e., Cardona, "Tuta" Cortés, Alberto Lorenzo Brenes, José Santos Delcore Alvarado, Alberto Quirós Sasso, Marshall, and Figuls, p. 133.

41. Figueres, *Espíritu*, p. 125.

42. Ibid., p. 139; John Patrick Bell, *Crisis in Costa Rica: The 1948 Revolution* (Austin: University of Texas Press, 1971), pp. 132-33. Bell comments that Murray's "contribution to the cause of the Second Republic probably was exceeded only by that of Figueres himself" (p. 133).

43. Figueres, *Espíritu*, p. 144; Marshall interview.

44. Figueres, *Espíritu*, pp. 151-52.

45. Ibid., pp. 152-53.

46. Ibid., pp. 154-56; Bell, *Crisis in Costa Rica*, p. 136.

47. Figueres, *Espíritu*, pp. 154, 195-96.

48. *By Whom We Were Betrayed*, p. 37.

49. Figueres, *Espíritu*, p. 154; but see Gleijeses, *Shattered Hope*, p. 109.

50. Figueres, *Espíritu*, p. 155.

51. *By Whom We Were Betrayed*, pp. 38-39.

52. Figueres, *Espíritu*, p. 155.

53. Interview by author with Daniel Oduber, February 29, 1972; Ameringer, *Don Pepe*, p. 49.

54. Figueres, *Espíritu*, p. 146.

55. *Bohemia*, August 21, 1949, p. 80.

56. Letter, José Figueres to "Querido Primitivo," January 15, 1948, Figueres manuscripts.

57. Figueres, *Espíritu*, p. 174.

58. Ibid., p. 175.

59. Ibid., p. 198.

60. Ricardo Blanco Segura, *Monseñor Sanabria* (San José: Editorial Costa Rica, 1971), p. 174.

61. Oscar R. Aguilar Bulgarelli, *Costa Rica y sus hechos políticos de 1948: Problemático de una década* (San José: Editorial Costa Rica, 1969), p. 226.

62. Figueres, *Espíritu*, pp. 208-9.

63. Ibid., pp. 220-21.

64. Ibid., p. 220.

65. Ibid., p. 221.

66. Ibid.

67. Alberto Baeza Flores, *La lucha sin fin* (Mexico City: B. Costa-Amic, Editor, 1969), p. 271.

68. Manuel Mora Valverde, *2 cartas de Manuel Mora a Calderón Guardia y José Figueres* (San José: Imprenta Elena, 1969), pp. 19-21.

69. Aguilar, *Costa Rica y sus hechos políticos de 1948*, pp. 241-44.

70. Ibid., pp. 251-52.

71. Baeza, *La lucha*, pp. 287-88.

72. U.S. Central Intelligence Agency, *The Caribbean Legion*, ORE 11-49 (March 17, 1949), Papers of Harry S. Truman, President's Secretary File, Harry S. Truman Library, Independence, Missouri.

73. Oduber interview; Ameringer, *Don Pepe*, p. 66.

74. Movimiento Liberación Nacional, *Los pagos*, p. 36.

75. Otilio Ulate, *Hacia dónde lleva a Costa Rica el Señor Presidente Figueres?* (San José: Imprenta Universal, 1955), pp. 18-20; Aguilar, *Costa Rica y sus hechos políticos de 1948*, pp. 267-68; *By Whom We Were Betrayed*, pp. 141-43.

76. "Hughes memorandum," Figueres manuscripts. Miguel Angel Ramírez used this identical phrase in an interview. See "La Legion del Caribe, Baluarte Democrático de América," *Bohemia*, August 14, 1949, p. 69.

77. Figueres, *Espíritu*, p. 318.

78. Movimiento Liberación Nacional, *Los pagos*, pp. 53, 71.

79. "Declaración rendida por Octavio Arana Jiménez, teniente ex-Guardia Nacional, ante la junta de investigación," October 9, 1948, OAS/OC (1949), Nicaragua.

80. *By Whom We Were Betrayed*, pp. 61-66.

81. Ibid., p. 67.

82. Movimiento Liberación Nacional, *Los pagos*, p. 36; "Declaración rendida por Guillermo Segundo Trejos Aguilar, ante la junta de investigación, en relación con los movimientos subversivos," November 3, 1948, OAS/OC (1949), Nicaragua.

83. *By Whom We Were Betrayed*, p. 71.

84. Alberto Bayo, *Tempestad en el Caribe* (Mexico, 1950), p. 120.

85. Figueres interview, February 17, 1972.

86. "Declaración rendida por el Señor Manuel Valle Urbina, teniente ex-Guardia Nacional, ante los oficiales investigadores," October 8, 1948, OAS/OC (1949), Nicaragua.

87. Ibid.

88. Ibid.

89. "Arana's statement," OAS/OC (1949), Nicaragua.

90. Ibid.

91. Ibid.

92. Ibid.

93. "Hughes memorandum," Figueres manuscripts.

94. Ibid.

95. Ibid.

96. Ibid.

97. "Arana statement," "Valle Urbina statement," OAS/OC (1949), Nicaragua.

98. Telegram 355, American embassy (Guatemala) to Secretary of State, August 20, 1948, in *Cuba, 1945-1949*.

99. Telegram 364, American embassy (Guatemala) to Secretary of State, August 25, 1948, in ibid.

100. Despatch 447, American embassy (Guatemala) to Secretary of State, September 2, 1948, in ibid.

101. Telegram 92, American embassy (San José) to Secretary of State, September 3, 1948, in ibid.

102. Figueres, *Espíritu*, pp. 319-20. During the author's extensive research for completing a political biography of José Figueres he did not encounter this note or any reference to it in lengthy and repeated interviews of Sr. Figueres.

103. "Arana statement."

104. Bayo, *Tempestad*, pp. 90-93.

105. Silfa, *Guerra*, 1:257-58.

106. Despatch 447, American Embassy (Guatemala) to Secretary of State, September 2, 1948, in *Cuba, 1945-1949*.

107. Silfa, *Guerra*, 1:259-60.

108. Ibid., p. 273.
109. Ibid., p. 274.
110. *New York Times,* October 16, 1948.
111. Silfa, *Guerra,* 1:278.
112. *New York Times,* November 2, 1948.
113. *La Prensa Libre* (San José), November 27, 1948.
114. Movimiento Liberación Nacional, *Los pagos,* pp. 71–72.
115. Ibid., p. 72.
116. Ibid., p. 71.
117. Figueres, *Espíritu,* p. 318.
118. "Trejos Aguilar statement," OAS/OC (1949), Nicaragua.
119. Ibid.
120. "Estado Mayor," San José, January 29, 1949, OAS/OC (1949), Costa Rica.
121. Organization of American States, *Aplicaciones del Tratado Interamericano de Asistencia Recíproca, 1948–1960,* 3d ed. (Washington, D.C.: Union Panamericana 1960), p. 25.
122. Ibid., p. 19.
123. Ibid., p. 21.
124. Ibid., p. 24; telegram, OAS Committee (San José) to Pan American Union, December 19, 1948, OAS/OC (1949), Costa Rica.
125. Military Experts (San José) to Pan American Union, January 20, 1949, OAS/OC (1949), Costa Rica.
126. Memorandum, Octavio Arana J. to Oficial Comandante, September 7, 1948, OAS/OC (1949), Nicaragua. See Figure 4.
127. Ibid.
128. OAS, *Aplicaciones,* p. 25.
129. Ibid., pp. 26–27.
130. Ibid., pp. 27–30.
131. "Estado Mayor," January 29, 1949, OAS/OC (1949), Costa Rica.
132. "Registro de procedimientos de un consejo de investigación reunido en el cuartel general de la Guardia Nacional en el Campo de Marte, Managua, D.N., para inquirir sobre la captura de treintinueve ciudadanos de nacionalidad costarricense entregados a las autoridades de la República de Nicaragua," December 30, 1948, OAS/OC (1949), Nicaragua.
133. "Una declaración de Eladio Alvárez Urbina," in ibid.
134. Ibid.
135. "Una declaración de Claudio Malavasi Mora," in ibid.
136. "Una declaración de Alvaro Castro Herrera," in ibid.
137. "Una declaración de José Ramón Villalobos Jiménez," in ibid.
138. "Una declaración de José Manuel Solís Vargas," in ibid.
139. "Una declaración de Claudio Malavasi Mora," in ibid.
140. "Una declaración de Hugo Orozco Mora," in ibid.
141. Report, "For the Council of the Organization of American States from the Military Commission," January 21, 1949, OAS/OC (1949), Costa Rica.
142. Ibid.
143. *By Whom We Were Betrayed,* p. 108.
144. OAS, *Aplicaciones,* p. 39.
145. Ibid., p. 40.
146. Ibid.
147. Ibid., p. 43.
148. Ibid., pp. 44–46.
149. CIA, *Caribbean Legion,* p. 1.

1949: Luperón

1. U.S. Central Intelligence Agency, *The Caribbean Legion*, ORE 11-49 (March 17, 1949), papers of Harry S. Truman, President's Secretary File, Harry S. Truman Library, Independence, Missouri, p. 6.

2. Ibid., p. 1.

3. Nicolás Silfa, *Guerra, traición, y exilio*, 3 vols. (Barcelona: P. Manuel Girona, 1980), p. 278.

4. Angel Miolán, *El perredé, desde mi ángulo*, 2d ed. (Caracas: Avila Arte, S.A., 1985), p. 486.

5. Tulio H. Arvelo, *Cayo Confites y Luperón: Memorias de un expedicionario* (Santo Domingo: Universidad Autónoma de Santo Domingo, 1981), p. 109.

6. Ibid., p. 111.

7. CARIB (Ciudad Trujillo), Report No. 4, May 1958, p. 48.

8. Arvelo, *Cayo Confites y Luperón*, p. 120.

9. Ibid., pp. 121-22.

10. Ibid., p. 131.

11. Ibid., p. 121.

12. Ibid., p. 122.

13. Ibid.

14. Ibid., pp. 141-42; handwritten notes [Charles C. Hauch], Dominican Republic, Organization of American States, Organ of Consultation, *Situation in the Caribbean, 1950*, documents pertaining to Haiti, Cuba, Guatemala, and the Dominican Republic, Columbus Memorial Library, Washington, D.C. Hereafter cited as OAS/OC (1950), [Country].

15. *Bohemia*, August 21, 1949, p. 89.

16. Alberto Bayo, *Tempestad en el Caribe* (Mexico, 1950), pp. 165-70.

17. Comisión Interamericana de Paz, "Situación en el Caribe, respuesta del gobierno de la República Dominicana," OAS/OC (1950), Dominican Republic, p. 7.

18. Despatch 52034, Manuel Tello to Luis Quintanilla, February 9, 1950, OAS/OC (1950), Guatemala/Mexico.

19. Ibid.

20. Ibid.

21. Arvelo, *Cayo Confites y Luperón*, p. 131.

22. Ibid., p. 132.

23. Ibid.

24. Ibid., p. 134.

25. Ibid., p. 135.

26. Horacio Ornes, *Desembarco en Luperón: Episodio de la lucha por la democracia en la República Dominicana* (Mexico: Ediciones Humanismo, 1956), pp. 153-54; Piero Gleijeses, *Shattered Hope: The Guatemalan Revolution and the United States, 1944-1954* (Princeton: Princeton University Press, 1991), p. 114. Gleijeses writes that Arévalo "helped persuade senior Mexican officials to permit [the] refueling."

27. Draft memo, February 1950, OAS/OC (1950), Guatemala/ Mexico; handwritten notes [Charles C. Hauch], OAS/OC (1950), Dominican Republic.

28. Arvelo, *Cayo Confites y Luperón*, p. 139; *Bohemia*, August 21, 1949, pp. 89-90.

29. *Bohemia*, August 21, 1949, p. 90.

30. Arvelo, *Cayo Confites y Luperón*, p. 140.

31. U.S. Foreign Broadcast Information Service, *Daily Report: Foreign Radio Broadcasts*, February 14, 1949, p. D2.

32. Stenographic transcript of taped testimony (behind closed doors) of Dominican ambas-

sadors Joaquín E. Salazar and Arturo Despradel before the Investigating Committee of the Organization of American States, OAS/OC (1950), Committee File. Hereafter cited as "Testimony of Salazar and Despradel."

33. Silfa, *Guerra,* 1:291.

34. Ibid., 2:251.

35. Miolán, *El perredé,* pp. 116, 469.

36. Organization of American States, *Aplicaciones del Tratado Interamericano de Asistencia Recíproca, 1948-1960,* 3d ed. (Washington, D.C.: Unión Panamericana, 1960), pp. 106-7.

37. Ibid.

38. Ibid., p. 107.

39. "Testimony of Salazar and Despradel."

40. Ibid.

41. Cable, President Trujillo to President Carlos Prío Socarrás, May 3, 1949, OAS/OC (1950), Dominican Republic.

42. Memorandum [Prío to Trujillo], in ibid.

43. "Testimony of Salazar and Despradel."

44. Arvelo, *Cayo Confites y Luperón,* p. 141.

45. *Bohemia,* August 21, 1949, p. 59.

46. CIA, *Caribbean Legion,* p. 1.

47. *Bohemia,* August 21, 1949, p. 90.

48. Arvelo, *Cayo Confites y Luperón,* pp. 144-45.

49. Bayo, *Tempestad,* p. 171; Despatch 819, American Embassy (Havana) to Secretary of State, June 24, 1949, U.S. Department of State, *Confidential U.S. State Department Central Files: Cuba, 1945-1949,* ed. Michael C. Davis (Frederick, Md.: University Publications of America, 1987).

50. *Bohemia,* August 21, 1949, p. 90.

51. Ornes, *Disembarco en Luperón,* p. 154.

52. Silfa, *Guerra,* 1:290.

53. Miolán, *El perredé,* p. 115.

54. Gleijeses, *Shattered Hope,* pp. 62-67.

55. Handwritten notes [Charles C. Hauch], OAS/OC (1950), Dominican Republic.

56. Note, Colonel Ramiro Gereda Asturias to Colonel Francisco Barriga Riva, June 20, 1949, OAS/OC (1950), Guatemala/Mexico.

57. Ornes, *Disembarco en Luperón,* pp. 35-37.

58. Arvelo, *Cayo Confites y Luperón,* p. 160.

59. Ibid., p. 161.

60. Ibid., p. 167.

61. Ornes, *Disembarco en Luperón,* p. 46; Arvelo, *Cayo Confites y Luperón,* pp. 180-81.

62. Arvelo, *Cayo Confites y Luperón,* p. 170.

63. Ibid., pp. 170-71.

64. Ornes, *Disembarco en Luperón,* p. 56.

65. Arvelo, *Cayo Confites y Luperón,* p. 179.

66. Ibid.; Ornes, *Disembarco en Luperón,* p. 128.

67. "Cronología de las informaciones dadas por las autoridades de la República Dominicana sobre los sucesos de Luperón" [Enrique C. Henríquez file], OAS/OC (1950), Cuba.

68. Letter, Federico to Querido Padre, June 11, 1949, in ibid.

69. Arvelo, *Cayo Confites y Luperón,* p. 212.

70. Ornes, *Disembarco en Luperón,* pp. 88-94.

71. Ibid., pp. 156-57.

72. Arvelo, *Cayo Confites y Luperón,* pp. 262-63; Enrique V. Corominas, *In the Carib-*

bean Political Areas, trans. L. Charles Foresti (New York: Cambridge University Press, 1954), p. 72.

73. Arvelo, *Cayo Confites y Luperón,* p. 229.

74. Ibid., p. 238.

75. Ibid., p. 228.

76. Ibid., p. 238; Ornes, *Disembarco en Luperón,* p. 175.

77. Arvelo, *Cayo Confites y Luperón,* pp. 181–82.

78. Cited in "Dominican reply," August 15, 1949, OAS/OC (1950), Dominican Republic.

79. Corominas, *In the Caribbean Political Areas,* pp. 51–52.

80. Ibid.

81. Ibid., p. 53.

82. Ibid., pp. 58–59.

83. "Testimony of Salazar and Despradel."

84. Corominas, *In the Caribbean Political Areas,* p. 59.

85. Ibid., p. 71.

86. Ibid., p. 70.

87. OAS, *Aplicaciones,* p. 106.

88. "Dominican reply," August 15, 1949, OAS/OC (1950), Dominican Republic.

89. Corominas, *In the Caribbean Political Areas,* p. 74.

90. Ibid., p. 76.

91. Ibid., pp. 77–78.

92. Ibid., p. 84.

93. Ibid., p. 85.

94. Ibid., p. 88.

95. Otilio Ulate, *Hacia dónde lleva a Costa Rica el Señor Presidente Figueres?* (San José: Imprenta Universal, 1955), p. 15.

96. *New York Times,* August 21, 1949, sec. 4, p. 6; ibid., August 26, 1949, p. 18.

97. "The 14 Conclusions of the Inter-American Peace Committee, Approved on September 14, 1949," in U.S. Department of State, *Peace in the Americas,* Publication 3964 (Washington, D.C., released October 1950), pp. 5–6.

98. Ibid., p. 6.

99. Ibid.

100. Ibid., p. 27.

101. Ibid., p. 26.

102. Ibid., p. 27.

103. *Bohemia,* August 14, 1949, p. 68.

104. Ibid.

105. Ibid., p. 69.

106. Ibid., p. 68.

1950: The OAS Puts on the Lid

1. Piero Gleijeses, *Shattered Hope: The Guatemalan Revolution and the United States, 1944–1954* (Princeton: Princeton University Press, 1991), p. 115.

2. Nicolás Silfa, *Guerra, traición, y exilio,* 3 vols. (Barcelona: P. Manuel Girona, 1980), p. 290.

3. Handwritten notes of interview with Enrique C. Henríquez [by Charles C. Hauch], February 1950, Cuba, Organization of American States, Organ of Consultation, *Situation in*

the Caribbean, 1950, documents pertaining to Haiti, Cuba, Guatemala, and the Dominican Republic, Columbus Memorial Library, Washington, D.C. Hereafter cited as OAS/OC (1950), [Country].

4. Copy, "Pasquín," *Prensa Libre* [Havana], October 11, 1949, OAS/OC (1950), Cuba.

5. Organization of American States, *Aplicaciones del Tratado Interamericano de Asistencia Recíproca, 1948-1960,* 3d ed. (Washington. D.C.: Unión Panamericana, 1960), p. 108.

6. Ibid.

7. Handwritten notes of interview with Enrique C. Henríquez [by Charles C. Hauch], February 1950, OAS/OC (1950), Cuba.

8. Ibid.

9. Ibid.

10. Statement of Héctor Incháustegui Cabral, January 21, 1950, OAS/OC (1950), Dominican Republic.

11. Ibid.

12. Ibid.

13. Ibid.

14. Ibid.

15. OAS, *Aplicaciones,* p. 109.

16. Statement of Héctor Incháustegui Cabral, January 21, 1950, OAS/OC (1950), Dominican Republic.

17. Letter, Paul Giacometti to Members of the Investigating Committee of the OAS, Ciudad Trujillo, January 27, 1950, OAS/OC (1950), Dominican Republic; OAS, *Aplicaciones,* p. 98.

18. Letter, Paul Giacometti to Members of the Investigating Committee of the OAS, Ciudad Trujillo, January 27, 1950, OAS/OC (1950), Dominican Republic.

19. Ibid.

20. Ibid.

21. Ibid.

22. Ibid.

23. Ibid.

24. Ibid.

25. Ibid.

26. Stenographic transcript of taped testimony (behind closed doors) of Dominican ambassadors Joaquín E. Salazar and Arturo Despradel before the Investigating Committee of the OAS, January 18, 1950, OAS/OC (1950), Committee File. Hereafter cited as "Testimony of Salazar and Despradel."

27. Ibid.

28. Handwritten notes of interview with Enrique C. Henríquez [by Charles C. Hauch], February 1950, OAS/OC (1950), Cuba.

29. "Mensaje: Dirigido al Congreso Nacional por el presidente de la República Dominicana, Generalisimo Dr. Rafael Leonidas Trujillo Molina," December 26, 1949, OAS/OC (1950), Dominican Republic.

30. OAS, *Aplicaciones,* p. 58.

31. Ibid.

32. Ibid., p. 63.

33. Ibid., p. 99.

34. Ibid., pp. 68-69.

35. Silfa, *Guerra,* 1:100-101.

36. OAS, *Aplicaciones,* p. 69.

37. Ibid., p. 71.

38. Ibid., p. 72.

39. Ibid., pp. 72-73.

40. Ibid., p. 73-74.

41. Ibid., pp. 74-75.

42. Ibid., pp. 75-76, 80.

43. "Testimony of Salazar and Despradel."

44. Ibid.

45. Ibid.

46. Ibid.

47. Ibid.

48. Ibid.

49. OAS, *Aplicaciones,* p. 99.

50. Ibid., p. 98.

51. Ibid., p. 100.

52. Handwritten notes [Charles C. Hauch], OAS/OC (1950), Dominican Republic.

53. Ibid.; Tulio H. Arvelo, *Cayo Confites y Luperón: Memorias de un expedicionario* (Santo Domingo: Universidad Autónoma de Santo Domingo, 1981), pp. 149-50, wherein Arvelo also refers to "Major Sardi" as assisting the expeditionaries at Lake Izabal.

54. Comisión Interamericana de Paz, "Situación en el Caribe, respuesta del gobierno de la República Dominicana," OAS/OC (1950), Dominican Republic, pp. 8-9.

55. Handwritten notes [Charles C. Hauch], OAS/OC (1950), Dominican Republic.

56. Ibid.

57. Ibid.

58. Arvelo, *Cayo Confites y Luperón,* pp. 266-67.

59. Ibid., p. 269.

60. Letter, Angel Morales et al. to Ambassador José A. Mora, Havana, January 16, 1950, OAS/OC (1950), Cuba.

61. Ibid.

62. Ibid.

63. Ibid.

64. Petition to "Excelentisimos señores miembros de la Comisión del Organo de Consulta Provisional de la Organización de Estados Américanos," Havana, February 7, 1950, OAS/OC (1950), Cuba.

65. Ibid.

66. OAS, *Aplicaciones,* p. 108.

67. Note, "Rubén de León García, Ministro de Gobernación, por la presente," February 10, 1950, OAS/OC (1950), Cuba.

68. Memorandum, Charles C. Hauch, February 23, 1950, OAS/OC (1950), Guatemala/Mexico.

69. Note, Colonel Ramiro Gereda Asturias to Colonel Francisco Barriga Riva, June 20, 1949, OAS/OC (1950), Guatemala/Mexico.

70. Note, Ismael González Arévalo [Guatemalan Foreign Minister] to José A. Mora, February 11, 1950, OAS/OC (1950), Guatemala/Mexico.

71. Note, José A. Mora to Señor Ministro [González Arévalo, Guatemalan Foreign Minister], February 10, 1950, OAS/OC (1950), Guatemala/Mexico. Mora made a similar request to the Guatemalan ambassador in Washington, Antonio Gaubaud Carrera, on February 25, 1950; ibid.

72. Memorandum, José A. Mora to Lieutenant Colonel Jacobo Arbenz, February 11, 1950, OAS/OC (1950), Guatemala/ Mexico.

73. OAS, *Aplicaciones,* p. 100.

74. Ibid., p. 102.

75. Ibid., p. 103.

76. Ibid., p. 105.

77. Ibid.

78. Ibid., p. 108.

79. Ibid.

80. Ibid., p. 109.

81. Ibid.

82. Ibid., p. 110.

83. Ibid.

84. Ibid., pp. 110-11.

85. Ibid., p. 111.

86. Ibid.

87. Ibid., pp. 111-12.

88. Ibid., pp. 113-14.

89. Ibid., pp. 114-16.

90. Ibid., p. 116.

91. Ibid., pp. 118-19.

92. Letter, Partido Revolucionario Dominicana to José A. Mora, Havana, March 31, 1950, OAS/OC (1950), Cuba.

93. Ibid.

94. OAS, *Aplicaciones,* p. 134.

95. David Rock, "Introduction," in David Rock, ed., *Latin America in the 1940s: War and Postwar Transitions* (Berkeley and Los Angeles: University of California Press, 1994), p. 9.

96. Ruth Berins Collier, "Labor Politics and Regime Change: Internal Trajectories versus External Influences," in Rock, ed., *Latin America in the 1940s,* pp. 68-70.

97. Quoted in Corinne Antezana-Pernet, "Peace in the World and Democracy at Home: The Chilean Women's Movement in the 1940s," in Rock, ed., *Latin America in the 1940s,* p. 179.

98. Michael Warner, ed., *CIA Cold War Records: The CIA under Harry Truman,* History Staff, Center for the Study of Intelligence, Central Intelligence Agency (Washington, D.C., 1994), pp. 173-75.

99. Ibid., p. 223.

100. John C. Dreier, *The Organization of American States and the Hemisphere Crisis* (New York: Harper & Row, 1962), p. 129.

101. Ibid., p. 69.

Selected Bibliography

Primary Sources

Figueres, José. Private Papers. Consisting of papers, correspondence, memoranda, documents, and press clippings. San José, Costa Rica.

Núñez, Benjamín. Private Papers. Consisting of papers, documents, correspondence, and press clippings. San José, Costa Rica.

Organization of American States. *Aplicaciones del Tratado Interamericano de Asistencia Recíproca, 1948-1960.* 3d ed. Washington, D.C.: Unión Panamericana, 1960.

———. Organ of Consultation. *Situation in the Caribbean, 1949.* Documents pertaining to Costa Rica and Nicaragua. 3 boxes. Columbus Memorial Library. Washington, D.C.

———. Organ of Consultation. *Situation in the Caribbean, 1950.* Documents pertaining to Haiti, Cuba, Guatemala, and the Dominican Republic. 4 boxes. Columbus Memorial Library. Washington, D.C.

U.S. Central Intelligence Agency. *The Caribbean Legion.* ORE 11-49 (March 17, 1949). Papers of Harry S. Truman. President's Secretary File. Harry S. Truman Library. Independence, Missouri.

U.S. Department of State. *Confidential U.S. State Department Central Files: Cuba, 1945-1949.* Edited by Michael C. Davis. Frederick, Md.: University Publications of America, 1987. Microform: internal affairs, decimal no. 837; foreign affairs, decimal nos. 737 and 711.37.

———. *Consultation among American Republics with Respect to the Argentine Situation.* Memorandum of the United States Government [Blue Book]. Washington, D.C., 1946.

———. *Foreign Relations of the United States: Diplomatic Papers.* Washington, D.C.: U.S. Government Printing Office. Selected vols.: 1947, vol. 8; 1948, vol. 9; 1949; 1950, vol. 2.

———. *Peace in the Americas.* Publication 3964. Washington, D.C., 1950.

U.S. Foreign Broadcast Information Service. *Daily Report: Foreign Radio Broadcasts.*

Vega, Bernardo, ed. *Los Estados Unidos y Trujillo. Colección de documentos del Departamento de Estado y de las Fuerzas Armadas Norteamericanos. Año 1946.* 2 vols. Santo Domingo: Fundación Cultural Dominicana, 1982.

———. *Los Estados Unidos y Trujillo. Colección de documentos del Departamento de Estado y de las Fuerzas Armadas Norteamericanos. Año 1947.* 2 vols. Santo Domingo: Fundación Cultural Dominicana, 1984.

Secondary Sources

Aguilar Bulgarelli, Oscar R. *Costa Rica y sus hechos políticos de 1948: Problemático de una década.* San José: Editorial Costa Rica, 1969.

Ameringer, Charles D. *The Democratic Left in Exile: The Antidictatorial Struggle in the Caribbean, 1945-1959.* Coral Gables: University of Miami Press, 1974.

———. *Don Pepe: A Political Biography of José Figueres of Costa Rica.* Albuquerque: University of New Mexico Press, 1978.

Arvelo, Tulio H. *Cayo Confites y Luperón: Memorias de un expedicionario.* Santo Domingo: Universidad Autónoma de Santo Domingo, 1981.

Baeza Flores, Alberto. *La lucha sin fin.* Mexico City: B. Costa-Amic, Editor, 1969.

Bayo, Alberto. *Tempestad en el Caribe.* Mexico, 1950.

Bell, John Patrick. *Crisis in Costa Rica: The 1948 Revolution.* Austin: University of Texas Press, 1971.

Bohemia (Havana). 1948-1952.

Bosch, Juan. *Poker de Espanto en el Caribe.* Santo Domingo: Editora Alfa & Omega, 1988.

———. *33 artículos de temas políticos.* Santo Domingo: Editora Alfa & Omega, 1988.

Braden, Spruille. *Diplomats and Demagogues: The Memoirs of Spruille Braden.* New Rochelle: Arlington House, 1971.

Briggs, Ellis. *Farewell to Foggy Bottom: The Recollections of a Career Diplomat.* New York: David McKay Company, 1964.

By Whom We Were Betrayed . . . And How. [1955].

Cañas, Alberto F. *Los 8 años.* San José: Editorial Liberación Nacional, 1955.

CARIB. Fourteen Issues (Reports). Ciudad Trujillo, April 1958-October 1958.

Castro Esquivel, Arturo. *José Figueres Ferrer: El hombre y su obra.* San José: Imprenta Tormo, 1955.

Clark, Paul Coe, Jr. *The United States and Somoza, 1933-1956: A Revisionist Look.* Westport, Conn.: Praeger, 1992.

Corominas, Enrique V. *En las areas políticas del Caribe.* Buenos Aires: Editorial El Ateneo, 1952.

———. *In the Caribbean Political Areas.* Translated by L. Charles Foresti. New York: Cambridge University Press, 1954.

Crassweller, Robert D. *Trujillo: The Life and Times of a Caribbean Dictator.* New York: The Macmillan Company, 1966.

Dozer, Donald Marquand. *Are We Good Neighbors? Three Decades of Inter-American Relations, 1930-1960.* Gainesville: University of Florida Press, 1959.

Dreier, John C. *The Organization of American States and the Hemisphere Crisis.* New York: Harper & Row, 1962.

Figueres Ferrer, José. *El espíritu del 48.* San José: Editorial Costa Rica, 1987.

Gallegos, Gerardo. *Trujillo: Cara y cruz de su dictadura.* Madrid: Ediciones Iberoamericanas, 1968.

Gleijeses, Piero. "The Death of Francisco Arana: A Turning Point in the Guatemalan Revolution." *Journal of Latin American Studies* 22 (October 1990), pp. 527-52.

———. "Juan José Arévalo and the Caribbean Legion." *Journal of Latin American Studies* 21, no. 1 (1989), pp. 133-45.

———. *Shattered Hope: The Guatemalan Revolution and the United States, 1944-1954.* Princeton: Princeton University Press, 1991.

Green, David. *The Containment of Latin America*. Chicago: Quadrangle Books, 1971.

Immerman, Richard H. *The CIA in Guatemala: The Foreign Policy of Intervention*. Austin: University of Texas Press, 1982.

Macaulay, Neill. *The Sandino Affair*. Chicago: Quadrangle Books, 1967.

Mecham, J. Lloyd. *A Survey of United States–Latin American Relations*. Boston: Houghton Mifflin Company, 1965.

Miolán, Angel. *El perredé, desde mi ángulo*. 2d ed. Caracas: Avila Arte, 1985.

Movimiento Liberación Nacional. *Los pagos de la Guerra de Liberación Nacional*. San José: Editorial Liberación Nacional, 1953.

Ornes, Horacio. *Desembarco en Luperón: Episodio de la lucha por la democracia en la República Dominicana*. Mexico: Ediciones Humanismo, 1956.

Pepper, José Vicente. *I Accuse Braden*. Ciudad Trujillo: Editora Montalvo, 1947.

Phillips, Ruby Hart. *Cuba: Island of Paradox*. New York: McDowell, Obolensky, 1959.

Rock, David, ed. *Latin America in the 1940s: War and Postwar Transitions*. Berkeley and Los Angeles: University of California Press, 1994.

Schlesinger, Stephen, and Kinzer, Stephen. *Bitter Fruit: The Untold Story of the American Coup in Guatemala*. Garden City: Doubleday, 1982.

Schneider, Ronald M. *Communism in Guatemala, 1944–1954*. New York: Frederick A. Praeger, 1959.

Silfa, Nicolás. *Guerra, traición, y exilio*. 3 vols. Barcelona: P. Manuel Girona, 1980.

Suchlicki, Jaime. *University Students and Revolution in Cuba, 1920–1968*. Coral Gables: University of Miami Press, 1969.

Ulate, Otilio. *Hacia dónde lleva a Costa Rica el Señor Presidente Figueres?* San José: Imprenta Universal, 1955.

Whitaker, Arthur P. *The United States and Argentina*. Cambridge: Harvard University Press, 1954.

Interviews

During the course of his career and in research directly related to this topic the author interviewed a number of the persons who figure prominently in this work: Rómulo Betancourt, Juan Bosch, José Figueres, Frank Marshall Jiménez, Angel Miolán, Benjamín Núñez, Daniel Oduber, Genovevo Pérez Dámera, Aureliano Sánchez Arango, and Otilio Ulate.

Index

Acheson, Dean, 115
ACNA. *See* Cuban-North American Airways
Act of Chapultepec, 16, 18
AD. *See* Democratic Action party
ADC. *See* Caribbean Democratic Action
Agostini, Jorge Felipe, 39
Aguila Ruiz, José, 39
Alemán, José
  and Cayo Confites, 36-37, 38, 39, 40, 45, 46, 51, 54, 55, 57, 61, 132
Alemán-Grau-Alsina bloc (BAGA), 36-37
Almoina, José, 7
Alonso, Cruz
  and Caribbean intrigues, 127
  and Cayo Confites, 34, 35, 39, 42
  and Luperón, 96, 98, 99, 101, 102
Alvárez Urbina, Eladio, 91
American Popular Revolutionary Alliance (APRA), 1, 2, 3, 28
APRA. *See* American Popular Revolutionary Alliance
Arana, Francisco, 62, 70, 72
  and Luperón, 104-5, 127
  assassination of, 112, 131
Arana Jiménez, Octavio, 81, 82, 83, 84, 85, 88
Arbenz, Jacobo, 62, 70, 85
  and Luperón, 95, 99, 105
  and 1950 crisis, 131
  overthrow of, 137, 139
Arévalo, Juan José, 4, 5, 31, 34
  and Carlos Prío Socarrás, 83, 85
  and Cayo Confites, 42, 57
  and José Figueres, 65, 66, 67, 70, 76, 161 n. 21
  and Juan Gregorio Colindres, 84, 85
  and Juan Rodríguez, 61-62

and Luperón, 95, 99, 101, 102, 105, 109, 110, 111, 123-24, 127, 130-31, 163 n. 26
and 1950 crisis, 121
Argüello, Rosendo, Jr.
  and José Figueres, 62, 64, 65, 66, 68, 70, 71, 84, 86, 92
  and liberation of Nicaragua, 80, 81, 83, 88
Argüello, Rosendo, Sr., 62, 66, 81, 83
Armour, Norman, 41
Army of National Liberation (Costa Rica), 69, 71, 74
Arvelo, Tulio
  and Cayo Confites, 44, 45, 55
  and Luperón, 96, 98, 99, 100, 103, 106, 107, 109, 110, 127
Auténticos. See Cuban Revolutionary party-*Auténtico*
Avila Camacho, Manuel, 104
Avila Camacho, Maximino, 104

Báez, Mauricio, 23, 25
Báez Bone, Adolfo, 71, 91
BAGA. *See* Alemán-Grau-Alsina bloc
Batista, Fulgencio, 3, 140
Bayo, Alberto, 80, 98-99
Bello, José María, 88
Berle, Adolf, 12
Betancourt, Rómulo, 2, 3, 4, 7, 8, 31, 33, 83, 85, 96, 121, 123
Beauvoir, Vilfort, 123, 126
Bonilla Atiles, José A., 22-23, 26, 32, 100, 104, 105
Bordas, Diego, 44
Bordas, Luis, 40, 44
Bosch, Juan
  and Cayo Confites, 34, 39, 42, 45, 47-48, 57-58

and founding of PRD, 27–28, 29, 30, 31, 32, 33
and José Figueres, 65, 83
and Luperón, 96, 98, 99, 100, 101, 102, 103
and 1950 crisis, 118, 120, 121, 128
Braden, Spruille, 9, 13, 16, 59, 117, 138
  background of, 11–12
  and Juan Perón, 16, 17, 18
  policy of, 12, 14, 20, 21, 22, 25, 26
Braden Corollary, 11–12, 14, 18, 42
Brett, George H., 21
Brewster, Owen, 18
Brierre, Jean, 120, 126
Briggs, Ellis O., 12, 13, 15, 16, 21, 23, 26, 42, 82, 117
Browder, Edward, 113, 156 n. 88
Butler, George H., 13, 14, 15, 16, 19, 24, 26, 117
Byrnes, James, 12, 13, 15, 18, 20, 22

Caamaño, Fausto, 46
Calderón Guardia, Rafael Angel, 63, 64, 65, 68, 72, 74, 87
Calderón Salcedo, Manuel, 106, 108
Camacho, Arturo, 104
Camejo, José Enrique, 52
Caminero, José, 118, 133
Cardona, Edgar, 69, 80
Carías Andino, Tiburcio, 5
Caribbean Democratic Action (ADC), 120, 121
Caribbean Legion
  activities of, 124, 130, 133, 136
  assessment of, 137–38, 139, 140
  in Costa Rica, 75, 77, 80, 81, 82, 84, 86, 87, 88, 90, 91, 92, 93
  and Francisco Arana's assassination, 121, 131
  and Luperón, 95, 100, 101, 104, 106, 111, 113, 114, 116
  origin of term, 9, 73–74
Caribbean Liberation Movement, 76, 82
Caribbean Pact, 66–67, 75–77
Casey, Edward, 58, 59, 60
Castillo Armas, Carlos, 137
Castro, Fidel, 40, 56, 58, 137
Castro, Manolo, 30, 38, 40, 42, 49, 54, 55, 56, 58, 59, 60, 113, 132
Castro Herrera, Alvaro, 91

Cayo Confites
  arms of, 35–36
  description and location of, 43
  significance of, 9
Cayo Güinchos, 56
Cayo Santa María, 55
Central American Air Transport (TACA), 70
Central American Democratic Union (UDC), 64
Central Intelligence Agency (CIA), 47, 103, 137, 138, 139
Chamorro, Emiliano, 62, 65, 66
Chewning, John W., 106, 108
CIA. See Central Intelligence Agency
Club Unión, 6
Cold War, in the Caribbean, 115, 117, 138, 139
Colindres, Juan Gregorio, 62, 65, 67, 68, 84, 85
Connally, Tom, 18
Conservative party (Nicaragua), 6
Córdova Boniche, José Félix, 106, 109, 137
Corominas, Enrique V., 111
Corrigan, Frank P., 41
Cortés, Fernando, 69
Cortés, León, 64
Cortés, Max ("Tuta"), 69, 70
Cosenza, Francisco, 70, 99
Costa Rica–Nicaragua dispute (1948–49), 85–93
Costa Rican civil war (1948), 9
CTAL. See Latin American Workers Confederation
CTC. See Cuban Confederation of Labor
Cuban Confederation of Labor (CTC), 23
Cuban–North American Airways (ACNA), 34
Cuban Red Cross, 118, 119
  and L'Amelie affair, 120, 122, 124, 130, 133
Cuban Revolution, 139
Cuban Revolutionary party-Auténtico (PRC-A), 2, 3, 28, 30, 31, 139
Cuello, Leovigildo, 29, 39, 128
Cummings, Homer, 19–20

Daniels, Paul C., 88, 111, 115, 124, 126
Davies, Joseph E., 19
Davis, Nathaniel, 74, 83
Del Castillo Altamirano, José María, 104
Del Valle, Alfredo, 99
Democratic Action party (AD), 2, 3, 4, 28, 31

Democratic Youth (JD), 24, 25, 26
De Moya, Manuel, 20
De Moya, Rafael Oscar, and Haiti, 122, 123,
    126, 127, 132
Despradel, Arturo, 40, 41, 54, 125, 126
Díaz, Juan, 52
Dominican Antifascist Democratic Union
    (UDAD), 29
Dominican party, 33
Dominican Revolutionary Central Committee
    (Cayo Confites), 39-40, 57
Dominican Revolutionary party (PRD)
    founding of, 27, 28, 29
    and 1950 crisis, 128, 136
Dreier, John C., 15-16, 139
Dulles, John Foster, 139
Dupuy, John, 122, 127

Eisenhardt, Karl, 113, 156 n. 88
Escalante, Otto, 70
Espinosa, José Ramón, 67-68
Esquivel, Mario A., 114
Estévez, Antonio Jorge, 110
Estimé, Dumarsais, 52, 122, 126, 132, 135

Fallas, Carlos Luis, 71, 72
Feliú Arzeno, Miguel, 105, 106, 109, 110,
    127
Fernández, Eufemio
    and Cayo Confites, 38, 39, 44, 56
    and Luperón, 83, 96, 98, 99, 100, 101,
        102, 104, 110, 112, 127, 130, 131, 132,
        140
    and 1950 crisis, 120
Fernández Alverdi, Jacobo, 99
Fernández Ortega, Eufemio. See Eufemio
    Fernández
Fiallo, Federico, 15
Fiallo, Viriato A., 15, 31, 33, 41, 55
Figueres, José
    antidictatorial policy of, 109, 111, 137
    background of, 9, 62, 63-65
    and Caribbean Pact, 66-67, 75, 76, 77,
        95
    and Costa Rican civil war, 68-75
    and Juan Rodríguez, 75, 84
Figuls, Fernando, 69
Findley, Marion, 99
Flying Tigers, 49, 55
Forrestal, James, 47
Fors, Alfonso Luis, 47

Fourteen Conclusions, 114-15, 117
Free Dominicans, 120

García Carrasco, Félix, 101
García Godoy, Emilio, 21, 50
García Granados, Jorge, 42
Gazón, Evangelina, 7-8
Gazón, Henry, 7-8
Generation of '28 (Venezuela), 2-3
Generation of '30 (Cuba), 2
Giacometti, Paul, 120, 121
Girón, Gustavo, 105
Gómez, Juan Vicente, 2, 4
Gómez, Manuel, 81, 82, 91
González, Ignacio, 99
González Muñoz, Rafael P., 40-41, 42, 47
Good Neighbor Policy, 11, 17
Grau San Martín, Ramón, 3, 7
    and Cayo Confites, 36, 39, 42-43, 46, 47,
        50, 51, 54, 55, 56, 57, 61, 123, 132
Gutiérrez, Guillermo, 124

Haiti
    and Cayo Confites, 52-53, 56
    and L'Amelie affair, 120, 121, 125, 126
    and Luperón, 101, 102
    and 1950 crisis, 122, 123, 124, 132, 135
Hannifin, Jerry, 73
Harrington and Richardson Arms Company, 95
Hauch, Charles, 83, 124, 127, 128, 131
Haya de la Torre, Víctor Raúl, 1, 2, 3, 28
Hemingway, Ernest, 60
Henríquez, Enrique Cotubanamá ("Cotú")
    background of, 27-28
    and Cayo Confites, 39, 43-44, 53
    and L'Amelie affair, 118, 119, 120, 121,
        125, 126, 127, 133
    and Luperón, 98, 99, 100, 102, 108
    and 1950 crisis, 129, 130
Henríquez, Rodolfo, 118, 119, 133
Henríquez Vásquez, Federico Horacio
    ("Gugú")
    and Luperón, 100, 106, 107, 108
    death of, 118, 119
Hernández, Manuel ("Pipi"), 30
Herrera, Pablo, 104
Hillenkoetter, Roscoe, 47, 157 n. 130
Hosford, Bob, 104
Hotel San Luis, 34, 40, 96, 99, 100, 101,
    112, 116
Hughes, James K., 82-83

IAPC. *See* Inter-American Peace Committee
Imbert, Antonio, 108
Incháustegui Cabral, Héctor, 40, 52, 119
Indo-American Maritime Company, 102
Inter-American Commission of Military Experts, 90, 92
Inter-American Peace Committee (IAPC)
and the "Fourteen Conclusions," 114–15, 117, 122
and Luperón, 111, 112, 113, 114, 124, 129
Inter-American Treaty of Reciprocal Assistance. *See* Rio Treaty
Internal Front (Dominican Republic), 33–34
and Luperón, 96, 98, 100, 101, 108, 110
Investigating Committee (OAS)
and 1948 Costa Rica–Nicaragua dispute, 88, 89, 90, 92
and 1950 crisis, 124, 128, 130, 131
report of, 132, 133, 134

JD. *See* Democratic Youth
Jiménez Grullón, Juan Isidro, 27–28, 29, 31, 32, 128
Jiménez Pichirilo, Ramón Emilio, 101

Kundhardt, Hugo, 106, 107, 108

La Lucha Sin Fin, 63, 68, 69, 71
Lamarche, C. M., 41
L'Amelie affair, 118, 119, 120, 121, 126, 130, 133
Latin American Workers Confederation (CTAL), 28, 100
Lawyer, Thomas, 58
Leger, Love, 120, 126
Lescot, Elie, 31, 32
Leyton, Alfonso, 106, 107
Liberal party (Nicaragua), 6
Liberation Army (Luperón), 103, 106
Liberation Army of America (Cayo Confites), 35, 40, 43, 47
Liberation Army of the Caribbean, 9, 77
Liberation Army of the Caribbean and Central America, 67, 70
Liz, Alexis, 40, 45, 128, 136
Lombardo Toledano, Vicente, 29, 100, 127
López Contreras, Eleazar, 4, 7, 41
López Henríquez, José, 104
Lovett, Robert, 47, 50, 58

Luperón, Bay of, 100, 107
Lyceo Lawn Tennis Club (Havana), 129–30

Machado, Gerardo, 2, 3
Magloire, Paul, 120, 126, 135
Magnolia Plan, 73
Mainardi Reyna, Virgilio, 27, 88, 128, 136
Maize Plan (Plan Maíz), 70
Malavasi Mora, Claudio, 91
Manzanares, Gustavo, 62, 66, 81, 84, 86
Marianao, battle of. *See* Orfila shootout
Marinello, Juan, 23
Maroot, Habert Joseph, 107, 108
Marrero Aristy, Ramón, 23–24
Marshall, George C., 18, 42–43, 47
Marshall Jiménez, Frank, 69, 71, 72, 73, 80
Martín, Daniel, 99
Martínez Bonilla, José Rolando, 106, 109, 127
Masferrer, Rolando
and Cayo Confites, 38, 40, 44, 45, 51, 54, 55, 56, 58
and Luperón, 102, 125
McLaughlin, Charles A., 20
Medina Angarita, Isaías, 3, 4
Mejía Lara, Alfredo, 62, 70
Messersmith, George, 18
Miolán, Angel
and Cayo Confites, 39, 43–44, 45, 48, 57
and founding of PRD, 27–28
and Luperón, 101–2, 104
and 1950 crisis, 128, 136
Mora, José, 124, 128, 129, 136
Mora, Manuel, 69, 74
Morales, Angel
and Cayo Confites, 34, 39–40, 51
and 1950 crisis, 118, 128
politics of, in exile, 25–26, 29, 31, 33
Morazán, Francisco, 62, 67, 70, 83, 91, 131, 132
Morgan, William A., 20
Morín Dopico, Antonio, 53
Moscoso, Alfonso, 124, 130
MSR. *See* Revolutionary Socialist Movement
Murphy, Edward William, 34, 58
Murray, Alexander, 69, 162 n. 42

National Guard (Nicaragua), 6
Norweb, R. Henry, 41, 42, 47, 48, 49, 52, 57, 58, 59
Núñez, Benjamín, 74
Núñez, Guillermo ("Macho"), 70

OAS. *See* Organization of American States
Oduber, Daniel, 75, 81, 86
Orfila shootout, 53–54, 58, 60
Organization of American States (OAS)
  and Haitian-Dominican dispute, 122, 123, 124
  and 1948–49 Costa Rica–Nicaragua dispute, 87, 88, 89, 90, 92, 93
  and 1950 crisis, 130, 134, 135, 136, 139
Orlich, Francisco ("Chico"), 69, 73
Ornes, Horacio
  and Costa Rican civil war, 70, 73, 74, 76, 91
  and Luperón, 100, 103, 104, 106, 107, 108, 109, 110, 111, 112, 127
Ortega, Presentación, 70
Ortega Frier, Julio, 41
Ortega Suárez, Luis, 118, 133
Osawa, George, 53
Osuna, Antonio, 99
Osuna, Gregorio, 99

Pact of Friendship (Costa Rica and Nicaragua, 1949), 93
Pact of the Mexican Embassy (Costa Rica), 74
Pact of Ochomogo (Costa Rica), 74
Pasos, Carlos, 62, 64, 84
Paulino, Anselmo, 122, 123, 132
Peña Batlle, Manuel Arturo, 15, 53
Pepper, José Vicente, 7
Peralta, Ismael, 68
Pérez Cabral, Romano, 39, 128
Pérez Dámera, Genovevo, 7–8, 46, 54–55, 57, 59
Pérez Jiménez, Marcos, 140
Perón, Juan, 11, 16–18, 21, 34
Picado, Teodoro, 63, 68, 74, 88
Pink Carnation Plan (Plan Clavel), 73
Plan Clavel. *See* Pink Carnation Plan
Ponce, Federico, 4
Popular Socialist party (Cuba), 23
Popular Socialist party (Dominican Republic), 23–24, 25
Popular Union party (Dominican Republic), 15
PRC-A. *See* Cuban Revolutionary party-*Auténtico*
PRD. *See* Dominican Revolutionary party
Prío Socarrás, Carlos
  and Caribbean Legion, 83, 85, 130
  and Cayo Confites, 30, 38
  and Luperón, 96, 98, 102, 109, 111, 131
Prosper, Marcaisse, 126

Quintanilla, Luis, 88, 123, 124
Quirós, Rodolfo, 69

Rafaela Herrera Company, 80. *See also* Río Conejo
Ramírez, Alberto, 106, 107
Ramírez, Miguel Angel
  background of, 38, 44–45
  and Cayo Confites, 45, 48, 51, 57, 58
  and Costa Rican civil war, 67, 70, 71, 72, 74, 76, 77, 83, 84, 86, 88, 90, 91, 92, 163 n. 76
  and Luperón, 100, 103, 104, 113, 116, 132
  and 1950 crisis, 118, 120, 121, 128
Raudales, Ramón, 68
Revolutionary Insurrectional Union (UIR), 40, 53, 56, 58
Revolutionary Socialist Movement (MSR), 37, 38, 40, 44, 46, 53, 54, 55, 56, 57, 59
Reyes, Heriberto, 68
Reyes Valdés, Salvador, 106, 108
Río Conejo, 80, 81, 84, 86
Rio Treaty, 18, 42, 87, 93, 111, 123, 124, 139
Rivas Montes, Jorge
  background of, 5, 44, 51
  and Costa Rican civil war, 62, 67, 70, 71, 73, 88, 91
  death of, 137
  and Luperón, 100, 116, 131
Rivera Delgadillo, Carlos, 87
Roca, Blas, 23–24
Rockefeller, Nelson, 16
Rodríguez, José Horacio
  background of, 33, 60, 66
  death of, 137
  and Luperón, 98, 99, 115–16
  and 1950 crisis, 128
Rodríguez, Juan ("Juancito")
  background of, 9–10, 32–33, 154 n. 36
  and Caribbean Pact, 66–67, 75, 76
  and Cayo Confites, 34, 35, 36, 39–40, 41, 42, 45, 55, 56, 57, 60
  and Central American intrigue, 61–62, 67–68, 83, 85, 93
  and Costa Rican civil war, 70, 74, 75, 77, 84, 86
  death of, 137
  and Luperón, 95, 96, 98, 99, 100, 102, 103, 104, 115–16, 127, 132
  and 1950 crisis, 118, 120, 121, 127, 128

Rodríguez García, Juan. *See* Juan Rodríguez ("Juancito")
Rodríguez Larreta, Eduardo, 8, 16, 17, 26
Rodríguez Lora, Sebastián, and Haiti, 122, 123, 126, 127, 132
Rodríguez Vásquez, José Horacio. *See* José Horacio Rodríquez
Roland, Astrel, 122, 127, 132
Román Durán, Antonio, 96, 99, 103
Ruiz, Fabio, 52, 54
Ruiz, Iván, 52, 54

Salabarría, Mario, 53-54
Saladrigas, Carlos, 3
Salazar, Joaquín E., and 1950 crisis, 123, 124, 125, 126
Sanabria, Víctor, 72
Sánchez, Buenaventura, 52, 128, 136
Sánchez, Francisco ("El Indio"), 62, 70, 88, 91
Sánchez Arango, Aureliano, 121
Sandinistas, 62, 67-68
Scherer, George F., 13, 15, 19-20, 22, 25, 26, 31-32
Scruggs, George Raymond, 107, 108
Selva, Alejandro, 106, 108
Servio Ducoudray, Félix, 128
Silfa, Nicolás, 34-35, 36, 38, 43-44, 84-85, 86, 101, 104, 118, 122, 136
Smith, Hollis B., 38, 39, 44, 51, 52, 55, 58, 113, 155 n. 60
Solís Vargas, José Manuel, 91
Somarribas Tijerino, Enrique, 71
Somoza García, Anastasio, 5, 6, 8, 11, 95, 137, 140
  and Caribbean Legion, 85-86
  and dispute with Costa Rica (1948-49), 87, 88, 93
  and José Figueres, 74, 75, 86, 87
Sosa Navarro, Mario, 62, 70
Spalding, Hobart, 124, 130
Special Commission on the Caribbean (OAS)
  charge to, 135
  reports of, 135, 137
Spignolio, Fernando, 110
Stamets, George H., 20
Starke, Ludwig ("Vico"), 73, 91
Stella, José Ramón, 22-23
Suárez, Fernando, 110

TACA. *See* Central American Air Transport
Tercero, José María, 51, 71, 91

Tijerino, Toribio, 62, 65, 66, 67, 68
Torres, Edelberto, 64, 65, 81
Trejos Aguilar, Guillermo Segundo, 86-87
Tró, Emilio, 53-54, 58, 159 n. 183
Trujillo, Rafael
  and Cayo Confites, 40, 46, 50, 51, 57, 60
  and Luperón, 95, 98, 101, 102, 104, 108, 109, 111
  nature of rule of, 5, 6-7, 8, 11, 12, 13, 14, 15, 18, 21, 23, 24, 25, 41, 42
  and 1950 crisis, 117, 118, 120, 121, 122, 124, 127, 129, 134, 135, 137
  plots against, 30, 31, 32, 33
  and Spruille Braden, 11, 12, 13, 14, 19, 20, 21, 22
Truman, Harry, 13, 20, 115

Ubico, Jorge, 4
UIR. *See* Revolutionary Insurrectional Union
Ulate, Otilio, 63, 68, 75
United Front for Dominican Liberation (FULD), 29
United States
  Caribbean policy of, 10
  and Rafael Trujillo, 12, 13
  See also Spruille Braden, Ellis O. Briggs, George H. Butler, and John C. Dreier
University Reform, 1, 2
U.S. Public Roads Adminstration, and Villa Mills (Costa Rica) facility, 69

Valenzuela, René, 105
Valle Urbina, Manuel, 81, 83, 85, 88
Valverde, Carlos Luis, 68, 70
Valverde Vega, Fernando, 69, 80
Vandenberg, Arthur, 18
Velásquez, Antonio, 84
Villalobos Jiménez, José Ramón, 91
Villegas, Silvio, 88

Waddell, Rupert, 56, 58
Wanguemert, José Luis, 40-41, 44, 48
War of National Liberation (Costa Rica), 70, 75. *See also* Costa Rican civil war (1948)
Warren, Avra, 82
Welles, Sumner, 17
Wells, Ralph, 104
Wright, James H., 54

Zepeda, Pedro José, 62, 64, 66
Zuleta Angel, Eduardo, 124